Advance Praise

"In a vigorous, excoriating rebuttal of current myths about the impact of the Europeans upon the Americas, Jeff Fynn-Paul shows how evidence has been manipulated in the interest of political activists whose understanding of the past is corrupted by their obsession with issues of today."

–David Abulafia, Professor Emeritus of History at the University of Cambridge and Author of *The Discovery of Mankind: Atlantic Encounters in the Age of Columbus* (2008)

"*Not Stolen* offers a brave, bold, direct contradiction of the fashionable story that European colonial endeavor in the Americas was nothing but a litany of theft, racism, enslavement, and genocide. Anyone who wants to know the whole, nuanced, humanly plausible truth about the encounters between Europeans and native American peoples should read this important book."

–Nigel Biggar, CBE, Regius Professor Emeritus of Moral Theology at the University of Oxford and Author of *Colonialism: A Moral Reckoning* (2023)

"*Not Stolen* is a dazzling work of history that corrects every modern shibboleth about the alleged evils of European colonization in the New World. One distortion, myth and outright lie after another is sharply rebuked with uncomfortable facts: Cortes did not commit genocide but was respected as a liberator by many Mexican tribes; native Americans were not peaceful environmentalists but hunted many species to extinction; American Thanksgiving resulted from Indian tribes seeking protection from their rivals; 95 percent of Indians survived the Trail of Tears; the U.S. government went to great lengths to inoculate Indians against smallpox. And so on. A significant and necessary book, coming at a time when the history profession is dominated by people who prefer ideology to facts."

–Bruce Gilley, Portland State University and
Author of *The Last Imperialist: Sir Alan Burns'*
Epic Defense of the British Empire (2021)

NOT STOLEN

The Truth About European Colonialism in the New World

JEFF FYNN-PAUL

BOMBARDIER
B O O K S

Published by Bombardier Books
An Imprint of Post Hill Press
ISBN: 978-1-64293-951-4
ISBN (eBook): 978-1-64293-952-1

Not Stolen:
The Truth About European Colonialism in the New World
© 2023 by Jeff Fynn-Paul
All Rights Reserved

Cover Design by Hampton Lamoureux
Map by Lennart Visser

Post Hill Press
New York • Nashville
posthillpress.com

Published in the United States of America
1 2 3 4 5 6 7 8 9 10

CONTENTS

A NOTE ON THE COVER

Our cover illustration, which depicts Dutch governor Peter Minuit's famous purchase of Manhattan Island in 1626, is a painting by the British-American illustrator Alfred Fredericks (1853–1926). Like many paintings of its day, it contains historical anachronisms that make it an easy target for modern critics, who may reflexively condemn it as a sentimental whitewashing of the genocidal theft of Indian land.

But Fredericks' painting reveals a more nuanced story to those who look past the hype. For one thing, the painter's brush carefully portrays the Natives' individuality, humanity, and dignity. Respect for the Indians and their way of life was surprisingly common amongst European-Americans in the later nineteenth century. The Scouting movement was founded on the idea that Indians were role models of bravery, intelligence, honesty and other virtues. Many thousands of Americans dedicated their careers and fortunes to the betterment of Native lives.

Moreover, the focus of the painting is the purchase of Manhattan—by mutual consent. By most definitions, a sale is the opposite of theft. It would be misleading to suggest, as many critics do, that the Natives were cynically taken advantage of when they parted with the island for twenty-four dollars worth of "trinkets." Dutch administrators studiously recognized Native land claims as a matter of policy. To the Indians themselves, the mosquito-ridden island was of little value, whereas the "trinkets" they were offered—including textiles, metal tools and weapons—were so life changing that many tribes intentionally relocated near the coast in order to trade more easily with the newcomers. They even fought wars with other tribes in order to be closer to the Europeans and their trade goods. In any case, neither party had any conception of what the island would become 200 years later, and judgments based on hindsight miss the point entirely.

This book tells the real story of 500 years of Settler-Native relations in America. The facts show that faddish labels such as "genocide" and "stolen land" are not only historically inaccurate—they do far more harm than good, including to the very people they are meant to protect.

MAPS AND FIGURES

THE RADICAL ASSAULT
ON WESTERN HISTORY

On June 18, 2020, protesters in Portland, Oregon, pulled down a statue of George Washington. With a mixture of ferocity and jubilation, the mob hacked at the effigy until they detached the bronze head of the first American president. On the base of the toppled statue, they spray-painted the words: "GENOCIDAL COLONIST." Across the Western world, statues of Columbus, Lincoln, Churchill, and other traditional heroes met similar fates.

The world has grown accustomed to seeing dictators' statues treated in this way. Such behavior is understandable since dictators, by definition, must sustain their power through a mixture of violence and intimidation. The novelty in 2020 was that for the first time, democratically elected leaders of major Western nations were being treated—by their fellow citizens—as though they had been mass murderers and archvillains of history.

The base of the Portland protesters' charge is that the United States is fundamentally illegitimate. It is a stolen country, wrested with sadistic violence from the Native Americans. In their view, the so-called Age of Discovery was no reason for celebration. On the contrary, it set in motion a global tragedy of the first magnitude, in which European settlers fanned across the globe, spreading the contagion of European culture like zombies spreading an apocalyptic disease. Agents of a cancer-like system based on patriarchy, oppression, and exploitation, European colonists devoured every human and natural resource in pursuit of unlimited capital. Inspired by the belief that natives were fundamentally inferior to themselves, Europeans held that natives had no real rights to property, or even to life itself. When they met any resistance from the New World's original inhabitants, European settlers intentionally spread disease, enslaved the survivors, and exterminated anyone else with ruthless efficiency. With the "Indian question" thus solved, settlers swooped in and occupied the ground left by their murdered victims. Enriched by the spoils of the dead, Europeans had the audacity to call themselves "agents of civilization."

This view of European colonialism, once held by only a few radicals, has recently become dominant across the globe. It seems that every pundit and authority from Britannica.com to science.org to the *Washington Post* to PBS to Vice President Kamala Harris have hopped on the "stolen ground" bandwagon.[1] According to Disney and the writers at Marvel Studios, the United States is so fundamentally tainted that no "person of color" should feel comfortable defending either the United States or its institutions. A Jamaican-American philosophy professor named Dr.

---

[1] These can be found at "American Indians: Loss of Land to the United States," *Encyclopedia Britannica*, https://www.britannica.com/video/212505/Shrinking-Native-American-lands-in-the-United-States-indigenous-peoples; Lizzie Wade, "Native Tribes Have Lost 99% of Their Land in the United States," *Science*, October 28, 2021, https://www.science.org/content/article/native-tribes-have-lost-99-their-land-united-states; Negiel Bigpond and Sam Brownback, "It's Long Past Time for Our Country to Apologize Publicly for What It Did to Native People," *Washington Post*, July 6, 2021, https://www.washingtonpost.com/opinions/2021/07/06/native-peoples-an-apology-never-spoken-is-no-apology-all/; Kira Kay and Jason Maloney, "Why Native Americans Are Buying Back Land That Was Stolen from Them," *PBS NewsHour Weekend*, October 16, 2021, https://www.pbs.org/newshour/show/why-native-americans-are-buying-back-land-that-was-stolen-from-them; Martin Pengelly, "Kamala Harris: European Colonizers 'Ushered in Wave of Devastation for Tribal Nations,'" *Guardian*, October 12, 2021, https://www.theguardian.com/us-news/2021/oct/12/kamala-harris-shameful-history-european-colonization-indigenous-peoples-day.

Jason Hill was recently told by a passionate student that there can be no morality in America, because:

> America was and continues to be located on stolen lands. This land was forged in genocidal conditions to eliminate Native Americans from the continent...we lived on their stolen land without their permission...we have yet to admit that genocidal policies neutralized any possibility for an ethical space. The United States of America, she declared, was irrevocably tainted as a country. No American could claim to ever have a legitimate ethical identity short of giving back stolen lands to the Native Indians; or, paying them for all illegally acquired lands.[2]

After the student had finished, nearly every other student in the classroom came forward to agree with the original speaker. The students' opinion on the matter was virtually unanimous. When the professor attempted to probe the basis of the students' beliefs, they responded by stating that their version of events was an incontrovertible historical fact.

The students in Professor Hill's lecture hall may believe their version of history to be based on "self-evident truth." In fact it is anything but. The proof is that only a few years ago, most people thought very differently about the fundamentals of American history. As recently as 2016, when Bernie Sanders was challenging Hillary Clinton for the Democratic nomination for president, he visited Mount Rushmore accompanied by a bevy of CNN reporters. To showcase his patriotism to Democratic voters, Sanders looked up at the four presidents on the mountain and said: "This is a monument to four great presidents. This is America at its very best...just the accomplishment and the beauty, it really does make

---

[2]   Quoted by DePaul University professor Jason Hill in "Genocide, Stolen Land, and Other Lies about America," The Atlas Society, May 11, 2022, https://www.atlassociety.org/post/genocide-stolen-land-and-other-lies-about-america.

one proud to be an American." The CNN reporter beside him went on to gush about the "majesty of the moment."

As late as 2016, then, both liberal and conservative Americans could still appeal to a shared undercurrent of "American" values. Just four years later, even that tenuous connection appeared to be fraying. In the fall of 2020, another CNN reporter stood in front of Mount Rushmore. Affecting a disgusted, dejected tone, she pronounced it to be nothing more than a monument to "slave owners, on stolen ground." Two wildly opposing visions of American history now dominate our cultural discourse, and since the facts of history have not changed, then the odds are that at least one of these narratives is based more on ideology than fact.

By most measures, the United States provides its citizens with more prosperity and opportunity than any nation on Earth. It has the highest per capita wealth of any major nation; the largest average house size after Australia; and despite what the majority of academics and Twitter users seem to believe, it consistently ranks among the most tolerant societies in history.[3] The United States has been at the global vanguard of civil rights and equality legislation ever since its Founding Fathers established the first modern democratic republic in 1776. Staggering progress towards equality has been made in the last few decades alone. Our collective accomplishments, of which we ought to be so proud, have been painstakingly chronicled by authors such as Stephen Pinker, whose books *Enlightenment Now* and *The Better Angels of Our Nature* present page after page of convincing data to this effect.

American democracy is built on European foundations; it is the product of a long march of Western civilization. Its hallmark is a public with the maturity to solve disputes by discussion rather than vio-

---

[3]   According to a 2016 survey reported by the *Washington Post*, the United States ranked in the global top ten in terms of racial tolerance. According to Sam Harris, fewer than one in one million police stops in the United States results in a controversial killing of a black person, and this figure had been declining every year between 2000 and 2020. According to the UN's Gender Inequality Index, the US ranks fifteenth out of 189 countries in terms of gender equality, ahead of Austria, France, and Spain. According to the Gay Travel Index, the US is ranked thirty-first out of 202 countries worldwide in terms of tolerance and safety for gay people.

lence—a remarkable achievement in global history, which has made the United States the envy of the world and the bane of tyrants for going on 250 years.

Logic would dictate that a history which produced so much opportunity and so many advances in human rights cannot be totally depraved or fundamentally tainted by five hundred years of relentless racism, genocide, and land theft. All of us know that many American presidents and public figures have had positive impacts on world events. Yet today nearly every historian with a public platform, every journalist, and every social media pundit seems unanimous in their conviction that America and the West have been uniquely depraved. They charge that the enslavement of Africans and the extermination of Indigenous People were "holocausts" and "genocides" equal in scale and intent to anything perpetrated by Nazi Germany or Stalinist Russia. Moreover, they argue that these massacres were not exceptional in American history but indicative of the corrupted soul of America itself.

The economist and public intellectual Thomas Sowell summed up the importance of impartiality in history when he wrote:

> History is what happened, not what we wish had happened, or what a theory says should have happened. One of the reasons for the great value of history is that it allows us to check our current beliefs against hard facts from around the world and across the centuries. But history cannot be a reality check for today's fashionable visions when history is itself shaped by those visions. When that happens, we are sealing ourselves up in a closed world of assumptions.[4]

When we "seal ourselves up in a closed world of assumptions" we are retreating from reality and science into dogma and superstition. A retreat

---

[4] Thomas Sowell, "The Wright Stuff," reprinted in *The Thomas Sowell Reader* (2011).

from science to superstition is precisely what led Roman civilization into the Dark Ages; we may yet witness the dawning of a new Dark Age if we learn to discard truth the moment it clashes with our beliefs.

If anyone should be aware of the need to present history from multiple points of view, it should be the august membership of the American Historical Association (AHA). Yet when James Sweet, its president, in the summer of 2022, dared to suggest that American professional historians were becoming so enslaved to modern political discourses that they were in danger of losing their scientific perspective about the past he was publicly excoriated. A few days later, he was forced by the membership to make a groveling public apology. Thus, branded with a scarlet "AHA," his scholarly career is effectively over.[5]

The purpose of this book is to give some space back to those thousands of expert voices who seek to nuance the anti-European diatribe that has become dominant in recent years. There are still many centrist historians out there for whom science and fact trump "bandwagoning" and political tirades. The problem is, we never hear from them because—with examples like AHA President James Sweet standing so vividly before them—they live in fear of joblessness and social stigma. The book aims to give those historians' voices a new foothold so that we can begin to reclaim some of the reasonable center ground that, as Sowell points out, historians are duty bound to occupy.

This is not a book of historical revisionism or a rah-rah defense of all things European. Rather, it is a work of historical restoration. Its goal is to remind us what historians used to believe a few years ago, up to the time when historical reason was drowned by cultural hysteria sometime around the year 2016. Its aim is to clear away the tangled vines of radicalism that have been allowed to grow over the precious garden of our

---

[5] This bold attempt by an establishment historian to rebuke the profession for a lack of scientific objectivity—and the terrifying results—has been summarized by Peter Wood in his article "One Worldview Has Taken Over the Historical Profession," *The Spectator*, August 29, 2022.

democracy in recent years, choking out levelheadedness and objectivity in the process.

THE TRIUMPH OF RADICAL HISTORY

Let us be clear: this book is not in any way anti-Indian.[6] People concerned with identity tend to believe that modern economic and social woes stem primarily from racism. Identity historians assume that modern disparities between racial groups are the result of historical racism. They therefore believe that the only morally acceptable way to write history is to foreground exploitation of non-white people by white people. Only by detailing the history of how Native Americans were oppressed as a race by the European race can we hope to grasp the history of "systemic racism" and, by ending or overhauling that system, reach economic and social equality today. This book is based on the idea that such theories are not only wrong, but hopelessly simplistic and damaging to the people they purport to defend. Explanations of history that fetishize a single cause have not fared well in the past, and I am shocked that so many of my fellow historians have fallen in line behind a new one, yet again. Historical outcomes always have more than one cause. Identity historians teach Indian youth to think of themselves as perpetual victims, for whom European-Americans have only ever been genocidal enemies. This is patently untrue in a thousand ways, as this book will show. Worse, it teaches them to think of modern American capitalism and democracy as enemies, and to think of modern western economic and legal systems as oppressive, rather than what they really are: the greatest creators of opportunity and wealth the world has ever seen. I know of no more effi-

---

[6] In this book I will use the word "Indian" interchangeably with "Native American," "Indigenous," and other terms for the first inhabitants of North America. The term was declared culturally insensitive only a few years ago, mostly by non-Indian activists, and often over the protests of many Native Americans who actually preferred it. The titles of many books about Native Americans before about 2010 used the term "Indian" with no sense of shame or guilt. I will therefore continue to use it until such time as a majority of American Indians who correspond with me tell me they find it demeaning.

cient way to create poverty, despair and violence in native communities than to teach identity politics and identity history. Rather than being anti-Indian, then, this book is pro-Indian. It is a work of objectivity and compassion, born of a fierce conviction that democracy, science, and markets are the keys to guaranteeing human rights for all citizens, including the descendants of Native peoples, today and in the future. This book aims at reconciliation and the optimism of a shared and prosperous future, while its detractors encourage factionalism born of nihilism, despair, and a petty desire for point-scoring and personal gain.

Nor does this book seek to belittle the tremendous damage done to New World societies by European interlopers. Europeans in the New World perpetrated any number of atrocities on the Indigenous Peoples of the Americas. This is something which should always be acknowledged and handled with sensitivity. At the same time, we must recognize that such cruelty was not the axis around which all American history revolved. Most of the time, depravity was not the basis of European institutions or behavior. Reality has always been more complex than that.

Though we now find it difficult to believe, the extent of European cruelty toward Native Americans was well researched and publicized before the rise of social media. Thus it was common knowledge among historians that Europeans were responsible for population decline, forced conversions, provoking wars, countless treaty violations, the Trail of Tears, the California Indian massacres, the extinction of the buffalo, racial prejudice and discrimination, confinement on reservations, and continued marginalization of many Native groups. The questions under debate are not about whether these things happened, but why they happened, what the intentions of European thinkers and policymakers actually were, and whether the new fad for anti-European hyperbole is justified by the historical evidence.

The origins of today's radical anti-Europeanism—the same anti-Europeanism that has gone mainstream in the past few years—lie in the intellectual ferment of the 1960s and '70s. As New Left campus Marxism reached a high-water mark in the 1970s, Marxist historians began a concerted assault on the foundations of American history. The problem with American history from their perspective was that it made capitalism look too good: American democracy empowered the people; its melting pot welcomed everyone, albeit not without serious friction, and its economic system rewarded hard work more often than not. Marxist historians therefore determined to rewrite American history to show their version of the "truth": that America was a "system" rooted in unrelenting oppression.

The most famous of these '70s historians was Howard Zinn. The title of his magnum opus—*A People's History of the United States*—tells you everything you need to know about his point of view. In its opening chapter, Zinn not only trashes Christopher Columbus and all who sailed in his wake, he clearly sets out his Marxist vision of the world, which is perpetually divided into two opposing classes of conquered and conqueror. Zinn writes:

> The history of any country…conceals fierce conflicts of interest (sometimes exploding, most often repressed) between conquerors and conquered, masters and slaves, capitalists and workers, dominators and dominated in race and sex. And in such a world of conflict, a world of victims and executioners, it is the job of thinking people, as Albert Camus suggested, not to be on the side of the executioners.

Of course it is proper for historians to retell history from different points of view, including that of Native Americans and the slaves of the South. This increases scientific objectivity, and it serves as a basis for all good historical writing. Scathing criticisms of Columbus and his human rights abuses could already be found in the pages of many balanced historical accounts in the later nineteenth century.

But Zinn's radicalism goes beyond objectivity and straight into the arms of a rigid philosophical dogma. For one thing his key passage quoted above echoes, nearly word for word, the opening lines of chapter 1 of the *Communist Manifesto*:

> The history of all hitherto existing society is the history of class struggles. Freeman and slave, patrician and plebeian, lord and serf, guildmaster and journeyman, in a word, oppressor and oppressed, stood in constant opposition to one another, carried on an uninterrupted, now hidden, now open fight….

For Zinn and the radical revisionists who followed him, democratic compromise is basically impossible. Anything that looks like progress in a democracy—such as the Civil Rights legislation of the 1960s—simply masks the certainty of ongoing oppression. This is how Leftist radicals come to conflate democracy with totalitarianism—their ideology makes no distinction between the two. For these radicals, history can only be a zero-sum game where gains by one group lead to loss by the other. In Zinn's view, history always consists of precisely two groups: the oppressor and the oppressed. The "system" perpetuates conflict between these two groups, ensuring the domination of one group over another. In Zinn's pessimistic view, oppression rather than freedom was the very foundation of the United States and its Constitution.

Zinn's inclusion of "conquerors and conquered" and "dominators and dominated in race and sex" shows how already, by the late 1970s, the New Left had begun to adopt the Marxist story of identity and oppression to their own particular hobbyhorses. In this way, they hoped to make the old, white-boy, class-struggle Marxism more palatable to race and gender radicals of every faction. It worked. In order to hide the origin of their dogmas, they adopted the euphemism "critical theory," even though their belief in the futility of gradual, democratic reform remained the same.

Thus, critical feminist scholars "discovered" that history revolved around males oppressing females, while critical race theorists discovered that history revolved around the oppression and slavery of black people by white people. Post-colonial theorists accordingly discovered that history revolved around the oppression of Indigenous People by Europeans. Soon, critical "intersectionality" theorists lumped all these identity-based oppressions together, discovering that wealthy, straight, white European males were the ultimate oppressors in history, while poor, black, gay or gender-fluid Indigenous women of color were the ultimate victims. Such a simple vision. And, as we will show, just as totally, tragically wrong as when Karl Marx and other nineteenth-century radicals first articulated it.[7]

Fortunately for society at large, critical theory remained confined to the academy for several decades, and its main victims were liberal arts students. But the meteoric rise of social media unchained this seductive beast, letting it loose on an unsuspecting society unduly impressed by its purveyors' academic credentials. When articulated by women or "People of Color," most white male academics knew to shut up, lest—like James Sweet—they be censored as sexist or racist. Since the majority of history professors in the Western world happened to be white males—due in large part to the fact that European-Americans remained the majority demographic in Western countries—this meant that ignorant activists were able to silence reasoned historical criticism of their outlandish theories in one fell swoop. Eager for social and professional approval, most male historians lined up to cheerlead the new theories that painted themselves as born villains. Savvy activists piggybacked their critical theory onto the message of the Black Lives Matter (BLM) movement and soon *#metoo* and Indigenous rights movements spread their versions of the same message. The venerable term "Indian" became unusable—even

---

[7] This simple black and white, either/or vision of society underpins too many Leftist political platforms today. The Left argues for example that wage gaps between African Americans and "whites," and between women and men, are mostly due to personal and "systemic" prejudice and oppression. Any competent economist will tell you that most of these wage gaps are caused by skill gaps. The clear remedy is improved educational environments. In the absence of legislation or traditions prohibiting African Americans from taking certain jobs, the skill gap data provides a robust explanation for the problem of African American underachievement.

over the protests of many Indians. Activists tried to recast Thanksgiving as "Indigenous Holocaust Day" and have met with remarkable success in many quarters.

By the 2010s, a clutch of older historians such as Roxanne Dunbar-Ortiz began to capitalize on the rising popularity of their decades-old critical theory narratives. Her *Indigenous Peoples' History of the United States* (2014)—note the homage to Zinn—argues that US history revolves around the oppression of Native Americans. The 1619 Project, concocted by a group of activist journalists at the *New York Times*, also sought to rewrite American history, this time with slavery as its foundational idea. In recent years, dozens of similar works have been appearing every month, often to critical acclaim. These narratives have been filling the minds of Western journalists, bureaucrats, and politicians with the same old 1970s theories, dressed in alluring new clothes.

The result of their stunning success has been a radical change in the public's perception of global history. Europe and the West used to be revered not only as the cradle of democracy, but as the home of the Renaissance, the Scientific Revolution, the Industrial Revolution, constitutional government, women's suffrage, global abolitionism, the Geneva Conventions, the United Nations, human rights, the research university—in short, the foundation of much that is good in modern life. Buoyed by social media successes, activists have worked tirelessly to cast European society in as negative a light as possible. They have also downplayed the numerous historical horrors that were perpetrated by non-Europeans, including the horrors of slavery within Africa, the horrors of Islamic slavery in Africa—which saw up to ten million Africans trafficked across the Sahara over many centuries—of modern genocides in Asia that have created tens of millions of victims, of longstanding antifeminism in India, and a host of truly awful histories besides. The activist campaign against Europe and Europeans has been so successful that even the likes of Beethoven and Sir Isaac Newton are now considered monsters by many on the Left.

Show me a historian who lacks a healthy skepticism of fads like critical theory and I'll show you a historian who is not doing their job. They can be as contrary as they want—but facts, rather than ideology, must come first for their work to qualify as science rather than propaganda.

THE ARGUMENT OF THIS BOOK

Our central argument is that the recent fashion for extreme anti-European allegations is too extreme for rational, balanced, scientifically minded people to take seriously. Widely accepted charges such as "genocide," mass murder, the primacy of racism and slavery, and the idea that the United States and Canada are illegitimate because they were founded on "stolen ground" were confined to the radical fringes of the historical profession as recently as a decade ago. Yet via the mechanism of social media the most extreme views have captured the historical profession, rendering it helpless to counteract charges that most of us used to acknowledge were disingenuous, even unhinged. Throughout the book it will be demonstrated that many of these claims can be traced to a handful of radical authors such as Roxanne Dunbar-Ortiz, David Stannard, and Bruce E. Johansen. Particularly when it comes to Indigenous studies, a surprising number of these scholars got their PhDs at West Coast universities in the 1970s, when "Indian studies" was in vogue among white, Left-leaning suburbanites. With these dots having been connected, the new extremism is revealed as the long-discredited, decades-old Marxist dogma that lies at its base.

To make our case, we will address a number of common beliefs about European expansion in the New World over the past five hundred–plus years. The aim is to avoid downplaying the real evil done by Europeans, while deflating the hyperbole spread in recent years by radical historians and their disciples. In order to put contemporary debates about racism, genocide, and the like on a more scientific footing, we will provide context that is usually missing from popular accounts, thus enabling readers to make their own informed decisions.

We begin with the Age of Exploration. In Part I we debunk the idea that European explorers were the vanguard of a nefarious "system" of racism, capitalism, white supremacy, or colonialist exploitation. We provide population figures to show that charges of genocide have been exaggerated to the point of meaninglessness, and we provide testimonials and proof that Europeans arrived in the New World ready to believe that Amerindians were of the same race as themselves, beautiful to look at, and mentally equal or superior to Europeans.[8] We also look at the true death toll of the conquest of Mexico and dismantle the awkward theoretical construct of "settler colonialism."

In Part II we turn to the Native Peoples of the Americas themselves. Our goal is to remind contemporary audiences what everyone (including Native American leaders) used to know—New World Natives were not saints. Like every other society, Native America produced saints and sinners in equal measure. Here we address questions such as whether the Aztecs and Incas were technologically equal to Europeans (as claimed by Charles C. Mann and his numerous admirers), whether Native Americans were peaceful and without knowledge of slavery or other forms of exploitation, whether Native Americans had special insight into the environment, whether their societies were less hierarchical than European ones, and whether Native Americans invented democracy, only to have the Founding Fathers steal the credit from them.

In Part III we turn to the era of displacement in the United States, with an eye to untangling the tension between policy, intention, and the realities of frontier life. These chapters address questions such as: Is it ethical to celebrate Thanksgiving? Did Pocahontas get along with the Jamestown settlers, or did the English behave despicably toward the Virginia Indians? How much Indian land was really stolen by the English colonists? Were the Founding Fathers racist architects of settler colonialism? Did Europeans intentionally spread disease among the Indians? Did they intentionally starve them by killing all the buffalo? Can the Trail of

---

[8]   "Amerindian" is used by anthropologists to denote indigenous people of the New World.

Tears be classed as a genocide? And how do we reckon with the Indian massacres that accompanied the California Gold Rush?

Finally, in Part IV we visit some contemporary issues such as Native-themed holidays, reparations, and the schooling of Indigenous children, which have been turned into cultural and political footballs in recent years by a handful of interested parties. These chapters address questions such as: Is it ethical to educate an Indigenous person in the "dominant" culture? Is it "cultural appropriation" to use Indian names or wear Indian costumes? And: Should the US pay further reparations to the Amerindians?

In the end, we conclude that America was not "stolen," any more than Europeans were the inventors of slavery or colonialism. Like every modern society, the United States is the result of complex historical factors that resist easy categorization, and we slide into nihilistic generalizations only at great peril to the health of our democracy.

I

THE AGE OF DISCOVERY

CHAPTER 1

INTREPID EXPLORER OR GENOCIDAL MANIAC? THE COMPLEX CASE OF CHRISTOPHER COLUMBUS

*Columbus was a thief, and invader, an organizer of
rape of Indian women, a slave trader, a reactionary
religious fanatic, and the personal director of a
campaign for mass murder of defenseless peoples.*

—John Henrik Clarke, *Christopher
Columbus and the Afrikan Holocaust*

I n an episode of the TV series *Yellowstone*, Native American his-
tory professor Monica Dutton gives a lesson on Christopher
Columbus to a class of mostly white students at Montana State
University.[9] Professor Dutton reads aloud the following phrases from
Columbus's journal:

---

[9]   *Yellowstone* stars and is produced by veteran filmmaker Kevin Costner, whose tendencies
to mythologize the American West were previously established in *Dances with Wolves*—a
film to which we will return in due course.

"[The Natives] willingly traded us everything they owned…. They do not bear arms and do not know them, for I showed them a sword they took it by the edge and cut themselves out of ignorance…. They will make fine slaves…. With fifty men we can subjugate them all and make them do whatever we want."

Dutton then singles out a white, baseball-cap-wearing "dudebro" named Trent:

"Trent, do you ever feel like making someone do what you want, whether they want to or not? It's a very European mentality. Stemming from the oppressive political and religious structures of the Renaissance. Kings and priests with absolute power ruling masses who have none. That was the mentality of the man who discovered America. And it's the mentality our society struggles with today. What you know of history is the dominant culture's justification of its actions. But I don't teach you that."

Professor Dutton has a point about the political uses of history. Most societies do paint a flattering portrait of their past and tend to justify or airbrush their crimes. Historical revisionism is therefore often a necessary corrective.

But it is also possible to go too far in the other direction. Thus, the idea of Christopher Columbus as the carrier of a peculiar European depravity founded on hierarchy, oppression, patriarchy, racism, capitalist exploitation, and a delight in cruelty and torture has become mainstream in the historical profession, and by osmosis among the public at large.

The image of Renaissance Europe as a place of absolutist hierarchy and oppression began with certain radical historians in the 1970s and has mushroomed in recent decades until it has become the mainstream interpretation of European culture. Beginning with books such as Francis Jennings's 1975 *The Invasion of America: Indians, Colonialism, and the Cant of Conquest*, this story has since made it into mainstream textbooks such as Peter Charles Hoffer's *The Brave New World: A History of Early America*, which we will visit in more detail later. Columbus himself has emerged as a symbol of this cultural invasion—the most destructive force ever to propagate itself across the planet.

In this view, Columbus embodies the European penchant for killing and enslaving nonwhite peoples wherever they are found. Throw in the notion that he was also the founder of modern capitalism, the first imperialist, the first colonizer, the bringer of patriarchy to the New World, and the instigator of mass environmental destruction, and Columbus becomes a nearly perfect embodiment of everything hated by the Left today.

On the surface, this vision of Columbus seems consistent with what most people think they know about New World history: Europeans created colonies that stole Indian land and pushed the Native peoples nearly to extinction; they were racists who engaged in slavery on a massive scale; they set up exploitative proto-capitalist trading systems, were rapacious and careless exploiters of natural resources, and imported alien technologies that lie at the root of modern environmental disaster.

But it is one thing to recognize that the interlopers who followed Columbus caused a great deal of suffering and quite another to suggest that they were the vanguard of a uniquely evil European "system" of oppression that has lasted from that day to this. A system that moreover remains the root of most suffering endured by minorities and women today. According to this view, if only Indigenous institutions and mentalities had triumphed over European ones, rather than the other way around, the world today would be a veritable utopia, where all races and genders live in harmony with nature and one another. Because that, in their idealized view, is what New World society was like before Columbus arrived.

This modern consensus resembles the portrait presented by the editors of the fringe academic journal *Social Justice*. In the introduction to their 1992 Columbus-themed issue, the editors had the following to say (italics mine):

> Columbus and subsequent invaders set in motion a world-historic process of European colonization, by which a nascent *capitalist system* expanded monumentally across the earth—in the Americas, Africa, and Asia. It was a process based on human and environmental *exploitation*, the legacies of which continue to this day. The *merciless assault on indigenous peoples* served as the *bedrock* upon which *Western culture* and the *capitalist economy* were built in the Americas.
>
> Human society had seen *racism* before, but nothing could approach the forms it took on this continent as the *capitalist process* unfolded....
>
> We can also say that the planet had been mistreated before, but nothing could approach its post-1492 fate.... Simply put, today's environmental crisis results from *500 years of unbridled capitalist exploitation*. "Progress" has not come without a staggering price, if it can be called progress at all.

In this view the wellspring of Western civilization is the oppression of Natives. A more radical statement could hardly be made, and yet this is now what passes for mainstream historical opinion. Notice how this view of history is carefully crafted to lump together the hot button issues of the modern Left. Classical Marxism did not give a fig about racism, or gender issues, or environmentalism, but as communism imploded after the fall of the Soviet Union in 1989, Leftists broadened their definitions of "oppression" in a deliberate move to broaden their appeal to these minority and activist groups. The resulting worldview is so rabidly anti-white, anti-male, and anti-European that it challenges the idea of human progress itself.

WHAT DID COLUMBUS THINK OF THE INDIANS?

How do we untangle the truth about Columbus in the face of so much vitriol? Let us begin by unpacking the supposed quotations from his journal that are cited in *Yellowstone*. This passage may be found quoted all over the internet and has now become widely accepted as a shocking confession of truth about Columbus's motives. Yet almost every word is misleading, based on mistranslation and distortion of what Columbus meant to convey.

We may skip over the fact that our modern version of Columbus's journal is an extract from a lost original, meaning that we will probably never know the navigator's actual words. Even so, the passage in question—which is also cited in Zinn's influential *People's History*—is actually a pastiche of lines that appear several pages apart in Columbus's original account. Presented as a single passage, they make the speaker look a lot worse than he was.

Dutton quotes Columbus as saying "they will make fine slaves." But Columbus did not use the Spanish word for slave (*esclavo*). In the original Spanish, the line she is quoting goes: "*Ellos deben ser buenos servidores y de buen ingenio, que veo que muy presto dicen todo lo que les decía*," which most translators render as: "they will make good servants, as they are very clever, and quickly understood everything which was said to them." Even in the context of an aristocratic system that seems unjust by modern standards, servants are very different from slaves. Moreover, elsewhere in the *Diario*, Columbus uses the term "*servidores*" to mean "subjects of the Crown" rather than personal servants. He uses this context because Columbus was addressing the journal not to himself, as modern readers might assume, but to his patrons Queen Isabella and King Ferdinand of Spain.

Monica's monologue neglects to mention Columbus's glowing appraisal of Indigenous intelligence and their capacity to learn, which can be found in the very same sentence. She also leaves out the passage where Columbus observes how fortunate the Spanish would be to welcome such intelligent people as fellow Christians and subjects of the crown.

It is therefore reasonable to suggest that what he meant was nearly the opposite of what Monica (and Howard Zinn) implies. Rather than consigning the Indians to perpetual enslavement on the grounds of irredeemable racial inferiority, Columbus was advocating their admission into European society as spiritual, racial, and social equals, based on his understanding of them as fellow descendants of Adam and Eve. (On which more appears in chapter 3.)

We know in hindsight that things did not turn out very well for the Caribbean Indians, so this may sound far-fetched to modern ears. But it is an indisputable historical fact that many Spaniards, including well-placed figures such as Columbus and Queen Isabella herself, did hope to welcome the Indians as fellow citizens and subjects at many points during the early history of the Spanish Empire.

Monica Dutton's quotation also contains the line: "They willingly traded us everything they owned." This quote appears to support the stereotype of Natives as guileless and easy to take advantage of: innocent, childlike, naive, generous, naturally communistic, ignorant of the evils of private property or exploitative labor hierarchies. In reality, Columbus's impression of Native generosity underwent a rapid series of transformations. When the first Natives willingly traded pieces of gold for a few glass beads, this was because to them, the beads were so rare and unusual that they were worth more than any gold that they could find. Nonetheless, a few encounters later, we find Columbus deliberately sending his secretary and other reliable lieutenants to oversee trade between his men and the Indians, in order to ensure that the Spanish did not take undue advantage of the Natives. Soon, however, the Spanish were complaining that the Natives had already learned to drive a hard bargain and would no longer part with things the Spanish found precious or useful without charging a high price.

In other words, the Natives quickly showed as much cunning as any merchants, anywhere on Earth. These initial encounters should be seen for what they were: the first exchanges in a market that was not yet fully understood by either side. As modern economists know, a major component of any market is information. What we see in this instance—as in others throughout the colonial period—is the ability of Native Americans to rapidly adapt to changing market conditions in order to maximize their own advantage. They did not stay naive, any longer than the Europeans with whom they traded.

Let us move away from the cherry-picked quotations favored by anti-Columbus campaigners and turn to what he actually said about the Native Americans as a people or "race." In his first weeks in the Caribbean, Columbus was astonished by the lushness of the landscape and the variety of the trees and animals, many of which had never been seen by Old World eyes before. About the Taino Indians he encountered, Columbus said:

> They are very well made, with very handsome bodies, and very good countenances. Their hair is short and coarse, almost like the hairs of a horse's tail. They wear the hairs brought down to the eyebrows, except a few locks behind, which they wear long and never cut.... They are all of fair stature and size, with good faces, and well made. I saw some with marks of wounds on their bodies, and I made signs to ask what it was, and they gave me to understand that people from other adjacent islands [Caribs?] came with the intention of seizing them, and that they defended themselves. I believed, and still believe, that they come here from

the mainland to take them prisoners. They should be good servants and intelligent, for I observed that they quickly took in what was said to them, and I believe that they would easily be made Christians, as it appeared to me that they had no religion.[10]

He also reported:

Your Highnesses may believe that there is no better nor gentler people in the world. Your highnesses ought to rejoice that they will soon become Christians, and that they will be taught the good customs of your kingdom. *A better race there cannot be*, and both the people and the lands are in such quantity that I know not how to write it…. I repeat that the things and the great villages of this island of Española, which they call Bohio, are wonderful. All here have a loving manner and gentle speech, unlike the others, who seem to be menacing when they speak. Both men and women are of good stature. It is true that they all paint [themselves], some with black, others with other colours, but most with red. I know that they are tanned by the sun, but this does not affect them much. Their houses and villages are pretty, each with a chief, who acts as their judge, and who is obeyed by them. All these lords use few words, and have excellent manners. Most of their orders are given by a sign with the hand, which is understood with surprising quickness."[11]

---

[10] Christopher Columbus, *The Journal of Christopher Columbus (During His First Voyage 1492–93)*, ed. Clements R. Markham (Oxfordshire, UK: Routledge, 2016), entry for October 11, 1492.

[11] Columbus, *Journal*, entry for December 24, 1492.

Columbus's favorable views about the physical and mental characteristics of the New World peoples were not unique. The Spanish scholar Peter Martyr d'Anghiera collected stories about the Indigenous inhabitants of the Caribbean from a number of men who sailed with Columbus and other early adventurers. In their collective opinion, these Caribbean islanders showed a number of admirable traits, including graceful customs and rhetorical sophistication. After reporting on their skills as weavers of cotton, Martyr writes:

> It is in the manufacture of [ceremonial stools] that the islanders devote the best of their native ingenuity. In the island of Ganabara which, if you have a map, you will see lies at the western extremity of Hispaniola and which is subject to Anacauchoa, it is the women who are thus employed; the various pieces are decorated with representations of phantoms which they pretend to see in the nighttime, and serpents and men and everything that they see about them. What would they not be able to manufacture, Most Illustrious Prince, if they knew the use of iron and steel?

Peter Martyr, who was a chief tutor at the Spanish Court with a major influence on elite opinion, was convinced that the Indians of the Caribbean would prove equal to Europeans in skill and productivity, if only they were given the same technology and skills.

In sum, the earliest accounts of Columbus and other Spanish adventurers present a complex picture of both Caribbean society and European intentions. Most conclude that at least some groups of Indians were equal or superior to Europeans in terms of physical beauty, intelligence, and potential for future development. They also believed that some groups of Indians were more fearsome, physically uglier in their opinion, and had less praiseworthy customs. Of one thing we can be sure: this complex picture smashes through easy stereotypes like those proffered by the majority of modern pundits.

WHO WAS THE REAL COLUMBUS?

Christopher Columbus was born in Genoa in 1451, as the Italian Renaissance was reaching a crescendo. Contrary to what Monica Dutton and many of her real-world colleagues might claim, Renaissance Europe was no more hierarchical, patriarchal, or oppressive than any other major civilization. In fact, it was a good deal less so. In Columbus's day, European society was a chaotic patchwork of jurisdictions and political systems. This included dozens of the world's only functioning small-scale republics. Many scholars have credited this political fragmentation with creating a fertile ground for entrepreneurialism, a crucible of clashing institutions that eventually gave birth to modern capitalism. It was messy, and it was risky, but it created unequalled opportunities for social mobility, along with technological and scientific advancement.

Just a few decades after Columbus landed in the New World, Spain was rocked by a series of urban revolts led by the *comuneros*, in which citizens demanded constitutional rights, liberties, and freedoms. One looks in vain for similar occurrences in the contemporary Islamic or Asiatic worlds. Moreover, Western Europe was the only major society that allowed women to hold supreme political power: Queen Isabella of Spain and Queen Elizabeth I of England are only the most famous examples. European society gave administrative and economic power to women at every level of society, from duchesses down to tailors' widows. The female literacy rate in Renaissance Europe far outstripped anywhere else in the world; Catholicism allowed women to become powerful abbesses; some Protestant sects allowed women to become preachers. Western Europe was—already by Columbus's day—easily the most "feminist" city-dwelling culture the world had ever known.

It was into this world of chaos and opportunity that Christopher Columbus was born, and he took full advantage of it. His father wanted him to become a cloth weaver like himself, but young Cristoforo abandoned the workshop in favor of an adventurous life at sea. As a traveling merchant and budding entrepreneur, Columbus showed good knowledge of the long-distance cloth trade and experienced some early success. In his twenties, he immigrated to Lisbon, where he spent ten years at the heart of Europe's growing community of Atlantic explorers and married into a wealthy family of Italian immigrants who had been ennobled by the Portuguese crown. His father-in-law—the lord of one of the newly organized European estates on Porto Santo, a previously uninhabited island off the coast of Morocco—served as an example of local lordship and estate management that loomed large in Columbus's mind.

After many years spent badgering the Iberian monarchs to let him lead an expedition across the Atlantic in search of a passage to Asia, Columbus set sail from Seville in August 1492. Two months later, he sighted land on the other side of the Atlantic, likely an island in the modern-day Bahamas. Two weeks later he was at Cuba, and a month after that, he landed at Hispaniola, a large island that today hosts the nations of Haiti and the Dominican Republic.

It was in these islands that Columbus encountered the Taino Indians, part of a larger group sometimes known as the Arawaks. The Tainos, in turn, were in the midst of being driven off their islands by the ruthless, cannibalistic Caribs, who were working their way up the Leeward Islands chain from South America. It was his encounters with the Tainos that caused Columbus to write the journal entries that we have already examined above.

After losing his flagship *Santa Maria* on a sandbar, Columbus had no choice but to leave some of his sailors behind. He christened the castaway settlement La Navidad and told them that he would return the following year. By February he was back at the Portuguese-held Azores. He returned to Spain in March, where he received a hero's welcome.

On his first voyage, Columbus's main goal was to produce proof that he had reached the great trading cities of Asia, described so lavishly by the Italian traveler Marco Polo some two hundred years before.

Columbus was extremely disappointed to find the Bahaman islanders going about naked and "poor in everything," as he put it. He asked these people for directions to China, but they kept pointing him to the source of their own legends, a great kingdom of gold that lay to the southeast. When Columbus later reached Cuba, he convinced himself (and tried to convince his men) that he had found the Asian mainland.

Also in Columbus's mind was the hope that, given proper instruction, the Great Khan (the emperor) of China might prove willing to convert to Christianity. This would make him an invaluable ally against the Muslims whose successes after the fall of Constantinople in 1453 threatened to drive the Christians off the face of the Earth.

The question of just how religious Columbus really was has exercised scholars throughout the modern era. On the one hand he was eminently practical, a crass businessman and self-promoter who recognized that the use of religious rhetoric would have a positive effect on the pious Isabella. On the other hand, he himself became increasingly religious as he got older, though this was tinged with a sense of himself as an agent of providence who united previously disparate people around the world.[12]

In his journal Columbus advocated restraint when it came to introducing the Indians to Christianity, writing that "they were a people who could be more easily freed and converted to our holy faith by love than by force." Even in late medieval Spain, voluntary conversion was usually preferred. While academics tend to think of Christian missionaries as agents of repression, the fact is Christianity has caused countless individuals to dedicate their lives to bettering the lot of Native groups in

---

[12] Francis Jennings in his *Invasion of America: Indians, Colonialism, and the Cant of Conquest*, pp. 5–6, sets up Spain as a "crusading society" that had been shaped by the Reconquista. This view was common in his day, but it has long since been debunked by scholars working on the topic. In the popular mind, this stereotype of Spaniards as religious zealots still has a lot of traction.

the New World, from Columbus's day through the present.[13] Bartolomé de las Casas, whom we will meet later, was only the tip of the charitable iceberg in these early decades, a small army of Christian clergy and others whose selflessness and decency are now completely overlooked. Columbus and many others believed that, if shown good treatment, the Indians would accept Christianity in due time. On a pragmatic note, Columbus also recognized that people who did not have their own scriptures, such as Jews and Muslims, had proven historically more receptive to Christianity. In the end, his perception was correct. Throughout his subsequent governorship of the Caribbean, despite his numerous incompetencies and misdeeds, Columbus was never a consistent advocate for forced conversion, any more than Isabella herself.

Upon his return to Spain, Columbus found the Spanish monarchs in Barcelona, where he misleadingly informed them that the lands he had discovered were "infinitely fertile" and contained ample amounts of gold and valuable Asian spices. As William and Carla Phillips put it, Columbus knew that "his reputation and his future success would depend on the profitability of the lands he had discovered."[14] More specifically, he hoped to rule over his island kingdom as a sort of count or duke, whose family would share in his prestige. With all the subtlety of a used car salesman, he described Cuba as an island larger than Great Britain, whose interior possessed "great mines of gold and other metals." He further suggested that his tiny colony of La Navidad was "in the best position for the mines of gold...and for trade with the mainland... belonging to the Grand Khan, where there will be great trade and gain."

In order to exploit the connections he created with the New World, the entrepreneurial Columbus proposed the creation of a series of trad-

---

[13] The dominant academic reading of Christian missionizing activity is based on the writings of French theorist Michel Foucault (1926–84), who is credited with inventing the notion that "all discourse is power." One implication of this theory is that no missionizing, however well-meaning, is simply "good" or "kind." It is also an attempt by one group to gain power over another. While cynical, this view contains enough elements of truth to keep a lively debate going.

[14] William D. Phillips and Carla Rahn Phillips, *The Worlds of Christopher Columbus* (Cambridge, UK: Cambridge University Press, 1992), 185.

ing posts in the Caribbean. The idea was to trade with Natives for their most valuable products, using a string of permanent coastal forts as bases for trade. This was hardly a novel idea: Columbus simply embraced the trading-fort model that the Italians had been using in the Black Sea for centuries. This trading-fort model had recently been exported to the West Coast of Africa with great success. It would soon be adopted by the Portuguese in India, Malaysia, East Africa, and the Persian Gulf.

Many people fault Columbus for setting up these trading forts, as if he should have known that this would soon prove devastating to New World civilization. But in the Black Sea, in West Africa, and in the Portuguese Indian Ocean Empire, these trading forts had only a very limited effect on local peoples. In all these places, Europeans were confined to their coastal enclaves by local rulers for many centuries, and the major effect of the European presence was to enrich both Europeans and locals via the creation of new trading networks. Given European experience throughout the Old World, in which Indigenous populations continued to thrive after contact with Europeans, neither Columbus nor anyone else could have foreseen the collapse in New World population levels that would result from European presence in the Caribbean.

The Spanish monarchs recognized that Columbus was an opportunist and prone to hyperbole, but they nonetheless granted him the title Admiral of the Ocean Sea as the promised reward for his exploits. Enticed by the potential of this New World, and the prospect of opening a direct trade route to China, they sent him out in 1493 with a much larger fleet of seventeen ships, with the purpose of reinforcing the fledgling colony at La Navidad. Columbus's brother Diego accompanied him on this voyage, with the idea that he could act as governor and help establish a Columbus family dynasty.

Columbus arrived to find La Navidad in ruins, its people having been murdered by the supposedly peaceful islanders. He therefore founded a second colony, which he called La Isabela. But with ships and intelligence reports now arriving in Spain from the New World every few months or so, the Spanish monarchs soon realized that the Caribbean offered less in the way of quick riches than Columbus had promised.

They also quickly came to understand that Columbus was a terrible estate manager. La Isabela was badly situated and had limited sources of fresh water; there was also a lack of domestic animals after the starving inhabitants had slaughtered them for meat. In the end, many colonists either ran off to live with the Indians or sailed back to Spain in disgust. Meanwhile fights broke out among the settlers, and within a few years a full-scale rebellion was underway. Other colonists picked fights with the Indians, leading to a rapid collapse of any remaining goodwill and war with the Taino as early as 1494.

A few decades of Spanish maladministration and repression were sufficient to drive most of the Taino Indians from the islands altogether. Most accounts assume that the Tainos pitifully gave up and died in droves at the hands of sword-wielding Spanish adventurers, but this theory assumes that the Indians were stupid and lacking in agency—which they most certainly were not. Given their proven ability to canoe from island to island, and also to spread news quickly over long distances, it seems likely that most of the supposed "victims" of the Spanish invasion simply fled as Spanish repression got out of hand.

Many Taino women, meanwhile, settled down as wives of the Spanish newcomers, knowing that this would afford them considerable protection. Enthusiastic miscegenation on both sides led to a rapid increase in the mixed-race "mestizo" population of the islands—not to mention a tolerance for mixed-race people that persists to this day.

Desperate to prove that the New World could be profitable for Spain, Columbus allowed his men to enslave some of the "rebellious" Indians on Hispaniola and sell them in the Seville slave market. He accordingly sent several hundred of these back to Spain, though nearly half of them died (along with their European captors) when their ship was lost in an Atlantic storm.

This single incident was to prove the sum total of Columbus's slaving activities, though even his admirers such as the chronicler Bartolomé de Las Casas would regard it as the darkest stain on his entire career. Whether he would have enslaved more Indians or not given the chance to do so, the practice of selling them in Spain was quickly squelched by order of the queen, who regarded the Taino as subjects and therefore ineligible for enslavement. When she learned that about three hundred Tainos had been sold, she had the Indians tracked down, ransomed from their owners, and sent back to their homes in the New World. In fact, she was furious with Columbus, since she had made it clear that he was not to enslave the Natives; after this, she quickly sought ways to limit his power.

Meanwhile, Columbus made numerous concessions to the disgruntled colonists in a misguided effort to placate them, including a fateful decision to replicate the labor-service practice owed by peasants on Iberian estates. This became the basis of the much-disparaged *encomienda* system, whereby Natives were subjected to forced labor by their Spanish landlords. Moreover, the labor-service concession, which worked reasonably enough back in Iberia, was roundly abused in the Caribbean. Many colonists interpreted it as a license to round up and forcibly relocate bands of Indians, leading to further strife, atrocities, mass flight, and rapid social disintegration.

No one should be under any illusion as to whether the Spanish sometimes treated the Indians with incredible cruelty. According to various accounts, they devised games to determine whether individual Indians should live or die; they tested the sharpness of their swords by lopping off Indians' heads at random, and mutilated them in any number of ways. At the same time, this needs to be seen in the light of Indian cruelty toward their own captives, both European and Indian, which as a rule was crueler and more torturous than that inflicted on them by the Spanish. It also needs to be seen in the light of the mixed-race relationships—and children—that were already being produced within a few years of the Spanish arrival.

When Isabella's inspector Francisco de Bobadilla arrived at the islands in 1500, he found open rebellion among Spanish and Indian factions against Columbus and his brother. As he sailed into the harbor, Bobadilla saw that the admiral was in the process of hanging more than a dozen Europeans who had refused to submit to his authority. He immediately ordered Columbus and his brother removed from power and sent them home in chains.

Though he was later released, Columbus was never given another governorship. After a disastrous fourth voyage in which he discovered the mouth of the Orinoco River in Venezuela, only to be shipwrecked for over a year on the coast of Jamaica, Columbus returned home in a state of extreme mental agitation. In these later years he was given to fits of mystical prophecy and religious extremism that lasted until his death.

WAS COLUMBUS A MASS MURDERER?

According to popularly accepted figures, Columbus and the Spanish administrators of the islands are held responsible for the deaths of up to eight million Indians. We will look in greater detail at the charge of Taino genocide in the next chapter. But this is undoubtedly a wild exaggeration.

The idea that Columbus killed millions of people on Hispaniola is an unfortunate legacy of the writings of the aforementioned friar de las Casas, who saw firsthand the mistreatment of the Natives at the hands of Europeans during those first lawless decades. Las Casas's most famous work, *On the Destruction of the Indies*, was a polemical tract designed to create maximum sympathy for the Indians in Spain.

It worked, and his persistence paid off with the passage in 1542 of the New Laws of the Indies for the Good Treatment and Preservation of the Indians, which overhauled the encomienda system and led to a gradual stabilization of Colonist-Indian-mestizo relations. By the end of the sixteenth century, most forced labor in New Spain had been replaced by wage labor, with African slaves remaining a small minority of unpaid workers in many Latin American countries.

Las Casas's sympathy for the Indian plight did not prevent him from being a great admirer of Columbus. He went out of his way to portray Columbus as a protector of the Indians rather than a scourge. This is another inconvenient truth that has been swept under the rug by modern polemical treatments. Las Casas's main target was not Columbus himself, but the Spanish adventurers and ne'er-do-wells who came after him in search of an opportunity to get rich quick. It was Las Casas who suggested that Hispaniola might have had up to three million people in 1491, a figure that most serious demographers reject as absurd, while modern activists continue to broadcast it as widely as possible.

The Yale Genocide Studies Program is slightly more cautious than many advocates of the island genocide theory, though it still gives credence to the idea that over a million Tainos might have died at the hands of the Spanish on the island.[15] Yet even Howard Zinn, who understood the geography of Hispaniola and the limited ability of the Taino to produce food using their system of mound farming, accepted the far more realistic figure of two hundred and fifty thousand inhabitants on the island before Columbus's arrival.[16]

Furthermore, while it is true that thousands of people died as a result of Spanish maladministration and forced labor (perhaps up to twenty-five thousand over the course of fifty years), the number of Indigenous people killed in military engagements or wanton violence probably numbered about two or three thousand. The total number who were enslaved and sent back to Spain likewise appears to have been in the hundreds. Columbus himself was responsible for a tiny fraction of those killed through direct violence and mistreatment; as governor, he proved as likely to kill a European "rebel" as an Indigenous one. The great majority of those who died—easily over 90 percent—were victims of disease rather than cruelty.

---

[15] "Hispaniola," Genocide Studies Program, Yale University, https://gsp.yale.edu/case-studies/colonial-genocides-project/hispaniola.

[16] For this system, see M. E. Danubio, "The Decline of the Tainos: Critical Revision of the Demographical-Historical Sources," *International Journal of Anthropology* 2, no. 3 (1987), 241–245, https://link.springer.com/article/10.1007/BF02442235.

Genetic tests have revealed surprisingly large proportions of Taino Indian DNA among modern Caribbean islanders, a finding that has shocked (and disheartened) advocates of Spanish genocide. Genetic evidence provides irrefutable proof that many more Indians survived and intermarried than is popularly believed. According to a report published in Indian Country Today, up to 61 percent of all Puerto Ricans have been found to have Taino Indian blood.[17] This is a huge proportion, compared with only a couple of percent of Indian blood found in the US population at large. It suggests that Puerto Ricans have similar levels of Indigenous blood compared to other highly mixed peoples such as Mexicans, Guatemalans, and Bolivians; more will be said on this in the next chapter.

Moreover, research suggests that Taino genes were not at all inbred, confirming that Taino peoples mixed widely with people all around the Caribbean. Flight, intermarriage, and disease therefore are likely to account for over 90 percent of the missing Indians, and all of this points to the fact that charges of mass murder have been greatly exaggerated.

The reason why the real numbers of killed and enslaved were so low is that the Spanish government viewed the inhabitants of Hispaniola and other Caribbean islands as valuable subjects of the crown. Just as Queen Isabella would never send out an army of extermination against one of her own provinces except in extreme circumstances, so she continually admonished her officials to treat the Caribbean Natives with as much care as possible. Human beings were the greatest source of capital in Isabella's day. Like other feudal lords, Isabella wanted to maximize the population of her territories, not reduce it. In a world recently depopulated by the Black Death, European lords knew that the only way to reap revenue from an estate was to have it worked by numerous hands in longstanding agricultural settlements.[18] Geographers and travelers often

---

[17] Rick Kearns, "Indigenous Puerto Rico: DNA Evidence Upsets Established History," Indian Country Today, September 6, 2017, https://indiancountrytoday.com/archive/indigenous-puerto-rico-dna-evidence-upsets-established-history.

[18] Karl W. Butzer, "The Americas Before and After 1492: An Introduction to Current Geographical Research," Annals of the Association of American Geographers 82, no. 3 (1992), 345–368, https://www.jstor.org/stable/2563350.

judged the quality of a city and a kingdom based on how populous it was. Population density was equated with power and good administration.

SLAVES...OR SOCIAL SUPERIORS?

The Wikipedia article on the voyages of Columbus is unfortunately typical of modern bias and sloppiness on the topic.[19] It suggests, for example, that the seven Tainos brought to Spain by Columbus after his first voyage were brought back as slaves, mere samples of human merchandise. To the contrary, all seven Tainos whom Columbus had captured and kept as interpreters were accorded places of honor in the Spanish court. Many solemn processions were held to commemorate their arrival; they were feasted and paraded with pomp across Iberia like visiting dignitaries.

In the royal hall at Barcelona, the seven Natives were baptized in a high ceremony, with one being given the baptismal name Fernando de Aragon—the same name as the king of Spain—and another Juan de Castilla, after the heir to the Spanish throne. The king and crown prince also acted as godparents.

The Indian christened Fernando was a relative of the chief Guacanagarix; he was therefore treated as a nobleman by the Spanish court. As we will see, this willingness to treat Indian "lords" as analogous to European nobility—hence socially and biologically superior to European commoners—was a standard feature of European-Indian relations for the first two centuries of contact.

Columbus's accomplishments as a navigator and explorer are irrefutable and justly catapult him into the first rank of historical figures. For hundreds of years after Columbus, the mapmaking and geography he spurred acted as anchors for countless scientific advancements. It is no exaggeration to say that the European voyages of discovery remain foundational to all modern science and technology. Columbus was the

---

[19] "Voyages of Christopher Columbus," Wikipedia, https://en.wikipedia.org/wiki/Voyages_of_Christopher_Columbus.

first to bring New World peoples back into contact with the major civilizations of the Old World, and he is rightly remembered as a brash, colorful architect of modern globalism. He was also very much a man of his time and of his culture. He marveled at the wonders of the New World and had some of the sensibilities of a Renaissance artist. He appreciated the physical form and intelligence of some of the Caribbean Indians he encountered. He had the capacity for religious fanaticism, but for most of his life he was a religious opportunist who counseled moderation. He was greedy, to be sure, but like all good businessmen, he understood the need to play fair. He was willing to sell war captives as slaves, but only in some cases and only if circumstances allowed. His primary motive was the creation of a family dynasty, though he also wished to be remembered as an oceangoing successor to Marco Polo. As an administrator, however, he was disastrous. He was not particularly cruel by the standards of his day, but nor was he good at maintaining order or restraining his adopted Spanish allies from making life intolerable for the Tainos.

In sum, Columbus was no saint. He was a self-aggrandizing entrepreneur and a bad administrator who allowed anarchy to break out where some other men might have kept order. This ended up causing thousands of deaths and set the stage for more. At the same time, Columbus was an extremely brave and skilled navigator and a visionary who set the stage for modernity by uniting the two halves of planet Earth. The task of governing first contact between the Caribbean and European peoples was never going to be an easy one, and the fact that New World people proved so extremely susceptible to Old World disease could have been predicted by no one.

One thing that does no one any good is to exaggerate the numbers of Natives who died in the Caribbean, and to exaggerate the level of malice, racism, cruelty, greed, and zealotry borne by the Europeans. On all these counts, the slightest brush with the facts about Columbus and his career shows that the ideas articulated by Howard Zinn and his followers—including the writers of *Yellowstone*—are gross misrepresentations of what was in reality a complex and multifaceted historical encounter.

CHAPTER 2

DID EUROPEANS COMMIT GENOCIDE IN THE NEW WORLD?

*What happened on Hispaniola was the
equivalent of fifty Hiroshimas.*

—David Stannard, *American Holocaust*

L arge segments of the public now take it for granted that Europeans
committed full-scale genocide in the New World. Only a few
years ago, however, such claims were considered so extreme that
no one but a radical would take them seriously.

One of those radicals is David Stannard, emeritus professor at the
University of Hawaii. Stannard's 1992 book, *American Holocaust*, was
published by the highly reputable Oxford University Press. In this book,
Stannard set out to maximize the genocide element in the European
colonization of the New World:

> It took a little longer, about the span of a single human
> generation, but what happened on Hispaniola was
> the equivalent of more than fifty Hiroshimas. And
> Hispaniola was only the beginning. Within no more

than a handful of generations following their first encounters with Europeans, the vast majority of the Western Hemisphere's native peoples had been exterminated.[20]

Stannard's book was followed in 1997 by Ward Churchill's *A Little Matter of Genocide*, whose lurid descriptions of millions of Indigenous people being hacked apart by European blades make Stannard's claims look measured by comparison:

> During the four centuries spanning the time between 1492, when Christopher Columbus first set foot on the "New World" of a Caribbean beach, and 1892, when the Census Bureau concluded that there were fewer than a quarter-million indigenous people surviving within the country's claimed boundaries, a hemispheric population estimated to have been as great as 125 million was reduced by something over 90 percent. The people had died in their millions of being hacked apart with axes and swords, burned alive and trampled under horses, hunted as game and fed to dogs, shot, beaten, stabbed, scalped for bounty, hanged on meathooks and thrown over the sides of ships at sea, worked to death as slave laborers, intentionally starved and frozen to death during a multitude of forced marches and internments, and, in an unknown number of instances, deliberately infected with epidemic diseases.[21]

In Churchill's telling, wild-eyed Europeans rampaged across the New World in a five-hundred-year orgy of axe murdering, horse tram-

---

[20] David E. Stannard, *American Holocaust: The Conquest of the New World* (Oxford, UK: Oxford University Press, 1992).

[21] Ward Churchill, *A Little Matter of Genocide: Holocaust and Denial in the Americas 1492 to the Present* (San Francisco: City Lights Publishers, 1997).

pling, and meat hook hanging, most of which was done for the sheer joy of killing inferior brown-skinned people. Churchill leaves the impression that any Indian who got within one hundred miles of a settler was likely to meet a grisly fate.

Books like Stannard's and Churchill's were dismissed by mainstream historians as sensationalist drivel throughout the 1990s. Indeed, these books languished unread for decades, until the rise of social media began to reward the least cautious and most unscrupulous interpreters of Indigenous history. Stannard's *American Holocaust* now has upwards of five hundred reviews on Amazon, and the number grows by the month.

Stannard was roundly criticized at the time for exaggerating his population figures, a tendency that carried over into his later work. For example, he claims at the beginning of *American Holocaust* that one hundred and thirty-five thousand people were killed at Hiroshima. But even this easily checkable figure contains a basic error: one hundred and thirty-five thousand were the total *casualties* of Hiroshima, with an estimated sixty-six thousand dead and sixty-nine thousand injured. Lumping dead and injured together for rhetorical effect does not make a solid basis for analysis.

Ward Churchill, for his part, is still considered a hero in Indigenous activist circles. Yet he is infamous for calling World Trade Center workers "little Eichmanns" who deserved to die for working in a "capitalist" building. Churchill made national news when he got fired from UC Boulder for research fraud in 2007—a thing that almost never happens to university researchers. In fact, most people who have heard of Churchill know him as one of the most infamous academic frauds in modern history. He is also known for claiming to be one-sixteenth Indian in the early 1990s and then upping this fraction to three-sixteenths in the early 2000s.

As one looks into the rumor mill that is academic anti-Europeanism, it becomes apparent that many of the more egregious offenders are not trained historians at all. Rather, they are scholars from related fields such as literature, anthropology, and sociology who often think in metaphors rather than facts, and make the dreamer's mistake of believing that metaphors drive reality. Such writers feel even less tied to genuine historical sources than historians like Stannard, and indeed, nonhistorians often lack the linguistic and archival skills to make sense of historical source material.

A prime example of a nonhistorian who repeats his own metaphors until others accept them as fact is the Berkeley sociologist Ramón Grosfoguel, whose spate of publications on European genocide has gained him a cult following. Grosfoguel, whose specialty is theorizing in a highly esoteric fashion about the transfer of knowledge in Western universities, is another darling of the modern Left who came of age during the 1960s radical movement. He summarized one of his recent publications as follows:

> The epistemic privilege of Western Man in Westernized Universities' structures of knowledge is the result of four genocides/epistemicides in the long 16th century (against Jewish and Muslim origin population in the conquest of Al-Andalus, against indigenous people in the conquest of the Americas, against Africans kidnapped and enslaved in the Americas and against women burned alive, accused of being witches in Europe). The condition of possibility for the mid-seventeenth century Cartesian "I think, therefore I am" is the 150 years of "I conquer, therefore I am" (ego conquiro) [and] is historically mediated by the genocide/ epistemicide of the "I exterminate, therefore I am" (ego extermino)."[22]

---

[22] Ramón Grosfoguel, "The Structure of Knowledge in Westernised Universities: Epistemic Racism/Sexism and the Four Genocides/Epistemicides," *Human Architecture: Journal of the Sociology of Self-Knowledge* 1, no. 1 (2013), 73–90. https://www.niwrc.org/sites/default/files/images/resource/2%20The%20Structure%20of%20Knowledge%20in%20Westernized%20Universities_%20Epistemic.pdf

If Grosfoguel's rhetoric makes little sense to you, that is probably a good sign. In a nutshell, he is arguing that all Western philosophical advancements since the Renaissance were somehow founded on four genocides (which he also calls "epistemicides" since these victims' distinctive "ways of knowing" supposedly died with them). He thus concludes that the Cartesian Enlightenment was only possible because European males had murdered pretty much everyone else, including their own women.

Grosfoguel's fevered musings fly in the face of thousands of careful scholars who have traced the pedigree of European philosophy and science back to the Middle Ages and the ancient world, centuries before Grosfoguel's "genocides." Nor do these purported genocides qualify as anything of the sort. It is true that thousands of European women were persecuted as witches in sixteenth- and seventeenth-century Europe— but the total number of victims amounted to fewer than 0.02 percent of all women living in a given generation. A good number of male heretics were burned at the stake during the same centuries—would that count as an auto-genocide by the European patriarchy?

As for the mass extermination of Africans, the actual number of Africans enslaved by Europeans during the sixteenth century was only a few thousand, whereas the Islamic world had already enslaved millions over the better part of a millennium. African epistemic traditions were certainly not eradicated by Europeans at this time; compared with centuries of Islamic depredations and impositions, Europeans barely had any impact on African culture until the later nineteenth century. As for the "genocide" of Jewish and Muslim people in Al-Andalus, only a tiny percentage of these were physically exterminated; most were forced into conversion or exile. Nor did this constitute an epistemic holocaust, since the Jewish and Muslim knowledge from Al-Andalus remained influential in European culture and has continued to thrive across the globe. Grosfoguel's fourth genocide—that of the Indigenous Americans—will be dealt with below.

Despite the lunacy behind such fact-lite theorizations, a new generation of historians now treat polemicists like Stannard, Churchill, and Grosfoguel as authoritative interpreters of truth. This has prompted increasing numbers of copycat books, often written by professional "genocide" scholars who readily equate the settlement of North America (death toll by massacre: 10 to 20 thousand people over 300 years; less than 1 percent of the total population), with what happened in Cambodia under Pol Pot (death toll by massacre: 1.5 to 3 million people over 4 years; up to 45 percent of the population).[23] In this way, fads lead to publications, which convince people that the fad is backed up by authority. On June 30, 2021, the Executive Board of the Canadian Historical Association posted a "Canada Day Statement" to its website. This claimed a "broad consensus" among historians that European Canadians were guilty of genocide against Native Canadians. (In the fine print, they admit that the Canadian government did not commit mass murder against Indigenous people; the substance of their charge is that nineteenth-century attempts to provide schools and education for Indigenous children amounted to "cultural" genocide. We will take up this claim in a later chapter.) The ten-member activist board did not put their radical manifesto to a vote by the general membership of the Canadian Historical Association. Clearly, they feared that their supposed "consensus" would not extend to a majority of the members.

Confronted with this glaring hypocrisy, such scholars now accuse their critics of being "apologists for genocide." A typical example comes at the beginning of *The Dawn of Everything*, a 2021 book by the late anthropologist (and self-described anarchist) David Graeber. In this book, Graeber and his coauthor, David Wengrow, claim to have discov-

---

[23] See for example Alexander Laban Hinton, et al., eds. (Duke University Press,) 2014. Hinton is primarily a scholar of the Cambodian genocide. The figure of less than 10,000 Indians killed by massacre during all of American history is taken from the standard account by William M. Osborn, *The Wild Frontier: Atrocities During the American Indian War from Jamestown Colony to Wounded Knee*. (New York: Random House, 2009). Osborn incidentally says that more settlers than Indians were killed in massacres. This debate is addressed in later chapters. Osborn's figures are cited in: https://en.wikipedia.org/wiki/List_of_Indian_massacres_in_North_America

ered a new truth about human history—that humans are inherently good after all, and that it was only Western civilization that turned them evil, by corralling them into a capitalist system of exploitation and oppression. Taking bestselling author and civilizational optimist Steven Pinker to task, Graeber suggests that any history emphasizing positive sides of European civilization "can be read as a retroactive apology for genocide, since the enslavement, rape, mass murder and destruction of whole civilizations—visited on the rest of the world by European powers—is just another example of humans comporting themselves as they always had; it was in no sense unusual."[24]

I would turn the argument precisely backwards. Is Graeber willing to acknowledge and describe the far larger record of inhumanity, rape, genocide, mass murder, and destruction of civilizations that have been perpetrated by non-Europeans such as the Mongols? Though Graeber is no longer alive to answer, we know how he would have replied.

THE REAL POPULATION OF THE NEW WORLD

For over a hundred years, historians across the political spectrum shied away from calling European adventurism in the New World "genocide." The burden of proof therefore lies on those who would press that claim. But no new evidence has come to light that might plausibly shift the longstanding scholarly consensus against the use of this term, which has a very specific implication.

Stannard's claim of one hundred million Indigenous dead rests on a series of population figures advanced by the maximalist "Berkeley School" of the 1970s. The Berkeley School of Latin American demographers, which included the physiologist Sherburne F. Cook and the historian Woodrow Borah, was motivated to cast European colonialism and

[24] David Graeber and David Wengrow, *The Dawn of Everything: A New History of Humanity* (London: Penguin UK, 2021).

capitalism in the worst possible light by making pre-contact population figures as high as possible. Then as now, the Berkeley School's exaggerated claims fly in the face of serious archaeological study of pre-Columbian settlement.

How credible is this claim of one hundred million deaths—or even one hundred and twenty-five million, as Ward Churchill asserts? A review of the relevant literature shows that the majority of demographers and archaeologists estimate the population of the New World in 1491 at between fourteen and thirty-two million people. Even the most inflationary modern figures put the total at fifty million people or less.

Maximalists also attribute impossible population densities to certain subregions of the New World. One of the most commonly cited figures involves the population of Hispaniola, which as we have seen is where Columbus founded his first colony. Stannard airs Cook and Borah's patently absurd claim of eight million. Others repeat Las Casas's equally implausible figure of three million. The US government–funded website Native Voices makes the following claim in its time line of European conquest:

> AD 1493: Christopher Columbus, who needs to demonstrate the wealth of the New World after finding no gold, loads his ship with enslaved Taíno people. During the next four decades, slavery contributes to the deaths of 7 million Taíno. By 1535, the Taíno culture on Hispaniola is gone.[25]

Seven million dead sounds serious indeed. But are there any facts to back this up? The Tainos were a preliterate society. In the absence of written records, we must fall back on archaeology, geography, and what we know about the ability of farmers to produce food using various agricultural techniques.

---

[25] "AD 1493: Spanish Settlers Enslave the Taino of Hispaniola," *Native Voices: Native Peoples' Concepts of Health and Illness*, National Library of Medicine, National Institutes of Health, https://www.nlm.nih.gov/nativevoices/timeline/170.html.

The island of Hispaniola has a total area of about seventy-six thousand square kilometers. This is just over one half the size of England excluding Wales and Scotland, whose total area is about one hundred and thirty thousand square kilometers. It so happens that the population history of England is the best-studied for any country on Earth. Our best guess is that England in 1500 had only 2.1 million people, living on double the area of Hispaniola. (England's maximum capacity before the agricultural revolution of the seventeenth century was probably less than five million.) If Hispaniola really had seven million people in 1491, that would make its population roughly triple that of England at the time, and its population density about six times higher.

We also know that England by 1500 had one of the most advanced agricultural regimes on Earth, with widespread use of heavy ploughs and draft animals. Only certain rice-growing areas of China and India could outpace it in the number of calories produced per acre. England was almost entirely cleared of forests, and a significant portion of its land was either farmed or used for grazing. Meanwhile, the natives of Hispaniola were using stone tools and practiced a light form of hoe and mound farming in clearings. They grew very limited crops, ate little and conserved energy to make up for their poor diet, and employed no animal power or mills. In fact, they had no domesticated animals besides dogs, and owing to their lack of metal axes their island was heavily forested; coupled with the mountainous terrain, this means that only a small percentage was arable.

This is why archaeologists and other specialists believe that the real population of Hispaniola in 1491 was about two hundred thousand people while even the "maximalists" in this subfield argue for only three hundred thousand. By the time Las Casas first reported these figures in the 1510s, the original population of two hundred thousand had probably shrunk to about ninety thousand individuals due to a combination of disease, flight, and mistreatment—in that order. For the record, even if all these people had died at the hands of European cruelty, this would deflate Stannard's claims of "fifty Hiroshimas" down to less than a single atom bomb (according to his own exaggerated reckoning of one hundred and thirty-five thousand). Stannard's "genocide" on Hispaniola is thus objectively only one-fiftieth as serious as he claimed, and that is before we start looking at other factors.

According to a macro study of the archaeological evidence for native populations published by the historical demographer S. Ryan Johansson in 1982, abundant caution is required in making any general claim about Indigenous population decline in the New World.[26] Not only because of the flimsy evidence that makes any claim difficult to sustain, but also because demographic decline varied tremendously over time and space. Johansson writes:

> While there is general agreement that the shock of contact with invading Europeans led to substantial reductions among most aboriginal populations... in North America some groups were much less disrupted than others. Many original populations disappeared altogether, but whether or not their demise was primarily a function of short-run rapid disruptions caused by disease and/or warfare, or a slower process spread out over several generations involving assimilation in its various forms, remains uncertain. With the establishment of the reservation system in the nineteenth century a basis was provided for continued demographic and cultural survival. By the early twentieth century most reservations populations were beginning a demographic transition based on declining death rates and high fertility. Finally, all phases of native American demographic history are characterized by defective and inadequate

---

[26] S. Ryan Johansson, "The Demographic History of the Native Peoples of North America: A Selective Bibliography," *American Journal of Physical Anthropology* 25, no. 3 (1982), 133–52. https://onlinelibrary.wiley.com/doi/abs/10.1002/ajpa.1330250508

data which makes straightforward description or analysis perilous.

Such a scientific, no-nonsense approach is refreshing; it represents an ideal of objectivity sorely missing in recent "scholarly" analyses. Unlike many modern writers, Johansson recognizes that many groups survived long centuries with little or no impact and other groups were assimilated in various ways rather than succumbing to sudden or violent ends by disease or warfare.

Johansson even recognizes the value in the reservation system, which gave Indigenous populations greater protection under US law than they previously enjoyed. As we will see for early colonial Mexico, the congregation of Indigenous groups into areas where they usually enjoyed protection under the law has resulted in a continuous upswing in Indigenous population levels, and paradoxically provided a basis for the recovery of Indigenous culture in modern times.

POPULATION AND GEOGRAPHY

One popular claim making the rounds on the internet is that the New World "had more people than Europe in 1491." The main basis for this claim is the pseudoscientific book *1491: New Revelations of the Americas Before Columbus* by the science journalist Charles C. Mann, a prolific anti-Western propagandist. Proponents of this claim tend to use the wildly exaggerated figure of one hundred million people in the New World, which we debunk over the course of this chapter.[27] It is also intentionally misleading because it compares the New World not with the Old World as a whole but with Europe—a tiny corner of the Old World that was home to only about one-seventh of its population in

---

[27] Typical of these claims is a post by the technology guru Christopher Wink: "The Americas Were More Populated Than Europe at the Time of First Contact," christopherwink.com, https://christopherwink.com/2018/10/01/the-americas-were-more-populated-than-europe-at-the-time-of-first-contact/.

1491. So let's sidestep the sensationalism and look at the demographic facts as they stand.

At about forty-two million square kilometers, the New World is about half the size of the Old. Yet according to demographers, the New World contained only about 10 percent of the global population of four hundred and fifty million people in 1491, while the other 90 percent lived in Africa, Europe, and especially Asia.

Why was the New World population so small in proportion to its size? One of the major constraining factors was geography. In the premodern world, people could only live where there were abundant food supplies. The New World presented a difficult geographical challenge to the first people who migrated across the land bridge from Asia in the years before 10,000 BC. Much of North America was still covered by ice as late as 5000 BC, and the climate was decidedly chilly. Long winters and months of snow cover drove people farther south, where they could enjoy year-round ice-free conditions. The major Old World civilizations evolved under similar conditions, in semitropical and temperate regions such as the Nile Valley, Mesopotamia, and in the Indus and Yellow River valleys.

Unfortunately for the New World peoples, the area that was ice-free year-round was relatively small. Fully one-third of the New World land is locked up in Canada, Alaska, and Greenland—which were far too cold to support large populations. Most of the continental United States freezes pretty hard in the winters, and the world was in the grip of a Little Ice Age when Columbus arrived. Most of northern Mexico is desert. Central America and equatorial South America are mostly thick, impenetrable jungle. At the southern tip of the New World, Argentina and Chile also get cold in the winters. This leaves only a narrow territory at the edge of the rain forests in central Mexico and analogous territory in parts of the Andes Mountains, where conditions were right for the multiplication of premodern peoples.

Neither of these areas contained a major river valley like the Nile or Indus Rivers. Major civilizations tend to spawn around such river valleys, because they combine the advantages of year-round growing seasons with fertile ground and easy transportation. In South America the Amazon basin was too dense with jungle, while farther north, the Rio Grande was too arid. The Mississippi valley, though cold in the winter, was a little more promising. The Mississippian culture, one of the most advanced pre-Columbian civilizations in the continental US, evolved along the shores of this river system. When the Spanish under De Soto arrived in the area in 1541, this proto-civilization was at a low ebb. The maximum population supported by some of its cities was a few hundred people. Based on what happened in the Fertile Crescent and other Old World regions, we can speculate that, given another few thousand years, the Mississippi River system might have become a major hub of civilization.

Accidents of geography therefore made it likely that the New World would never have as many people as the Old. Furthermore, close to 80 percent of the New World population was located in two very localized regions: central Mexico and the northern Andes. The rest of the New World was thinly populated indeed, with all of North America north of the Rio Grande probably containing between one and three million people. Most of these were spread across the Mississippi, Appalachian, and Great Lakes regions, with few settled in the west and north, apart from a few Pacific coastal regions including California. Population densities in most of this area were usually less than one person per ten square kilometers.

By contrast, England had about ten people per square kilometer in 1500, which is a population density fully one hundred times higher than most of North America at the time. This is after the Black Death had been ravaging the European populations for a century and a half. The reason for this discrepancy in population densities is the difference in technology levels and capital. As primitive as English agriculture in the year 1500 might seem to us now, the English were still employing a much more efficient food-producing regime than the Appalachian-area Indians. This meant that English farmers could produce hundreds of times more calories per square kilometer. When we combine geography and technology, the predictable result was a far greater population density in much of the Old World than in all but a few parts of the New.

THE DEBATE OVER THE POPULATION OF MEXICO

Of all the New World peoples, only the Aztecs were in the process of developing a pictographic alphabet and writing system when the Europeans arrived. The Incans used a system of knots in strings, which might over time have evolved into written records. Still, no one kept census records that might serve as a guideline for us to estimate how many people lived in certain regions or towns.

This lack of records means that our population figures for pre-Columbian peoples are subject to a lot of guesswork. The principal method we use is to count how many settlements we have archaeological evidence for in a certain region. We then assume that there were many more settlements than we know about and make an educated guess about how many the total might have been. On top of this, we have to guess how many people actually lived in each settlement, in part by estimating how many might have been served by the buildings for which we have archaeological remains. You can easily see how, given this vague methodology of guesses multiplied by other guesses, demographers might end up with figures ten or more times higher than the probable number.

What no one disputes is that the major population centers of the New World were the same areas that housed the great Aztec and Inca civilizations—central Mexico and greater Peru. This can be seen from Map 2.1. It is agreed that central Mexico was home to half the total New World population in 1491. But again, due to a combination of thin evidence and politically motivated scholarship, experts' opinions on the actual Mexican population figure have varied wildly.

The full range of demographic estimates for the Mexican population, however, has been tabulated by Robert McCaa of the University of Minnesota.[28] This shows that by far the most common estimate for the number of Mexicans before Cortes arrived is between five and ten million people.[29] This would put the total population of the Americas at merely ten to twenty million people in 1491—a very reasonable assumption, considering the small amount of fertile, temperate land available, and the types of agriculture that were practiced.

While David E. Stannard and popular writers such as Charles C. Mann wax poetic about the teeming and sophisticated cities of the New World, the fact is only a tiny area was home to such cities; as we will discuss in a later chapter, the urban situation in the New World was analogous to parts of the Old World circa 3000 BC. And only in a very few regions of the rather small Aztec empire and environs were truly intensive farming methods in use.

Unsurprisingly, most online "authorities" ignore such realistic estimates. Instead, the estimate nearly everyone accepts for the Mexican population is the highest estimate that has ever been produced—the estimate put forth by Cook and Borah of the Berkeley School. Cook and Borah estimated that Mexico might have had between eighteen and thirty million people; to get this figure they used estimates and multipliers that most experts simply do not support. But because their estimate makes the Mexican civilization seem that much more magnificent, most writers today accept an average of their "maximalist" estimate—about twenty-five million people—as the true figure. They then double this to get an estimate of the entire New World population. From McCaa's data, we can see that the actual population of Mexico was probably only one-third as high as most people now assume, and the New World population accordingly much smaller.

---

[28] Data from Robert McCaa, "The Peopling of Mexico from Origins to Revolution," pub. online 1997, specifically from his Table 2: Demographic Disaster in Mexico, 1519–1595. To simplify the picture, we only reproduce his figures for "all Mexico." (Other estimates are for the central valley only and are therefore partial.)

[29] Throughout this book, I use the anglicized version of Cortes's name (omitting the accent) because this has long been standard practice when referring to him in English.

The earliest reliable records that we have for the Mexican population begin to appear more than a century after Cortes arrived in 1519. The Indigenous population of Mexico in 1600 was probably about 1.5 to 3 million people. If the population in 1517 had been twenty-five million people, then this makes it look as though the Spanish conquest had killed off 90 percent of the people in Mexico—some twenty-two million victims. If the population of Mexico in 1517 had only been 7.5 million, then, the Indigenous population probably plummeted by some 66 percent, but the total loss was more in the range of 5 million—only one-quarter as many people.

Before we lament these five million "dead" however, we need to understand something about the nature of historical demography: population decline in the aggregate does not equate to a horrible death for individual people. Most people who look at declining population figures in Mexico will assume that a decline from say, seven million people in AD 1500 to two million people in AD 1600 equates to five million Indians who died miserable deaths by disease, starvation, mistreatment, or murder.

Map 2.1. Population Distribution in the New World, 1491.

But long-term population decline in a region does not necessarily indicate anything of the sort. As historical demographers like S. Ryan Johansson point out, all you can say for certain about these estimates is that death rates exceeded birth rates. For example, in Europe between 1348 and 1500, the population of many regions fell by up to 80 percent over one hundred and fifty years. Some of this was because the Black Death became endemic, increasing child mortality. With fewer people reaching child-bearing age, fewer children were produced, creating a downward population spiral. Contrary to popular belief, however, Europeans of this time did not experience life as a relentless cycle of deaths from plague. Even during this time of major demographic decline, many people went their whole lives without witnessing a major outbreak of plague. Demographers studying the fall of Rome have found similar patterns of natural population decline due to cultural and political change, rather than violence.

The same pattern that disrupted post-Roman populations in Europe seems evident in post-Aztec Mexico. In sixteenth-century Mexico, population decline was also due to a combination of social, political, and economic factors. These were summarized by Hanns Prem in 1992.[30] In some regions, the impact of the Spanish incursion completely rearranged Mexican society. Some of this was due to active intervention on the part of the Spanish, but passive effects of new Spanish technology and methods were probably more decisive in the long run. The Spanish banned or transformed the old religious cults and dissolved many Indigenous political alliances. Trade routes, military recruitment patterns, and agricultural techniques were also transformed.

THE NEW WORLD POPULATION TODAY

Our final demographic argument against the claim of genocide is the most straightforward: The Americas today are simply teeming with the descendants of the Indigenous people who were alive in 1491.

According to data found in the Wikipedia article "Ethnic Groups in Latin America," which was compiled by Mexican professor Francisco Lizcano Fernández, Europeans remain a minority in every country that had a dense settlement of Indigenous people in 1491.[31] The pattern in the New World is similar to what happened during the European

---

[30] Hanns J. Prem, "Spanish Colonization and Indian Property in Central Mexico, 1521–1620," *Annals of the Association of American Geographers* 82, no. 3 (1992), 444–459, https://www.jstor.org/stable/2563355.

[31] As reported in Lizcano's "Composición Étnica de las Tres Áreas Culturales del Continente Americano al Comienzo del Siglo XXI" ("Ethnic Composition of the Three Cultural Areas of the American Continent at the Beginning of the 21st Century").

colonization of Africa, the Middle East, and Asia. In all those regions Europeans gained near-total political power for a time, but they continued to remain a small minority of the population. No one bothers to claim that Europeans committed "genocide" in these Old World regions; but in the New World and Australia, they take advantage of low initial population densities in some regions to press unsubstantiated claims of mass slaughter.

The heart of the greater Aztec population nucleus was in Mexico, Guatemala, El Salvador, and Honduras. Today the population in those countries is overwhelmingly mestizo, an attestation of the fact that Indigenous and European people have been intermarrying there for some five centuries.[32] In all these countries, non-mestizo Europeans are equal or fewer in number than non-mestizo Indigenous people. Meanwhile, Bolivia, Peru, and Ecuador were the heart of the greater Incan population nucleus. Just as in the former Aztec lands, today we find that "white" Europeans make up a tiny minority of the population in former Incan territory, at between about 10 and 15 percent. The rest are either mestizo or Amerindian. In all three of these countries about half the population is "pure" Amerindian.

Since these two population nuclei accounted for perhaps 80 percent of all New World people in 1491, the obvious conclusion is that Europeans did not slaughter or displace the great majority of Indigenous people in the New World. Today, geneticists have described the Mexican population as "the most genetically diverse place on Earth." Its population of one hundred twenty million people consists of eighty million mestizos, about twenty million Indigenous people, and about twenty million people of European descent. Likewise, fully sixty-eight native languages continue to survive in Mexico alone.

---

[32] The vast majority of mestizo births in these regions, today and in past centuries, have been to married couples. Some of these births will of course have been out of wedlock, and a small subset of these will have been the result of rape, but to imagine that most of these births were the result of violence is to completely misunderstand the nature of these societies since 1520. Communities were close-knit and male relatives keen for vengeance, meaning that the odds of getting away with violent rape without reprisal were low.

To anyone who cares to see, it could be argued that Mexico—the epicenter of European-Indigenous encounters in the New World—represents one of the most successful experiments in interracial mixing in recent global history. As we will see in subsequent chapters, this had been the case ever since the earliest contact between Spaniards and Indians in the Caribbean. As the historian Ida Altman put it in the *William and Mary Quarterly* in 2013:

> Ethnic complexity quickly came to characterize intimate relations, households, and families in the Caribbean...becoming a hallmark of emerging Spanish-American societies. The material culture of early Caribbean households; the presence of indigenous and then African women [as] wives, or mistresses, and mothers of ethnically and culturally mixed children...and the formation of family and kinship ties among people of differing ethnic or racial origin, all played a key role in shaping the new societies that came into existence after Europeans arrived in the Caribbean. Close connections between Caribbean and Spanish society...integrated [Taino] patterns of family and household...with the family and kin structures and traditions of Spain and the Mediterranean.[33]

This passage, incidentally, highlights just how profound is the ignorance of Latin American history on the part of many anglophone historians. Genocide, it wasn't.

In light of these cold, hard population figures, with tens of millions of mestizos and Amerindians living precisely where their ancestors lived five hundred years ago, where then is the "holocaust" of one hundred

---

[33] Ida Altman, "Marriage, Family, and Ethnicity in the Early Spanish Caribbean," *William & Mary Quarterly* 70, no. 2 (2013), 225–250, https://www.jstor.org/stable/10.5309/willmaryquar.70.2.0225.

million dead claimed by Stannard and others? Up to 75 percent of them never existed at all—they are a figment of the Berkeley School's fevered imaginations. In places such as Hispaniola, the pre-Columbian population is exaggerated by the media and government organizations by several thousand percent.

Of those Indigenous people who did "disappear" after 1491, most did not die a horrible death. Many were simply not born, because cultural upheaval tends to cause lower birth rates. Of those who actually died under adverse conditions introduced by Europeans, even Stannard recognizes that some 90 percent of Indigenous casualties of European intervention were due to neutral causes such as disease, rather than war. Nor as we will see in later chapters is there evidence that Europeans deliberately infected Indian populations with smallpox or other diseases.

It nevertheless remains true that tens of thousands of Indigenous people died of mistreatment and forced labor at the hands of early Spanish adventurers, and thousands more died as a result of battles and massacres relating to warfare and cruelty through the centuries. Far too many people died in horrible conditions. This has been known and acknowledged, for centuries. It should never be lost sight of, and it is absolutely not our purpose to belittle or explain away the many crimes committed by Europeans against the Indigenous people of the New World. But a balanced look at the big picture supports the majority of historians over the past one hundred years, who maintained that claims of "genocide" are inappropriate. Those who insist on using such terms are political agitators, whose work should not be accepted as the basis of historical fact.

CHAPTER 3

WERE EUROPEANS RACIST?

*Racist ideas were nearly two centuries old
when Puritans used them in the 1630s.*

—Ibram X. Kendi, *Stamped from the Beginning*

*White nationalism was inscribed in the
founding of the United States as a European
settler-colonial expansionist entity.*

—Roxanne Dunbar-Ortiz, *Not a Nation of Immigrants*

The opening lines of the *New York Times'* 1619 Project contain a clarion call for progressives to make racism the fulcrum of American history. The stated goal of the project is to place racism "at the very center of the story we tell ourselves about who we are as a country." In response, a veritable army of scholars have set off in search of the racist sinews of American history and of the European culture from which it was forged.

The publication of the "1619 Project" as a special issue of the *New York Times Magazine* came as a windfall to that handful of radical scholars whose aim had always been to paint America as essentially racist and white supremacist. As happened with other pet issues of the radical Left, books and articles on early American and European racism that used to be deemed too extreme for serious consideration have now been thrust front and center in American cultural discourse.

One of the unlikely academic stars of early New World racism studies is the historian Gerald R. Horne, who holds the Moores Professorship of History and African American Studies at the University of Houston. Horne has become a darling of the Left because of his unequivocal, uncompromising readings of American and European history as "stamped from the beginning" with an indelible stain of racism and white supremacy. Horne's 2014 book, *The Counter-Revolution of 1776: Slave Resistance and the Origins of the United States of America*, paints the American Revolution not as a war to establish democracy but as a war to preserve slavery.

Horne's take has been trumpeted by 1619 Project lead author Nikole Hannah-Jones, who wrote that "one of the primary reasons the colonists decided to declare their independence" from Britain "was because they wanted to protect the institution of slavery." This view has been thoroughly debunked by major historians of the American Revolution such as Princeton's Sean Wilentz, who observed, "I instantly wondered how anyone even lightly informed about the history of either slavery or the American Revolution could write that sentence."[34]

In a 2020 follow-up entitled *The Dawning of the Apocalypse: The Roots of Slavery, White Supremacy, Settler Colonialism, and Capitalism in the Long Sixteenth Century*, Horne goes further back in time to the origins of European expansionism in the New World. His opportunism can be gauged from the fact that his title deftly hits every progressive talking point. In this book, Horne places much of the blame for the origins of modern racism on England itself—a trend which we will see repeated in other writers. More specifically, he claims that the origins of modern racism can be found in the rise of England to global prominence, which he places in the sixteenth century. A typically rambling passage from his introduction explains:

---

[34] Sean Wilentz, "The 1619 Project and Living in Truth," *Opera Historica* 22, no. 1 (2021), https://www.opera-historica.com/pdfs/oph/2021/01/05.pdf.

[This is] a book about the seeds of the apocalypse...
which led to slavery, white supremacy, and settler
colonialism...planted in the long sixteenth century,
which eventuated in what is euphemistically termed
"modernity," a process that reached its apogee in
North America. In these pages I seek to explain the
global forces that created this catastrophe—notably
for Africans and the indigenous of the Americas and
how the minor European archipelago on the fringes
of the continent (the British isles) was poised to
come from behind....

Despite his meandering style, Horne is feted by major media outlets
including NPR and can boast dozens of interviews posted to YouTube.
Like many of his fellows, Horne views the past five hundred years as
an unmitigated catastrophe for all nonwhite people. Prominent New
Racialists such as Ibram X. Kendi follow Horne's line, which places the
origins of European racism at some point in the Renaissance between
the Middle Ages and modernity. Kendi's time line puts the origins of
European racism a century earlier than Horne—during the fifteenth century—which is convenient for him because it makes Columbus and the
other early explorers into ready-made vectors for Jim Crow–style racism.

Roxanne Dunbar-Ortiz is another radical scholar who has benefitted
from the runaway vision of Western civilization as racist. We have already
encountered her *Indigenous Peoples' History of the United States*, in which
she portrays US history as a story of uninterrupted racist genocide. In
Not a Nation of Immigrants, her main argument is that the success of US
imperialism was based on the systematic, racist exploitation of nonwhite
people. In Zinnian fashion she encapsulates her major talking points
thusly: "White nationalism was inscribed in the founding of the United
States as a European settler-colonial expansionist entity, the economy of
which was grounded in the violent theft of land and in racial slavery, and
with settlers armed to the teeth throughout its history."

In her eyes, Europeans were already violently racist when they came to the New World; their wealth was built on a nakedly racist and oppressive program of stealing land from brown people and enslaving nonwhites, and the United States is inevitably bad because of this early history.

Not to be outdone, a cadre of scholars who study ancient and medieval Europe have also pored over their obscure texts in search of proof that Europeans have been exceptionally prone to racism since the beginning. Prominent among these has been a pair of literary scholars, Geraldine Heng and Cord J. Whitaker, both of whom have been rewarded with prominent academic positions.

Heng is now Mildred Hajek Vacek and John Roman Vacek Professor of English and Comparative Literature with a joint appointment in Middle Eastern studies and an affiliate of women's studies at the University of Texas at Austin. Her book *The Invention of Race in the European Middle Ages* won a bevy of awards including the Association of American Publishers PROSE prize for world history. Whitaker, for his part, is associate professor of English literature at Wellesley College; his major book on the topic is *Black Metaphors: How Racism Emerged from Medieval Race-Thinking* (2019).

Notice that neither of these scholars is a historian: they are literature majors whose formal training in history was presumably limited to discussions of how to read Geoffrey Chaucer through the lens of critical theory. Despite these questionable qualifications, both authors have become scholarly stars in America. Their books have won awards intended for historians and have become standard reference points for scholars from multiple disciplines, who cite their often obscure textual inferences as "proof" that medieval Europeans were—if not fully racist—then at least comfortably proto-racist.

WHAT HISTORIANS USED TO THINK

The image of Western civilization painted by the new racialism is grim indeed. But how much of this picture gels with historical reality? Let us begin by looking at a time line of European racism.

But first we need a working definition of what racism means. This can be simple or enormously complicated, depending on one's goals, so we'll choose a middle ground.

The simplest definition is that racism is a belief system in which one group of people is felt to be inherently inferior by nature. (We will leave aside the fact that aristocrats throughout history have believed themselves biologically superior to nonaristocrats, without any reference to race.) Modern racialists have expanded upon this simple definition to encapsulate as much thought, behavior, and culture as possible, which is why it seems that everyone and everything, including the US Constitution, is now decried as racist by someone or another. According to modern critical race theory, institutions that were set up by a particular racial group, and which historically have been used to oppress other people on the basis of race, can be considered "racist" until such time as those institutions are radically overhauled. Thus the United States government is held by many to be racist because it was constructed by white people and has been used as an instrument of oppression for Indigenous and black people at various times in the past.

While this is a broad definition indeed, it is still based on the idea that the people who set up institutions are thinking in essentialist categories—i.e., they not only believe that races are distinct, but that some are inherently inferior to others or should be subjugated on that basis.

It is also useful to look at what serious historians were saying about the long-term history of European racism before the rise of BLM in the 2010s. Before that time, mainstream historians treated the long-term history of race and racism as a fringe topic of interest only to radicals who wished to stir up trouble. The obvious reason for this is that modern conceptions of race only emerged in the later nineteenth century, and most historians knew that the further back you went in time, the less meaningful the modern terms "race" and "racism" actually become.

Like everyone else, I have been so bombarded with the notion that race is fundamental to human history that I was shocked to open a number of articles from the early 2000s to find authors who openly wondered whether studying the history of "race" is a worthwhile pursuit for a serious scholar. One reason they cite is that society had made so much progress in race relations up to about 2010 that the issue was considered passé. It is worth recalling that in the 2000s, mainstream ideas about race in American society were centered on "colorblindness." This was Martin Luther King's mantra that in the future, racial prejudices would simply fade into the background.

It seems almost impossible to imagine that as late as 2011, a young scholar at the University of Toronto could begin a scholarly book review with the question: "Is it still important to study the history of racism?"[35] Today, such a question would never be publicly raised; and if it was, the author's career would be canceled before they could pack up their desk. In 2005 another scholar, Fergus Millar, publicly dismissed a book purporting to find racism in ancient Greece as follows:

> Is racism, as opposed to other ills such as economic imperialism or religious fanaticism, really the most urgent moral and social issue in the contemporary world? However profound inter-group prejudices may be, and however liable to lead to ethnic conflicts, the overall movement of the last half-century has been in the direction of the removal of racial barriers to citizenship, civil rights, voting rights, educational opportunity, and social acceptance. Think only of Germany, South Africa, Australia, and the southern

---

[35] Sciltian Gastaldi, "The Origins of Racism in the West," *Renaissance and Reformation/Renaissance et Réforme* 34, no. 4 (2011), 138–141, https://www.academia.edu/51260482/The_origins_of_racism_in_the_West.

states of the United States. In the United States, whatever the social barriers to effective equality, citizens of African, Native American, Mexican, Chinese, and Japanese origins can rise to high positions in public or private life. How many states are there now in the world where biological origin, or race, constitute a legal barrier to citizenship, civil rights, and public office?[36]

This opinion, that tracing the history of racism was unnecessary in the modern world, and next to meaningless in the distant past, was also expounded by some of the most famous medievalists of the later twentieth century. In a 2001 issue of the *Journal of Medieval and Early Modern Studies*, Thomas Hahn asked some prominent scholars to weigh in on the issue of race and racism in medieval and early modern Europe. One of those, the eminent African American Princeton medievalist William Chester Jordan, responded with an article titled, "Why 'Race'?"

What is the purpose of giving the name race to a set of descriptors (language, law, customs, and lineage) that medieval writers attributed to contemporary social groups? What payoff is there in regarding medieval attitudes towards people of different "races" as "racist"?[37]

What indeed, unless one is hell-bent on discrediting Western civilization in the broadest terms possible? Professor Jordan has many choice words for academic opportunists who seek to advance their careers by appearing to be "with it" and "cutting edge" rather than building a reputation through genuine scholarship. He dismisses authors who purport to find racism in medieval and early modern sources as "presentists"—

---

[36] Fergus Millar, "Review Article: The Invention of Racism in Antiquity," *The International History Review* 27, no. 1 (2005), 85–89.

[37] William C. Jordan, "Why 'Race'?" *Journal of Medieval and Early Modern Studies* 31, no. 1 (2001), 165–173, https://muse.jhu.edu/article/16480/summary.

fake historians who make the amateur mistake of viewing and judging the past through the lens of the present. This charge of presentism, by the way, is the same one that AHA President James Sweet made against the 1619 Project authors in the summer of 2022.

More than twenty years ago, with a crisp air of contempt, Jordan dismissed such historians as "silly" and "performing" a game that was less about scholarship than "name dropping, convoluted sentences, cute turns of phrase, meditations on words used in deliberately strange ways." But even decades ago, Jordan saw which way the wind was blowing, and that it bode no good. He concluded that the people who wanted to see the European past as indelibly racist had already won, concluding: "If [historians] say medieval people were racists, then ordinary readers and people they talk to will conclude that the pedigree leads right to apartheid or antebellum slavery, and some of them will even find comfort in their own prejudices about…white Euro-Americans in general, saying 'They've always been racists.'" As Jordan predicted, this is precisely what has led to the crowning of Heng, Whitaker, and similar opportunists.

EUROPEAN RACISM AGAINST BLACKS AND INDIANS

The scholarly consensus still holds that Europeans were in fact *not* racist in the modern sense of believing some races to be distinct or essentially inferior, until the later nineteenth century. This makes good sense: before Charles Darwin published his work on evolution in 1859, it was not really possible to conceive of humans as having evolved in distinct genetic lines in the way we now take for granted. It was left to the Nazis to take this genetic-racist idea to its extreme, with their fantasy of dominating every other "inferior" race.

Fortunately, Western science continued to evolve past this point. By the 1960s, the earlier models of race that had motivated the Nazis were significantly outdated. For example, almost everything that led the Nazis to consider themselves "Aryan" or "Caucasian" was proven to be a late nineteenth-century fantasy. The history of racism in Europe is therefore surprisingly modern, and scientific racism, at least, was surprisingly short-lived.

If early modern Europeans were not technically "racist" in a Social Darwinist way, then other scholars have been keen to trace a European sense of "whiteness" some centuries earlier than Darwin. This slowly evolving sense of being lighter skinned resulted from increasing encounters with non-Caucasian peoples across the globe. Sometimes, but not always, the rise of "whiteness" is associated with a justification for the enslavement of Africans.

Even in the case of "whiteness," Europeans did not develop a clear sense of what this might mean until relatively late. Some authors claim that this occurred during the seventeenth century, while others maintain that this did not enter into common European discourse until the later eighteenth century. According to David Olusoga, writing in the *Guardian* in 2015, the roots of European racism against Africans can be "traced to those justifying slavery in the eighteenth century."[38] David R. Roediger, writing for the Smithsonian National Museum of African American History and Culture, repeats the consensus that Europeans did not really think of themselves as "white" until a few people started using the term in the seventeenth century, but the idea did not really catch on until the eighteenth century.[39]

The *Encyclopedia Britannica* likewise argues that the "myth of black inferiority" did not really take hold in Europe until the very end of the eighteenth century, particularly with the Haitian Revolution of 1791.[40] (The *Britannica* article does not remark on how much support the Haitians received from people across Europe and the Americas, includ-

[38] David Olusoga, "The Roots of European Racism Lie in the Slave Trade, Colonialism—and Edward Long," *Guardian*, September 8, 2015, https://www.theguardian.com/commentisfree/2015/sep/08/european-racism-africa-slavery.
[39] David R. Roediger, "Historical Foundations of Race," Smithsonian National Museum of African American History and Culture, https://nmaahc.si.edu/learn/talking-about-race/topics/historical-foundations-race.
[40] "Race: Human," *Encyclopedia Britannica*, https://www.britannica.com/topic/race-human/Building-the-myth-of-Black-inferiority.

ing US President John Adams, who gave them economic aid, weapons, and occasional help from the US Navy.)

Much of what many people now categorize as early "racism" was relatively innocent, insofar as it was an inevitable consequence of an emerging scientific view of the world. As modern science began to take off in the eighteenth century, a big part of the process was observation and categorization. Though it seems simplistic to us now, such categorization served the essential function of assembling vast datasets from which modern scientific theories could later spring. It is from this period that the great collections of seashells, insects, birds, rocks, and the like began to appear in the houses of wealthy Europeans. The mania for collecting stemmed from people's desire for completism—a desire to have an exemplar of every rock, every insect, and so forth, with the idea that this would help humanity to gain a complete picture of the world around us. This is the essence of a scientific mindset.

As Europeans were developing this obsession with collecting and categorizing everything under the sun, they were also attempting to categorize different groups of humans. It was from the late eighteenth and early nineteenth centuries that they began to sort humanity into "black," "red," "yellow," and "white" races, for example. Later on, anatomists noticed that some groups have consistently distinct skull shapes and facial features. When combined with nineteenth-century aesthetic and psychological theories, this led to the pseudoscience of physiognomy—the idea that you can judge a person's character from the way they look. While there might be just enough in human nature to serve as a springboard for this pseudoscience (casting agents for movies rely on these types of judgments all the time) the ridiculous excesses and moral pronouncements the Victorians made on this score now strike us as eminently cringeworthy.

Where does that lead us in terms of European prejudice against the Indians they found in the Americas? The historian Alden T. Vaughan summed up the longstanding consensus on European prejudice toward

Indians in a 1982 *American Historical Review* article with the following words:

> Not until the middle of the eighteenth century did most Anglo-Americans view Indians as significantly different in color from themselves, and not until the nineteenth century did red become the universally accepted color label for American Indians. To read later perceptions of Indian pigmentation into the first centuries of racial contact is fallacious, because, in general, it distorts the nature of early ethnic relations and, in particular, it obscures the evolution of Anglo-American attitudes toward the Indians.
>
> Anglo-Americans believed that American Indians were approximately as light-skinned as Europeans— with all its implications—and thus would be assimilated into colonial society as soon as they succumbed to English social norms and protestant theology.

Vaughan's statement lays out quite nicely what scholars have always known, namely that Europeans did not think of the Indians as biologically different from themselves, until more than 250 years after Columbus landed. If they thought of Indians as biologically inferior, this happened much later; it was widespread for only a short period, and we will see how even then such beliefs were far from universal.

SKIN COLOR AS A FUNCTION OF LATITUDE

If early European explorers and settlers did not believe that Amerindians were of a different race, what did their science and philosophy tell them? Most people looked first and foremost to their religion. Christianity is difficult to force into the category of "racist" philosophies, because Christian theologians taught that all mankind was a single human family descended from Adam and Eve. There was a longstanding tradition in Christian iconography that the Three Magi represented the three known continents of Asia, Africa, and Europe—they were accordingly represented in late medieval Europe with appropriate features and skin color. It was believed, however, that it was the mission of the church to unite all these people as one holy family in Christ, ideally with as much gentleness and persuasion as possible. The Cathedral of St. Barbara at Kutná Hora in the Czech Republic, for example, contains a mural in which all the people of the Earth are represented peacefully hearing and accepting the Gospel as one global people, including Natives of the Americas. It was this global vision of redeemed humanity that motivated Queen Isabella to welcome the Amerindians as subjects of the Crown of Castile, something the French kings were also to do with the Amerindians of Quebec.

The science of the day also said next to nothing about different "races" of people based on skin color. A tradition dating back to ancient times held that humans were essentially the same all over the globe, but that the closer they got to the sun (i.e., to the equator), the darker their skin became. It was believed that if light-skinned people spent enough time in the south, they too would become dark. It should come as no surprise that late medieval people, who classified both bats and bumble-bees as birds, were not attuned to any fine points of racial difference. The contrast with their far more scientific nineteenth-century descendants is tremendous.

The prevalence of geography and latitude rather than "race" or innate characteristics in early explorers' thinking is what led Columbus to conclude that the Indians he found in the Caribbean were about the same color as the Canary Islanders but not as dark as the sub-Saharan Africans.[41] Columbus reasoned that if he traveled farther south in the Americas, he would find darker-skinned people. His contemporaries

---

[41] Columbus, *Diario* entry for Saturday October 13, 1492.

also believed that as they traveled farther North in North America, they would find lighter-skinned Indians.

Based on the strength of this anti-racist prejudice, Europeans well into the seventeenth century believed that North American Indians were essentially the same color as themselves. They believed that the skin color of the Old and New World people was differentiated by latitude rather than by continent. Dozens of sources relate to us their belief that North Americans were "born white" as babies but only became darker due to exposure to the sun and the thick ointments spread over them by their parents. Evidence for this attitude is widespread as we shall see.

Writing in 2017, the scholar Joan-Pau Rubiés summed up these Christian and proto-scientific strains in European thinking on race in the following way:

> In early modern Europe and up to the mid-eighteenth century, cultural diversity was usually explained with reference to climate, religion and national genealogy, without any serious equivalent to the racist ideologies that arose to prominence throughout the late eighteenth and nineteenth centuries. While there were some examples of religious persecutions, discriminatory colonial polices and philosophical attempts to classify the peoples of the world which involved some racialist principles... [this was done] within the framework of a monogenist understanding of the history of humankind.

The term "monogenist" refers to the Christian teaching that humans were descended from common ancestors and would one day be united again under the church. It took several centuries for these prejudices against racism to be overcome to the extent that the more egregious nineteenth-century racial theorists managed to do.

RACISM AND SLAVERY

What about slavery? Influential writers such as Ibram X. Kendi suggest that the only evidence they need to prove early European racism against Africans and others is a European willingness to enslave these people. In Kendi's telling, Prince Henry of Portugal was a dyed-in-the-wool racist who made a 1444 auction of two hundred and forty African captives "into a spectacle to show the Portuguese had joined the European league of serious slave-traders of African people." Kendi further asserts that a chronicler of the time, Gomes Eanes de Zurara, wrote "the inaugural defense of African slave-trading, the first European book on Africans in the modern era," and the beginning of "the recorded history of anti-Black racist ideas."[42] (Kendi would seem to be ignorant of several centuries of Islamic anti-Africanism antedating Zurara, which we will touch upon below.)

Zurara's book has made the rounds in CRT circles because a few passages repeat stereotypes that became prevalent at a later date. This does not mean that it was typical for its time. Zurara does repeat the medieval belief that Africans were descended from Cain and therefore doomed to a life of subjugation to other people, a belief that was later used to justify slavery in the antebellum South.[43] However, context matters: Zurara notes with some dismay that his own Moorish captive offered to ransom himself with "five or six black Moors." Zurara was perplexed because he could not understand how a (lighter-skinned) Moorish noble would be willing to enslave fellow Moors (Muslims) just because they were black. He concludes by musing that the North African Moors must have been allowed by God to enslave black Africans because of the curse of Cain. Zurara does not necessarily approve of this behavior; he is simply trying to find an historical explanation for why black people seem always to have been enslaved by the lighter-skinned North Africans (and now by Europeans).

---

[42] Ibram X. Kendi, *Stamped from the Beginning* (New York: Bold Type Books, 2016), 23.
[43] Gomes Eanes de Zurara, *Chronicle of Discovery and Conquest of Guinea*, ch. 16.

Zurara's account also contains an instance of colorism, where he claims that those who were whiter were more fair and those who were darker were uglier.[44] However, he claims that no matter how ugly some of them might have been, that no heart "could be so hard as not to be pierced with piteous feeling to see that company" of slaves. Apart from his indictment of Zurara, whose "racism" is questionable, Kendi's narrative provides very little evidence of actual racism against Africans by the Portuguese. What it does do is provide a potted summary of how the Portuguese began to trade in African slaves from the 1440s, as though this was sufficient proof of racism. But this perspective is oblivious to the fact that Europeans before Columbus's day did not equate slavery with race—at all.

The further back you go into European history, the more the seemingly self-evident bond between slavery and racism dissolves into nothingness. Medieval Europeans thought of slavery in terms of religion not race. Christians made it legally permissible to enslave Muslims (though not Jews as a rule), and Muslims certainly made it permissible to enslave Christians. In many parts of the Mediterranean, both Christians and Muslims came from the same ethnic stock. This equating of enslaveability with religion caused many practical problems for slave owners, because (as we have seen in Portugal) the religious conversion of a slave put enormous social pressure on owners to free their slaves, at least by the second generation.

Even more embarrassingly for CRT scholars, there is abundant evidence that medieval and early modern Arabs were more racist toward Africans than Europeans were and from a much earlier date. William Chester Jordan provides the following examples:

> Consider the Muslim case. Avicenna (Ibn Sina) at the turn of the millennium wrote, "Those who are far removed from acquiring virtues are slaves by nature like the Turks and [N]egroes and in

---

[44] Zurara, ch. 25.

general people living in an unfavorable climate."
Or consider Ibn Khaldun, who would opine in the
fourteenth century, "The only people who accept
slavery are the Negroes, owing to their low degree of
humanity and their proximity to the animal stage."

The Arab world was importing slaves from Africa long before the
Europeans, and we know that medieval Arab merchants charged far less
for African than Caucasian slaves because they valued them less. Arabic
commentators regularly pronounced Africans to be stupid, lazy, ugly,
sexually predatory, and many other negative things besides. The *Arabian
Nights*, one of the most widely copied manuscripts in the late medieval
Islamic world, begins with a notorious description of a black slave as a
"big slobbering Negro with rolling eyes…a truly hideous sight" who goes
on to pleasure the debauched fair-skinned queen. As the critic Robert
Irwin put it:

> The sexual threat posed by black men, as well as
> the disparagement of their looks and intelligence,
> features in a significant number of the stories of
> the Arabian Nights, including 'King 'Umar ibn
> al-Nu'man and his family', 'Judar and his brothers',
> 'Gharib and Ajib' and 'Sayf al-Muluk'. These ugly
> passions can be found elsewhere in medieval Arabic
> popular literature. *Tales of the Marvellous and News
> of the Strange* is a rival story collection to the Nights,
> though much less well known. It includes 'The Story
> of Ashraf and Anjab and the Marvellous Things
> That Happened to Them', a sustained fictional
> exercise in racial abuse. The sadistic and villainous
> Anjab is described to Harun al-Rashid as follows:
> 'This man is black as a negro…with red eyes, a nose
> like a clay pot and lips like kidneys' and his mother

is no better looking for she 'was black as pitch with a snub nose, red eyes and an unpleasant smell.'[45]

It would take centuries before any Europeans would attain this level of eloquent prejudice against Africans. Indeed, there is plenty of evidence that the Europeans of Columbus's day were on the whole favorably inclined toward Africans. The patron saints of some European guilds were black Africans, certain black Madonnas were widely respected, the Magus Balthazar was regarded as a saint, and so forth.

The legend of Prester John was one of the most common depictions of Africans in medieval Europe. According to this legend, Prester John was a wealthy African-Christian king who lived on the other side of Egypt. This was a garbled conflation of the historical Christian kingdom of Ethiopia and the gold-strewing journeys of other African kings like Mansa Musa. European explorers hoped that they might contact this wealthy, powerful African Christian king, thereby gaining a valuable ally in their centuries-long struggle against Islam. They were pleasantly surprised when in the early fifteenth century, ambassadors sent by Ethiopian Emperor Dawit and his successors began to appear in Europe. Ethiopian delegations were repeatedly entertained by the pope and other European officials as honored guests and potential allies against Islam. The sources repeatedly praised Ethiopian learning and decorum, with little or no mention of "race." At one stage, the king of Aragon seriously considered a dynastic marriage between his children and the royal house of Ethiopia, which was thwarted mostly by the difficulty of passing through hostile Mamluk Egypt.[46] The lack of anti-African prejudice is palpable, and Kendi would have a difficult time explaining it.

---

[45] Robert Irwin, "The Dark Side of 'The Arabian Nights,'" *Critical Muslim* 13, no.1, https://www.criticalmuslim.io/the-dark-side-of-the-arabian-nights/.

[46] The remarkable story of Ethiopian contacts with late medieval Europe (together with evidence that religious solidarity rather than racial difference was the main factor in most people's inter-cultural calculations) is told in Verena Krebs, *Medieval Ethiopian Kingship, Craft, and Diplomacy with Latin Europe* (London, UK: Palgrave Macmillan, 2021).

As Europeans reached the preexisting slave markets of Asia, Africa, and the New World, one of the main questions that confronted them was which categories of their fellow humans could be legally bought and sold. The old answer, "Muslims and Pagans," was clearly no longer sufficient, given the bewildering variety of people they were now encountering.

As a result, the Spanish authorities began to rule that certain groups of people were enslaveable based not on their religion or race but on their customs. This is why they pronounced that the cannibalistic Carib Indians were legally enslaveable, while the great bulk of the Indigenous population of the New World—including the Tainos and Mexica Indians—were not. By practicing cannibalism, the Caribs were held to have broken a law of humanity so sacrosanct that they forfeited their natural right to freedom because of it. Even so, the number of Caribs actually sold into slavery during the sixteenth century probably did not exceed the low thousands.

From Columbus's time until the present day, Europeans usually stuck to this view that New World Indians should not be enslaved. This fundamental fact gives the lie to anyone who wishes to create a master narrative of European racism against all "People of Color." True, some Indians were taken as slaves in the very early period, but by the end of the seventeenth century the Spanish, Portuguese, French, Dutch, and English had all agreed that while Africans were enslaveable, American Indians were not.

A number of factors influenced this attitude against enslavement of Indians. The most important creator of precedent was Queen Isabella herself. Her pronouncement against enslavement of the Indians was reiterated by her Spanish successors including Charles V and Philip II. The second factor was a practical one—it was discovered that, perhaps because of their susceptibility to Old World diseases, Native Americans tended to waste away and die at a much higher rate than Africans when subjected to confinement and forced labor.

The racial hierarchy of slavery in nineteenth-century America placed Indians on a distinctly higher rung than African Americans, and, indeed, Indian racism against African-Americans is well attested. American Indians traditionally held slaves from rival tribes; thus, they thought nothing of purchasing and keeping Africans as slaves. When the Chickasaw Indians were forcibly driven toward Oklahoma, their black slaves numbered more than 20 percent of the Indian population. The Cherokee held African slaves equal to 10 percent of their total population.

EUROPEAN PRAISE FOR AMERINDIANS

Further complicating Kendi's ahistorical picture of Europeans as "anti-dark skinned" is the fact that from the earliest period of European exploration, there are no shortage of sources that describe American Indians in glowing terms. One of the first Spaniards to meet the Taino people described a Taino feast as follows:

> Out came...King Behecchio and the Queen, his sister Anacaona, singing their songs and dancing their dances, which they called *areytos*, things that were very pleasant and agreeable to see, especially when their numbers were great. Out came thirty women, who were kept as wives of King Behecchio, all completely naked, only covering their private parts with half-skirts of cotton, white and very elaborate in their style of weaving, which they call *naguas*, which cover from the belt to the middle of the leg. They were carrying green branches in their hands, singing and dancing and jumping with moderation, as is suitable for women, and showing great peace, delight, happiness, and the spirit of a party.[47]

---

[47] As dictated to Peter Martyr and quoted in Samuel M. Wilson, *Hispaniola: Caribbean Chiefdoms in the Age of Columbus* (Tuscaloosa: University of Alabama Press, 1990).

Elsewhere he says:

> As for the young girls, they covered no part of their bodies, but wore their hair loose upon their shoulders and a narrow ribbon tied around the forehead. Their face, breasts, hands, and the entire body was quite naked, and of a somewhat brunette tint. All were beautiful, so that one might think he beheld those splendid naiads or nymphs of the fountains, so much celebrated by the ancients.

Much later in the colonial period, English travelers throughout the colonies frequently remarked on the beauty of Native women, describing them as "sylvan nymphs," "enticing dryads," and other expressions of extreme beauty. They also appreciated the fact that many young Indian women proved willing to cavort with Englishmen. As one author put it:

> Although, as we will see, sexual interest in native women sometimes took the form of violent assault, it would be wrong to assume that the English advances were always unwelcome or that the advances always came from the English. Eighteenth-century observers noted with prurient fascination that young women in many Indian tribes were free to experiment sexually prior to marriage and eager to do so with white as well as native men.[48]

So much for the worship of "whiteness" as the epitome of beauty and grace. For those who argue that any instance of admiration is "fetishizing the black body," I would turn around and say: Can Europeans do anything right? If they call Amerindians ugly, they are criticized, and the same holds true if they do the opposite. And how can it be fetishiz-

---

[48] Richard Godbeer, "Eroticizing the Middle Ground: Anglo-Indian Sexual Relations along the Eighteenth-Century Frontier," in Martha Hodes, ed., *Sex, Love, Race: Crossing Boundaries in North American History* (New York: NYU Press, 1999), 91–111.

ing if they often hold Amerindians to the same ideals that they use for Europeans? Indeed, most early European portraiture of Indians is keen to show them looking more or less like classical Greek gods, as can be seen from the 1577 engraving of a Brazilian Indian and her husband in Figure 3.1.

Figure 3.1. A Brazilian Indian and her Husband.

Meanwhile, before the modern mania for finding negative racial attitudes took hold, a master's student at William and Mary looked into French attitudes toward the Quebec Indians and observed in eloquent prose:

> Not only did the French believe the natives to be fundamentally like themselves, they also found them

to be very attractive people. Many of the Jesuits wrote with admiration about the natives' physical appearance, stressing their robust health, attractive bodies, and youthful appearance. "They are of lighter build than we are; but handsome and well-shaped," commented Father Pierre Biard, superior to the Huron missions, in 1616. "You do not encounter a big-bellied, hunchbacked, or deformed person among them." Father Perrault agreed. He wrote in 1634 that "there is nothing anomalous in their physical appearance; you see well-formed men, good-looking, of fine figures, strong and powerful." And in 1653, Father Francesco Bressani wrote:

"They are not very dark, especially in their youth; they are strong, tall in stature, and well-proportioned: more healthy than we,—not even knowing the name of many diseases common in Europe.... They are not found either hunchbacked or dwarfed, or very corpulent, or with goiters, etc." [49]

French observers also found time to praise Indian mental characteristics and characters in the highest possible terms. To the Jesuits, the Indians seemed every bit as intelligent as Europeans. The missionaries found the Indians to be intelligent, neighborly, and stalwart people. And although they exhibited vices, these were ascribed to their lack of Christianity and civility, not their inherent character. Again Jones:

The Jesuit Father Biard noted in 1612 that the Indians "love justice and hate violence and robbery, a thing really remarkable in men who have neither

---

[49] The following is taken from the MA thesis of Jennifer A. Jones, 1994. The citation of a master's thesis is deliberate: this shows that both history students and their faculty supervisors were able to look much more dispassionately at questions of European racism in the 1990s than they are today.

laws nor magistrates." Father Perrault commented wryly that "as to their intelligence, if we may judge from their conduct and from their way of dealing with the French, they are not at a great disadvantage." Father de Peron agreed with Perrault's assessment of the Indians' intelligence. "They nearly all show more intelligence in their business, speeches, courtesies, intercourse, tricks, and subtleties, than do the shrewdest citizens and merchants in France," he observed. Many Jesuits noted approvingly that the Indians possessed a grave manner and natural modesty. Indeed, Perrault argued that the only thing "they do lack is the knowledge of God."

As for the later English colonists, we can cite the testimony of Daniel Pastorius, the founder of Germantown, Pennsylvania, who in 1700 wrote the following about the local Indians:

> The natives, the so-called savages…are, in general, strong, agile, and supple people, with blackish bodies. They went about naked at first and wore only a cloth about the loins. Now they are beginning to wear shirts. They have, usually, coal black hair, shave the head, smear the same with grease, and allow a long lock to grow on the right side. They also besmear the children with grease and let them creep about in the heat of the sun, so that they become the color of a nut, although they were at first white enough by Nature.[50]

---

[50] Pastorius's letter can be found at "Francis Daniel Pastorius Recalls the Founding of Germantown, 1685," ExplorePAhistory.com, https://explorepahistory.com/odocument.php?docId=1-4-2C6.

We may conclude with the remarks of the British colonist William Byrd, who wrote in his *Histories* in Virginia in the 1720s:

> All nations of men have the same natural dignity, and we all know that very bright talents may be lodged under a very dark skin. The principal difference between one people and another proceeds only from the different opportunities of improvement.[51]

CULTURE VS. RACE

William Byrd's comments make clear a final distinction that almost every modern commentator on race fails to notice, namely that someone can pass negative judgment on a culture without judging it in racial terms. We used to use words such as prejudice, bias, chauvinism, ethnocentrism, and many other things to describe these types of judgment. Rolling them all into "racism" obscures these important distinctions and diminishes our understanding of human behavior.

For example, David E. Stannard, in the introduction to *American Holocaust*, repeatedly denounces his fellow historians as "racist" when what he really means is that they were "culturist." Byrd was perfectly correct in stating that English colonists in the eighteenth century inherited a more advanced culture than the Virginia Indians. For example, the Europeans possessed advanced metallurgical knowledge, which had been circulating around the Old World for thousands of years. But there is a vast difference between a racist person and a realistic progressive like William Byrd. Just like Zurara's fifteenth-century Portuguese, Byrd was willing to believe that Indian youths would prove to be just as clever and capable of discipline and hard work as any English school child if they were only given the right opportunities. Ergo he was not racist. The same observation should be made about European attitudes toward

---

[51] Byrd is quoted in Godbeer, cited above.

Indian civilization. These were not fixed but continually evolving, and they varied from one person, and one country, to the next. Attitudes changed over time and only hardened into chauvinism as European societies stumbled into the modern era.

A BALANCED ASSESSMENT

Serious historians have always been aware that Europeans did not link slavery with race until centuries after they discovered the New World. Unlike contemporary Islamic society, early European explorers did not consistently associate Africans, Native Americans, or dark skin with negative traits. Colorism was apparently less prevalent in sixteenth-century Europe than in the Islamic world, or South Asia, or East Asia, where its long-term presence antedates European arrival and is incontestable. If Europeans believed that Native Americans were "born white," or "white by nature," this had less to do with their sense of superiority than with their scientific understanding that color was a product of latitude.

Even after European attitudes toward Africans took a negative turn under the influence of transatlantic slavery, their attitudes toward Amerindians as a "race" remained much more favorable and more fluid. Thousands of sympathetic descriptions attest to a spectrum of generous, charitable, humane, hopeful, optimistic, fraternal, universalist, and generally un-racist European attitudes toward Amerindians. Europeans were ready to compare them to classical dryads and naiads, or write approvingly of their physical and mental traits.

As we will see, over the centuries hundreds of commentators, preachers, and educators would reiterate the point that the only thing that made Amerindians different from Europeans was their cultural disadvantages. Oft-repeated statements to the effect that "the only good Indian is a dead Indian" generally stem from much later in history, often from brief, specific periods arising in the context of warfare and revenge.

We have also seen, conclusively, how the majority of serious historians believed until quite recently that chasing European "racism" prior to the eighteenth century was a fool's errand, favored only by opportunistic pseudo-scholars. In light of this overwhelming consensus, we can see that it is actually modern race baiters like Dunbar-Ortiz, Kendi, Horne, and Heng who are cherry-picking evidence. In their efforts to find the holy grail of systemic racism, they willingly conflate cultural chauvinism with racism, while deliberately sowing division and anger by portraying Europeans as racist monsters out of all proportion to their genuine sins.

CHAPTER 4

WERE THE CONQUISTADORS BLOODTHIRSTY ZEALOTS?

The Spanish conquistadors would dig large pits and fill them with sharp stakes. Then "pregnant and confined women, children, old men, as many as they could capture," were thrown into the pits, and left there—often impaled on the stakes—until the pits were filled and everyone had perished.

—Bartolomé de las Casas, quoted in
David Stannard, *American Holocaust*

The first Spanish explorers set foot in the future United States more than five hundred years ago and explored surprisingly large areas in a short amount of time. Florida was first explored by Juan Ponce de Leon in the 1510s. The Lower Mississippi was explored by Hernando de Soto in the 1530s and '40s. And the southwest was originally explored at about the same time by men such as Francisco de Coronado and Juan de Oñate. Finding no gold, cash crops, or large cities, they left most of this area untouched for several centuries afterwards.

Because these events constituted the first recorded historical activity in many US states, many Spanish explorers have been memorialized by state and local authorities across the US with statues, school names, and other honors. This could be seen as a nod to the (multiracial) Hispanic community in the United States and a recognition of their long history in the New World. Nonetheless, in recent years these memorials have come under increasingly heavy fire by a handful of Indigenous activists and their academic supporters. A spate of newspaper and magazine articles has also helped drum up public resentment against these early Spanish explorers and settlers. The accusations are drearily familiar.

On Twitter, Facebook, and other online platforms, descriptions of the most gruesome events from the entire conquest period—many of them popularized by Stannard's *American Holocaust*—get posted and go viral. With little or no understanding of the real scope of what they describe, activists angrily accuse Spaniards of impaling thousands of pregnant women and burning people at the stake, until one is left with the impression that this was the primary occupation of every Spaniard who set foot in the New World.

Spanish colonizers are portrayed in the national media as agents of "violence, theft, the erasing of Indigenous culture and forcible religious conversion." In 2020, *USA Today* published an interview with an Indigenous rights activist named Elena Ortiz who repeated the usual charges of genocide, white supremacy, and colonialist systems of systemic brutality which continue to this day.

> It is an act of violence to even have [statues of conquistadors] in our homelands...they represent the celebration of our genocide. [The conquistadors] brought with them not only...weapons of mass destruction, but also the imposition of the Catholic Church and the imposition of a patriarchal government on peaceful matrilineal societies. Those

colonially imposed systems exist to this day, and have impacted generations.

Ortiz writes as though her opinions represent the views of the majority of modern Americans with Indigenous ancestry. What *USA Today* neglects to mention is that Ortiz is chairperson of a local chapter of The Red Nation, which advertises its blog as a way to look at the world "through the lens of indigenous Marxism." Once again, we scratch the surface only to find fringe ideas being trumpeted as though they were mainstream and amplified by major media.

Around the same time that *USA Today* was giving Ortiz's Marxist radicalism a wide audience, NPR published an interview with Louie Dean Valencia-García, a historian who described himself as a senior fellow at the Centre for the Analysis of the Radical Right. In his interview, Valencia-García said that putting up a statue of a conquistador in an American city is analogous to putting up a statue of Satan or Judas in a church. (In fact, thousands of churches across the West do sport images of devils, demons, and sinners such as Judas, but Valencia-García has apparently never realized this.) Valencia-García has published a book called *Far-Right Revisionism and the End of History*, in which he claims, as editor, that anyone who speaks against his Far Left agenda is probably an apologist for the Far Right.

In 2000, a historian at University of San Diego by the name of Iris Engstrand published an article titled "How Cruel Were the Spaniards?," which was intended as a light pushback against some of the anti-Spanish sentiments that were increasing as postcolonial history took root during the 1990s.[52] The article points out a number of obvious and reasonable truths, such as that the conquistadors were people of their time who have been victims of stereotyping.

Such a balanced and insightful article would never be published today. Recent scholarly articles on conquistadors instead have titles like

---

[52] Iris H. W. Engstrand, "How Cruel Were the Spaniards?" *OAH Magazine of History* 14, no. 4 (2000), 12–15, https://www.jstor.org/stable/25163377.

"Fierce and Unnatural Cruelty," which play to stereotypes rather than engaging them in a critical manner.[53]

Defending the conquistadors might seem a Quixotic enterprise. Their reputation among the general public remains abysmal, and most people would have little problem comparing Cortes with the Devil himself.

But as Engstrand pointed out twenty years ago, one of the first problems with the anti-conquistador argument begins with our adoption of the word itself. In English we tend to lump the early Spanish under this umbrella term. We use this label for any Spaniard, whether they were missionaries, farmers, craftsmen, traders, or adventurers who had not the slightest intention of conquering anyone. Very often, the Spanish were attacked by the Natives on sight and had to defend themselves, as was the case with De Soto. When they could, many Spanish adventurers attempted to maintain good relations with the tribes they came across. It is a fundamental truth of history that most of the major battles of conquest in Mexico and Peru were fought and won not by the Spanish themselves but by Native troops who voluntarily allied with the Spanish against their longstanding tribal enemies. Considering how dependent the Spanish were on Indigenous people for supplies, information, and simple goodwill, their policy of creating such local alliances makes perfect sense.

The fact that the Spanish have been saddled with this label is a legacy of the anti-Hispanic "Black Legend" which long sought to put them in the most negative possible light. The odds are that most readers will never have heard of the Russian atrocities committed against Indigenous Aleuts in Alaska. Similar Russian excesses against Indigenous people in Siberia lasted for many centuries and were often as horrific and widespread as anything perpetrated by the Spanish in the New World. And yet—partly because the Left spent much of the twentieth century sympathizing with the USSR—the English-speaking world knows nothing about this egregious chapter in the history of anti-Indigenous violence.

---

[53] Inga Clendinnen, "'Fierce and Unnatural Cruelty'": Cortés and the Conquest of Mexico," *Representations* 33 (1991), 65–100, https://www.jstor.org/stable/2928758.

The purpose of raising the issue of Russian atrocities in Siberia is not to excuse the Spaniards; rather, it is to show the extent to which ideology drives us to magnify some atrocities while ignoring others that stand in plain sight. It is the job of an objective historian not merely to lament and lay blame for tragedies but to contextualize them and to compare them with similar events for the purpose of coming to a true understanding of their cause and context, the better to avoid their repetition.

THE REAL CORTES

In the English-speaking world, Hernan Cortes retains a reputation as a wily, bloodthirsty soldier of fortune who orchestrated the deaths of millions of Indigenous people and viewed the rest as so many potential slaves. The Spanish-speaking world has a much more nuanced view. The real Cortes was a complex man. Highly literate and educated in the law, he was fiercely determined and fearless on the battlefield. He was also a very skillful negotiator and a charismatic leader, and showed a preternatural skill for wartime logistics. After first visiting the Yucatan and then landing in Veracruz with an initial force of a few hundred men, Cortes ordered them to burn their remaining boats. His stated intention was to conquer the Aztec Empire, and he made it clear to his men that there would be no room for failure.

From these humble beginnings, Cortes would strike westward with his expedition toward the Aztec capital of Tenochtitlan, which was rumored to be a storehouse of untold riches. It was a journey of some two hundred and fifty miles through tropical forests and mountainous scrub, much of which was densely settled by New World standards. By September 1519 Cortes had reached the territory of the Tlaxcalan Indians; after they were defeated in battle, the Tlaxcalans were persuaded to join the Spanish in alliance against their mutual enemies the Aztecs. In October, however, the Tlaxcalans manipulated the Spanish into a battle with their longtime enemies, the Cholulans. After a ruse, the Tlaxcalans (by some accounts, they were helped by the Spanish) massacred the Cholulans by the tens of thousands. (A death toll which by the way dwarfs the total amount of Natives killed in massacres by whites during the entire history of the United States and Canada, but which appears perfectly acceptable to the likes of David Stannard and Roxanne Dunbar-Ortiz.)

By November, rumors of the Spanish exploits had impressed the Aztec leader Montezuma, who appears to have believed that Cortes had been sent from the gods as a sort of avenging angel.[54] Montezuma's unwillingness to anger the gods by attacking Cortes was one of the major reasons why the Spanish were welcomed into their capital, where they could pursue various intrigues and manipulate the Aztec power structures in their own favor. Accordingly, by mid-November, the Spanish were able to arrest and imprison Montezuma himself.

An uneasy truce lasted in Tenochtitlan for a period of some months, with Montezuma under house arrest, until Cortes was distracted by a second Spanish army approaching from the east. This army had been sent by the Spanish governor of Cuba, who hoped to displace Cortes and take the Aztec treasure for himself. Leaving Mexico City under his second-in-command, Cortes defeated his Spanish rival and incorporated the second Spanish army into his own.

When Cortes returned to Mexico City at the end of June 1520, he found the city in a state of chaos; Montezuma was wounded as he attempted to plead for calm after Cortes's return. When Montezuma died of his wounds, the Aztec people finally rose in open revolt against the Spaniards. Cortes and his men were forced to flee back to their allies at Tlaxcala under cover of darkness, though many of them were killed during a night they later called the "Night of Sorrows."

By September, the Aztecs were firmly in control of their city once again. But fortune turned against the Aztecs once more when a wave of smallpox spread across central Mexico; this claimed the life of the new

---

[54] NB: Throughout this text we will use common English versions of famous names (e.g., Montezuma, Pocahontas). This is done deliberately, on the grounds that most scholars who insist on alternative names or spellings for such figures (including those who would call Pocahontas "Amonute") fall squarely into William Chester Jordan's "academic poseur" category.

Aztec king, Cuitláhuac. During the winter of 1520–21, Cortes drew up plans to besiege Tenochtitlan using a number of boats to be constructed at the far edge of the lake surrounding Mexico City. By the end of April 1521, the boats were launched, and the city was besieged by the end of May. A few months later, in August 1521, a final king of the Aztecs, Cuauhtémoc, was captured by the Spanish, ending effective resistance. Cortes was governor of New Spain from this time until 1524; later he led an expedition to Honduras with a number of Native allies and in subsequent years explored as far north as the Baja peninsula.

How many Indigenous people died as a result of Cortes and his campaigns? A Google search on "How many Indigenous people did the Spanish kill" returns a figure of "EIGHT MILLION INDIGENOUS PEOPLE" in all capital letters—which Google at least has the decency to amend by suggesting (in much smaller font) that most of these died of disease. Other mainstream sources such as biography.com suggest that Cortes's main wars of conquest caused the deaths of "up to one hundred thousand" Indigenous people, which though still a lot is obviously much fewer than eight million. But even this reduced figure is not reliable, since it is very likely that the majority of Aztec deaths were caused by Cortes's Indian allies, most of whom were more than happy to kill the people who had been subjecting their families and ancestors to capture, torture, slavery, and sacrifice for several generations. Considering that the Spaniards' Indigenous allies often outnumbered them by a ratio of twenty to one, it stands to reason that most of the Aztecs who died in the campaigns were likely killed by Indigenous rather than European hands.

From any realistic perspective, Cortes's plan to conquer the Aztecs was a ridiculous proposition and should not have succeeded. He may have had a few dozen horses and crossbows and a small assortment of primitive firearms and cannon, but the region of Mexico into which he was marching contained dozens of cities and hundreds of thousands of people. The Aztec capital of Tenochtitlan was rumored to house two hundred thousand people, and the Aztec king could muster fifty thousand or more soldiers in battle. No matter how skilled the Spanish might have been or how impervious their steel armor was to native weapons, such numbers could easily overwhelm them in a pitched battle.

This is why recent biographies tend to portray Cortes as one of the world's luckiest men. At several points on his most famous expedition, he came within a hair's breadth of being overwhelmed and killed. Of course, we all know that you make your own luck, at least to some degree. Cortes understood this as well, which is why he determined to make and keep as many Indigenous allies as possible, a strategy he adhered to throughout his campaigns. Incidentally, this shows how the Indigenous people of Mexico could have—at any point—turned on Cortes and massacred him and his men. But many of them saw Cortes as a useful political opportunity, of which they were more than happy to take advantage.

It is therefore no exaggeration to say that Cortes did not conquer Mexico—his Indigenous allies did. His allies were volunteers not forced, and Cortes simply could not have prevailed without them. The Natives' actions might make little sense through the foggy lens of modern racialist thinking. But—then as now—New World people tend to think in terms of tribe rather than race. In the perspective of the intertribal rivalries that constituted the reality of Mexican power dynamics, an alliance with Cortes and his Spaniards sometimes made all the sense in the world.

The story of Marina, Cortes's Indigenous interpreter and lieutenant, epitomizes many of these points. Before reaching mainland Mexico from Cuba, Cortes and his expedition landed on the island of Cozumel, where they encountered tribes already friendly to the Spanish. They also met a handful of Spanish castaways, whose differing attitudes toward captivity neatly illustrate the broad spectrum of early Spanish attitudes toward the Natives. One of the castaways had married a Native woman and had completely integrated into the Indigenous lifestyle. He did not want to come along with Cortes and had no desire to go back to a European-controlled area. Another, however, was only too happy to see Cortes and immediately agreed to accompany him. Having learned some of the local language, he was able to act as an interpreter.

Not long after Cortes left Cozumel, a local chief offered Cortes twenty female slaves as part of a gift exchange. Cortes's acceptance of slave girls should not be read in an anti-European light. It was part of the local culture that chiefs, upon meeting, might exchange presents including slave girls. The persistent rumor repeated by the likes of Elena Ortiz that most Indigenous cultures were "matrilineal" therefore "feminist" and more empowering for women than European society is truly ridiculous, especially in the context of central Mexico circa 1520. Indigenous society, even more than in Europe, tended to treat women as prizes and trade goods, leaving individual women to get by as best they could. The twenty women offered to Cortes had already been (sex) slaves to Indigenous masters; many of them had been captured and purchased by Indigenous traffickers from across central and southern Mexico, whence they had been brought to regional slave markets.

One of these slave women, Malintzin, rechristened Marina by the Spanish, turned out to be fluent in Nahuatl, the lingua franca of the greater Aztec region. Some commentators suspect she had been raised as a noblewoman, which explained her ability to speak in the high dialect of the Aztec nobility. Whatever the case, Cortes quickly recognized her intelligence and raised her to a position of power and influence in his camp. After several crucial negotiations, Cortes recognized that he could rely on her to make the best decisions under pressure, and he soon let it be known that in his absence, both Spaniards and Indigenous people with questions or quarrels should treat her as his surrogate.

Marina was instrumental in helping Cortes negotiate with Montezuma, the king of the Aztecs, and Cortes reportedly said that he could never have accomplished the conquest of the Aztec kingdom without her. In making her his lieutenant and giving her clear political power, Cortes was simply reproducing a power structure that was common in Europe during his day but that was virtually unknown among Indigenous Mexican cultures. Who then should go down in history as "empowering female indigenous bodies"? The irony here is thick.

**Figure 4.1. Malintzin Helping Cortes to
Negotiate with Montezuma.**

Cortes and Marina worked together extremely well under pressure, and the attraction between them was palpable. The pair soon became lovers, despite the fact that Cortes was already married, and Marina bore him several children. Marina maintained a fierce loyalty to Cortes, and he returned the favor. The most famous of her children would become known as Martin Cortes "el Mestizo." In later years, Martin el Mestizo was honored with a place at the court of King Philip II and accompanied the king on several military campaigns. But Martin el Mestizo was also given the high noble title of marquis and extensive lands in Mexico, and he returned there in the 1560s to oversee his estates.

Figure 4.2. Martin Cortes (el Mestizo) as a Spanish Marquis.

In Mexico, Marina is known as La Malinche—which meant "sheaf of twisted corn"—and her reputation, like that of Cortes, is complicated. To Mexicans with an Indigenous-activist bent, La Malinche is the ultimate traitor—a sort of Benedict Arnold figure, who betrayed her race to the Europeans. Others are more sympathetic, recognizing that she was a clever woman making the most of the opportunities available to her. They also recognize that Mexico at the time was not a unified country but rather consisted of many warring tribes—including those who had taken her prisoner, enslaved her, and traded her like a beast. To whom should she have been more loyal than Cortes himself? La Malinche is also celebrated as the mother of all mestizos in Latin America, who as we have seen make up the majority of many national populations today.

Another Mexican group that has endured a mixed legacy are the people descended from the Tlaxcala Indigenous group, who as we have seen were instrumental in helping Cortes to conquer the Aztecs. As recently as 2021, an article in the *Guardian* reported that this group still struggles to overcome the sense—promoted by today's Left within

Mexico—that they are traitors to the Mexican people.[55] In the sixteenth century, the Tlaxcalans made up the bulk of the Indigenous allies whom Cortes eventually brought to the Aztec capital. The Tlaxcalan Indians had remained outside of the Aztec confederacy at the time of his arrival and were surrounded by tribes loyal to the Aztecs. They were therefore in a strategically precarious position, subject to constant attacks. The Tlaxcalans maintained a longstanding feud with the Aztecs, who had been responsible for many atrocities and injuries against them, and Aztec brutality helped push them into the arms of Cortes.

The Tlaxcalans in turn were largely responsible for the Cholula massacre, one of the bloodiest events of Cortes's campaign. According to an eyewitness account related in Nahuatl to Fray Bernardino de Sahagún, the massacre occurred as follows:

> Then [the Spaniards] asked them: Where is Mexico? How far is it? They [the Tlaxcalans] answered them: "It is not far now. Perhaps in three days you will arrive. It is a very good place. And [the Aztecs] are very valiant, great warriors, conquerors, who go conquering everywhere."

> But the Tlaxcalans in past times had been at war, had risen up with rage and anger against the Cholullans, They [the Tlaxcalans] disliked, hated, detested them; they would have nothing to do with them. So they told [the Spaniards]: "They [the Cholullans] are very evil, and they are our enemy. Those of Cholula are as valiant as the Mexicas. They are friends of the Mexicas."

---

55   David Agren, "Don't Call Us Traitors: Descendants of Cortés's Allies Defend Role in Toppling Aztec Empire," *Guardian*, August 13, 2021, https://www.theguardian.com/world/2021/aug/13/mexico-tlaxcala-aztec-empire-anniversary.

When the Spaniards heard this, they went to
Cholula, taking those of Tlaxcala and Cempoala
with them dressed for war. When they arrived, they
shouted for all noblemen, rulers, captains, chiefs,
and also the men of the town to assemble in the
courtyard of the gods [probably of the Temple of
Quetzalcoatl].

When they had all gathered, [the Spaniards and
their allies] blocked the entrances, all of the places
where one could enter. In the first moment, people
were murdered and beaten. Nothing like this was
in the minds of the Cholulans. Without swords or
shields they met the Spaniards. Without warning,
they were treacherously and deceitfully slain. They
were ambushed because the Tlaxcalans persuaded
[the Spaniards] to do it.[56]

So while the Spanish may have facilitated the massacre, it is clear
that it would not have happened had the Tlaxcalans not desired to make
this detour in order to avenge themselves against their hated enemies.
It seems that the Tlaxcalans suggested the ambush as the best method
for dealing with the Cholulan leadership and army. Other sources make
clear that the majority of perpetrators in the subsequent massacre were
Tlaxcalans, and some Spanish observers were horrified by the delight
taken by them in the slaughter of their defenseless Cholulan rivals.

For their aid in the subsequent conquest of Mexico, Cortes and the
Spanish government later allocated them a special status. They were literally ennobled—the entire tribe was granted the Spanish title of *hidalgo*.
This fact made them socially superior to most of the Europeans they
encountered. Europeans in the sixteenth and seventeenth centuries

---

[56] *Florentine Codex*, Book 12, Chapter 11 (Mexica), https://enl.wired-humanities.org/
fcbk12ch11.

believed that the quality of "nobility" made someone almost biologically superior to other people; they also believed that nobility could be passed on through one's blood via procreation. If the early Spanish were racist in any significant way, they believed that nobles were a sort of superior race within their own society. And yet, they proved willing to confer this status en masse to their Indian allies. None of this fits very easily with postcolonialist stereotypes about Europeans, colonization, racism, and the rest.

Further complicating matters, the Tlaxcalans were granted status as Indigenous allies of the state, which included the right to an independent administration of their homelands. This also gave them the full rights of Spanish citizens, meaning that they were able to buy, settle, and sell land anywhere in Mexico or elsewhere in the Spanish empire. The Tlaxcalans were exempt from labor service in the encomienda system and were preferred in military appointments to the army of New Spain.

This special status lasted until the independence of Mexico from Spain in the 1820s. The Tlaxcalan cities became a model for the Republicas de los Indios, which were set up across Mexico in the aftermath of the conquest as a reward to other Indigenous allies and as a deliberate attempt to protect Indigenous people from Spanish encroachment.

The Republicas de los Indios were jurisdictions in which only Indians could settle; even mestizos and mulattos (mixed-race people with African ancestry) were not allowed. These were areas with a separate juridical status and distinct customs from the rest of Mexico. They were characterized by communal ownership of land, annual elections of municipal and confraternity officers, a full ceremonial calendar including Catholic and native elements, a uniform head tax, and exception from all other taxation. The Indigenous inhabitants of the *republicas* were allowed to make their own laws and keep their own customs, as long as they did not egregiously contravene the doctrines of Christianity or the laws of the Spanish state.

The republicas were governed by councils that directly mirrored Spanish local and regional government. Town councils consisting of councilors called alcaldes were appointed; all these officials were Native people. They were allowed to administer in their own native languages, and thousands of documents written in Nahuatl and other languages exist from this long period of native self-rule.

We have seen that it is partly for this reason—the Spanish granting independent government and real political power to Native groups from the beginning of the conquest—that so many unmixed Indigenous people still survive in Mexico today. Meanwhile, many Native people chose to live and work outside of these republicas, and many mestizo people lived all across Mexico. Following the example of Martin Cortes "el Mestizo," Mexican mestizos were quickly accorded full rights as citizens.

ETHNIC HETEROGENEITY IN MEXICO

From the earliest years of Spanish Mexico, Indigenous and mestizo people were given places of honor in the Mexican hierarchy. Of course, colorism and racial labels were common, just as classism was. Today we seem to fetishize the one, while ignoring the other. But as in every historical society, many Spanish in Mexico were keen to reserve to themselves as many positions of privilege as they could. Racism did not necessarily take the forms that many activists expect, and the reality was that many influential Mexicans were Indians and mestizos from the outset. Later, a small but significant number of Africans and part-African mulattos also added to the genetic mix.

All this intermarriage meant that Mexico became the mixed-race society that it is today with surprising rapidity, just as occurred in the Caribbean. In such a plural society, we should not be surprised to find complex and accommodating racial attitudes. A recent dissertation studying a late sixteenth-century Mexican community concluded:

> In this region, most families were heterogenous bringing together *indios* and *negros*, *mulatos* [*sic*] and *mestizos*. Again, the family of Alonso Hernández is

a good example. He, a *mulato*, was married to an
india. His cousin was called a *mestiza*. Presumably,
one of his parents was a negro; certainly his uncle
Pedro was considered a negro. He shared ties of
godparentage with a *mulato* and an *india* as well as
with a *mestizo* and a *mulata*. The widespread practice
of intermarriage across these *generos de gente* and
equally diverse kinship ties suggests that for non-
Spaniards terms such as *indio, negro, mulato, mestizo*
had little relevance in the formation of relationships
within this region. Instead, these relationships and
the general portrayal of friendship, family, and
community within the testimony suggest that these
terms did not function as markers of inclusion or
exclusion…. Rather, a shared community existed
above and beyond these categories and not through
them or because of them.[57]

In other words, while Mexican scribes and notaries gave labels of
"Indian," "Black," "Mestizo," and "Mulatto" to various people, abundant
evidence suggests that few people acted on or cared about these labels in
day-to-day life.

This easygoing attitude toward racial difference, interracial marriage, and kinship for the first several centuries of colonialism in Mexico
is also illustrated in a peculiar class of artwork known as caste or "casta"
paintings.

[57] Robert C. Schwaller, *Defining Difference in Early New Spain* (dissertation submitted
to the Pennsylvania State University History Department, 2010), quote from p. 319,
https://etda.libraries.psu.edu/files/final_submissions/5109.

Figure 4.3. Casta Painting of Planter and Wife.

The phenomenon of caste painting became popular in Mexico during the early eighteenth century. Commentators note that this was a period when European society was becoming intensely interested in taxonomy of plant and animal species, and the ideas of the Swedish taxonomist Carl Linnaeus were electrifying the scientific world. The resulting classification of humans need not be seen in any more sinister a light than simple intellectual curiosity, as we noted in an earlier chapter.

A look at the various paintings suggests that they were indeed painted more out of curiosity, indeed as a celebration of difference, rather than anything negative.[58] In one painting, the Virgin Mary stands over all the mixed-race couples as a vulvic symbol of the Mother of All. She even has a baby peeking out from under her skirts, in case the symbolism wasn't clear enough. Meanwhile, the painting is graced along the bottom with a scientific depiction of various fruits.

---

[58] Susan Deans-Smith, "Casta Paintings," *Not Even Past*, November 9, 2011, https://notevenpast.org/casta-paintings/.

In Figure 4.3, a well-dressed planter is shown alongside his equally well-dressed Indian wife whose clothes are an obvious mix of Indian and European fashions. The couple is seen in the midst of their prosperous farm, a portrait of domestic and reproductive bliss. She is bashfully making eyes at her husband and showing off her child, who is portrayed as white, not to signal the dominance of the husband's "superior" racial heritage but according to the belief that Indian children were born white. The child is lovingly clinging to his mother.

While some casta paintings tend to emphasize male Europeans having children with non-European women, others were explicit in their depiction of European women marrying non-European men. In Figure 4.4, the first couple includes a primly dressed European lady wearing the full eighteenth-century regalia of skirts and petticoats, standing next to a noble Indian man wearing a loincloth and carrying a bow. The woman gives her spouse a shy but enamored look, and their child is painted to look proud like his father. The painter also portrays a European man coupled with a well-dressed African woman, alongside their mixed-race child; in all, eight different mixings are lovingly portrayed.

**Figure 4.4. Casta Painting Showing White
Women Marrying Non-White Men.**

Despite the fact that "whiteness" gradually came to be seen as superior in colonial Mexico, a cursory glimpse into the annals of Mexican history reveals a great number of Indian and mestizo elites. For example, Benito Juárez was a full-blooded Indian who rose to the presidency of Mexico in 1861, after having served as chief justice of the Mexican Supreme Court. Born of humble parents, Juárez's brilliance was noticed by a friar, who took him to Oaxaca at a young age and ensured that he got an education. He studied to become a lawyer and became involved in local politics. He began practicing law in 1834, allying himself with the liberal faction. This meant that he was anti-monarchist and pro-democracy. Unfortunately, French intervention on behalf of the Conservatives helped to topple the Mexican republic for which Juárez fought, and a pro-Catholic dictatorship was established in 1876. Plainly, religious and political divisions were more decisive at this stage than racial ones.

Figure 4.5. Mexican President Benito Juárez.

Other heroes of the various Mexican wars for liberation include José María Morelos and Vicente Guerrero. Morelos was registered as a European in his baptismal register, but his father's family was mestizo and he was widely acknowledged at the time to be such. Morelos began his career as a priest, who was goaded into becoming a revolutionary leader after the Catholic church and various Conservative factions took up arms in favor of an absolute monarchy. After Morelos was captured and executed, his compatriot Vicente Guerrero, himself both a mestizo and a mulatto, became commander in chief of the republican forces; he briefly ascended to the presidency of Mexico in 1829.

From all this evidence, it is clear that the conquistadors and the Spanish administrators created a society in Mexico that was not only racially plural but also was from the very beginning founded on principles of interracial fraternity; a place in which Indigenous rights were defended in law and very often in practice as well. By most measures, colonial Mexico was a more tolerant and heterogeneous society than any colony set up by the English.

CHRISTIANITY AND CULTURAL GENOCIDE

Another easy target for modern activists are the Spanish friars and other clergy who came to the New World supposedly with the objective of eradicating Native culture while forcing everyone to convert to Christianity. Lingering specters of the Spanish Inquisition make it easy for people to imagine giant autos-da-fé in which hundreds of Indigenous people were burned for refusing to submit to the faith of the conquerors. The British Museum website accuses the Spanish of "ruthless colonialism, forced religious conversion and the erasure of Indigenous knowledges and practices," as though such brutality was normative and Native agency was nonexistent.[59] According to Alan Riding of the Daily Beast, for example, Mexico followed a "bloody" path to Catholicization, in which Mexicans had "no choice but to embrace the faith," and in which "the brutality of the Inquisition" played a prominent role.[60] Following these leads,

[59] "An Indigenous Reframing of the Fall of the Aztec Empire," British Museum, https://blog.britishmuseum.org/an-indigenous-reframing-of-the-fall-of-the-aztec-empire/.
[60] Alan Riding, "A Bloody Tale of How Mexico Went Catholic," Daily Beast, February 21, 2016, updated April 13, 2017, https://www.thedailybeast.com/a-bloody-tale-of-how-mexico-went-catholic.

Anglophone students are regularly taught about Spanish atrocity in a hyperbolic fashion by their professors, which is reflected in their own writings on the topic. A student blog post on Georgetown University's Berkley Center for Religion, Peace, and World Affairs repeats that "the conquistadors used forced conversion, destruction and violence to subjugate the native people. Missionaries kidnapped children and converted them to Christianity. In addition, conquistadors killed local political leaders who resisted the conquest."[61]

Though we will say more about it in a subsequent chapter, Aztec religion was polytheistic, which absorbed many concepts from earlier Mesoamerican cultures, particularly the Maya. Though they believed in an ultimate god, they also worshipped many lesser deities who represented various concepts, objects, and places. One of the central concepts of their religion was that human blood was needed in order to keep the world from falling apart; the gods had given blood at the time of the world's creation, and humans were therefore obliged to give this blood back or risk the dissolution of the world. There was a great deal of entropy in their religious philosophy, meaning that continuous rituals (including human sacrifices) were necessary in order to keep the world operating on its present course. The symbolism of the skull was widespread in Mesoamerica, though skull worship was taken to new heights by the Aztecs and their allies. Aztec priests were seen as those responsible for providing gifts to the gods, while rulers were charged with providing proper numbers of sacrificial victims for their temples. When a people were conquered by a neighboring tribe, those who were not sacrificed would be forced to adopt the religion of the conquerors, though oftentimes important local deities would be incorporated into the calendars of the conquerors themselves.

The Spanish clergy in the New World acted quickly to destroy certain signs of the ancient religious practices that they deemed most egre-

[61] Jessica Frankovich, "Mexican Catholicism: Conquest, Faith, and Resistance," *JYAN Blog*, Berkley Center, Georgetown University, March 22, 2019, https://berkleycenter.georgetown.edu/posts/mexican-catholicism-conquest-faith-and-resistance.

gious, such as human sacrifice and the drinking of human blood. At the same time they were well aware that honey gained more converts than vinegar, so they proved willing to allow time for certain communities to come into conformity with Catholicism, even as they agreed to locate churches on the site of previous religious sites and to accommodate the worship of local deities into Catholicism's extremely malleable and useful pantheon of saints. (This was a common practice of the church throughout Europe and the New World.)

The lead inquisitor of early Mexico was the Franciscan friar Juan de Zumárraga, who was also the first bishop of Mexico (from 1530), and simultaneously held the title "Protector of the Indians." This combination of these offices in one man might sound ominous, but the reality was more benign. The Spanish crown gave Zumárraga the title of protector of the Indians knowing that a bishop's authority to intervene on the Natives' behalf was perhaps the only sort that other Spanish elites would heed.

The move proved a stroke of genius, because thousands of Indians came streaming to the bishop with grievances against Spanish landowners, and Zumárraga, being well chosen, gave them the impression that he was genuinely concerned for the protection and voluntary conversion of his flock. While he did bring inquisitorial charges against a total of 158 Spanish and Indian leaders during the first decade of his tenure, according to Patricia Lopes Don, author of *Bonfires of Culture: Franciscans, Indigenous Leaders, and the Inquisition in Early Mexico, 1524–1540*, after 1540 Zumárraga judged only eleven Inquisitorial cases, all of which involved Spaniards accused of various heresies (usually involving Protestantism).

Given that there were millions of Indians living in central Mexico at this time, the percentage of these persecuted by the Mexican Inquisition was tiny to the point of irrelevance. Over the course of his career, the bishop of Mexico went from very infrequent persecution of Natives for religious infractions to zero. According to Don, the apparent catalyst for Zumárraga's change of heart was a directive from the central government itself. A letter from the bishop of Seville, a member of the Spanish royal council, arrived in 1540 suggesting that the Native people "might be more persuaded with love than with rigor," suggesting that Zumárraga "should not apply to them the rigor of the law...nor confiscate their property" for ecclesiastical offenses.[62] In counseling this, the bishop was merely repeating the wishes of Queen Isabella, who had died several decades earlier.

Meanwhile, in December 1531 the Virgin Mary had appeared on multiple occasions to an Indigenous Mexican peasant named Chichimec. In part due to the positive reputation of Bishop Zumárraga, this miracle spread a genuine zeal for conversion among the Native peoples of central Mexico, who began to flock to various Christian sites seeking blessing and baptism from the friars. By some accounts there were several million converts already by 1536, with hundreds of thousands more Indians arriving every year.

These numbers are undoubtedly exaggerated, but the mass voluntary baptism of Indigenous Mexicans in early colonial Mexico is an established fact. The rapidity of the conversions and the numbers involved forced the Franciscan missionaries to adopt a fast track to baptism using mass catechisms and water only, which other religious orders eventually called into question for being too slapdash.

The reality of most Indian conversions in early central Mexico then is not what most activists, and sadly, many journalists and historians who ought to know better would like us to believe.

Moreover, to imagine that most Mexican Indians found it traumatic to be converted to Christianity is to fundamentally misunderstand the cosmology of the Indigenous people of central and southern Mexico. Very much like the ancient Greeks and Romans, these polytheistic people were used to the idea of syncretism—the practice of adopting new gods into their own pantheons. Late medieval Europeans, for their part, were not terribly sophisticated in their expectations of religious worship

---

[62] Patricia Lopes Don, *Bonfires of Culture: Franciscans, Indigenous Leaders, and the Inquisition in Early Mexico, 1524–1540* (Norman: University of Oklahoma Press, 2012), 175.

either and tended to demand little from their new converts. In France and Spain, bishops were often happy if a peasant could get through most of the Lord's Prayer.

Indigenous conversion in Mexico might therefore involve little more than lip service and a willingness to make the sign of the cross, though as was the case with Chichimec, it might also involve a profound personal devotion. Mexican Indigenous peoples found it all the easier to adapt to Catholic Christianity since most friars went out of their way to allow them to continue worshipping their favorite local deities in the guise of saints. Making liberal use of the fact that Catholicism allowed for thousands of saints to be patrons and intercessors on almost any theme, clever friars accommodated local sensibilities by allowing Mexican Catholicism to become a syncretic amalgam of the various belief systems.

This represents a well-established scholarly consensus about the introduction of Christianity into Mexico. The gold-standard *Cambridge History of the Native Peoples of the Americas* has this to say about the process:

> Pre-Hispanic religion had been a major force for expressing and reinforcing community unity, and Christianity proved a vehicle to continue this. Each town had a Christian patron saint, as did each residential subdivision (tlaxilacalli). The saint's name became part of the name of the town or ward: pre-Hispanic Culhuacan, for instance, became San Juan Evangelista Culhuacan. The saint's day of the town or ward was one of celebration, reinforcing community solidarity as much as religious belief. In general, the sites of the pre-Hispanic cults became the location of the Christian churches and chapels, important for the community. The pre-Hispanic sacred site at Tepeyac became the focus of first a local, then a regional, and finally a national

pilgrimage destination for the cult of the Virgin of
Guadalupe. In most indigenous towns, the churches
built on sacred sites continued to be a focus of native
identity through religious expression. The size of a
church and the elaborateness of its decorations and
furnishings were important to the native community,
visible signs of unity and prominence.[63]

Is this really "cultural genocide"? If so, much of this change happened voluntarily, over the course of several generations. Many avowedly
Native traditions continued to exist alongside Catholicism in Mexico
for centuries, until the more organized statism of the nineteenth century
helped to suppress them in a more systematic fashion.

Of course culture is more than religion; much of it is based on language. We will have more to say on these aspects of Indigenous culture
in the Americas later on. But racism, genocide, and cultural genocide are
not at all helpful descriptions of what went on when Indigenous peoples
and Spaniards met in colonial Mexico. The idea that the Spanish conquistadors were bloodthirsty religious zealots should therefore be seen as
a politically motivated exaggeration, originally brought to us courtesy of
la leyenda negra española.

---

[63] Sarah L. Cline, "Native Peoples of Colonial Central Mexico," in Richard E. W. Adams
and Murdo J. MacLeod, eds., *The Cambridge History of the Native Peoples of the Americas,
Volume 2*:2. (Cambridge, UK: Cambridge University Press, 2000), 187–222.

CHAPTER 5

IS EUROPE GUILTY OF "SETTLER COLONIALISM"?

*Settler colonialism is inherently predicated upon
a relationship of genocide that renders the whole
of a settler nation-state's existence genocidal.*

—Pauline Wakeham, "The Slow
Violence of Settler Colonialism"

In 1995, a German dental technician named Klaus Teuber published a board game titled Die Siedler van Catan. In the game, players attempt to build cities and farms on an uninhabited island until they gain a clear economic advantage over the other players. The game was an instant hit; it won the coveted "Game of the Year" prize in Germany and went on to sell millions of copies around the world. It was also a runaway hit in the United States, where it was published under the English title The Settlers of Catan. Easily the most influential board game of the past thirty years, Catan single-handedly launched the "Euro board game" craze of the early 2000s.

By 2015, however, The Settlers of Catan found themselves in troubled waters. Publisher 999 Games decided to drop all references to "settlers" and "colonists" in the game's title and instruction manuals and the game was rebranded simply as Catan.

Why all the hubbub? The problem is that the words "settler" and "colonist" had taken on such an enormous cultural baggage in the years between its first publication and the early 2010s, that 999 Games found itself inundated with complaints about how the game glorified colonialism in general and settler colonialism in particular. (This even though the imaginary island on which players built their colonies was uninhabited.) Once considered neutral terms, words like "settler," "colonist," and "imperial" had become toxic epithets in the cultural discourse. We have seen how in the aftermath of the George Floyd riots statues of George Washington were spray-painted with the term "colonist"—a word that now signaled to the faithful that Washington was to be considered a genocidal racist monster.

To the uninitiated, all this hullabaloo about settlers and colonialism might seem like a tempest in a teacup. To a large swath of the global English-speaking population, however, settler colonialism, to use the fashionable term, serves to undermine the very legitimacy of countries such as Canada, Australia, New Zealand, and the United States.

The idea of settler colonialism was popularized by the rogue Australian academic Patrick Wolfe, whose book *Settler Colonialism* was published in 1999, some four years after Klaus Teuber named his new board game. According to the doctrine of settler colonialism, Europeans who came to the New World, and to other areas such as Australia and New Zealand, engaged in a particularly egregious form of colonialism. For them, it has been alleged, the goal of colonization was not simply to dominate a subject people politically, culturally, and economically. In addition, it was infused with a racially motivated drive to replace or exterminate the Indigenous inhabitants altogether. We have seen how in *Not a Nation of Immigrants*, Roxanne Dunbar-Ortiz summarizes this alleged combination of racism, capitalism, and genocide by explaining that "white nationalism was inscribed in the founding of the United States as a European settler-colonial expansionist entity." Quoting Wolfe, the academic Dina Gilio-Whitaker calls settler colonialism a "social structure that continually reproduces itself in order to accomplish the elimination of the "Native."[64]

All this might take a minute to unpack, because it is laced with jargon and takes a number of theoretical assumptions for granted.

Wolfe's idea of settler colonialism grew out of the academic field of postcolonial studies, which was itself spurred by the publication of Palestinian scholar Edward Said's landmark book *Orientalism* in 1978. Said's book was one of the first in-depth critiques of Western narratives that until that time viewed the West as normative and primary, and the East as exotic and secondary. Edward Said had a point: until then, most Westerners *did* write as though Europe was the yardstick against which every historical value judgment should be made.

The blossoming of postcolonial theory gave new power and direction to a long-held view of European expansionism that saw the voyages of Columbus as the birth of global capitalism. A major proponent of this argument was the New York sociologist Immanuel Wallerstein. According to Wallerstein, Columbus's voyages marked the beginning of a "Modern World System" through which Europe exploited the nearly limitless resources and markets of the New World until it turned from a sleepy backwater into a globe-dominating economic powerhouse.

Noam Chomsky, unsurprisingly, described the rise of Wallerstein's "Modern World System" in less neutral terms. In his 1992 book, *Year 501: The Conquest Continues*, Chomsky marries it with the old Marxist take on colonialism. Europeans stole New World resources by force, rendering prosperous Natives poor and poor Europeans wealthy in the process. This "savage injustice"—here Chomsky plucks a phrase from Adam Smith—fed the capitalist monster until it became the dominant power in world history.

[64] Dina Gilio-Whitaker, "Fourth World Nations' Collision with Capitalism in the United States," *Fourth World Journal* 13, no. 2 (January 2015), 1–20, https://www.researchgate.net/publication/307465117_Fourth_World_Nations%27_Collision_with_Capitalism_in_the_United_States.

Many people who claim to write and speak on behalf of Indigenous people have since turned this longstanding anti-capitalist narrative into a rigid dogma. In their eyes, capitalism is what drove Europeans to sail to the New World in search of riches. Finding few developed markets or readily exploitable resources, they enslaved or killed the people and commodified the land, turning it into large plantations. This fostered a stage of proto-capitalism known as "primitive accumulation," which according to both Marx and Adam Smith was a prerequisite for the Industrial Revolution.

Newer versions of this narrative tend to place even more emphasis on race. According to modern theorists of primitive accumulation, Indigenous people were deemed useless if they could not serve as slaves or farm labor. European capitalists, acting as much out of racist contempt as greed, therefore marked them for destruction and replacement. They deliberately planted European colonies throughout the New World with the aim of removing or exterminating all Indigenous people who stood in the way of the total commodification of the continent.

As Dunbar-Ortiz put it in her 2014 *Indigenous Peoples' History of the United States*: "The form of colonialism that the Indigenous peoples of North America have experienced was modern from the beginning: the expansion of European corporations, backed by government armies, into foreign areas, with subsequent expropriation of lands and resources." The result of this racially motivated capitalist pressure was the phenomenon now known as "settler colonialism."

As with many popular ideas, the story of capitalist settler colonialism sounds compelling at first. It ties up five hundred years of European history in one tidy narrative. It focuses on catastrophes such as slavery, enforced mass migration, and environmental destruction. And it appeals to the emotions with loaded terms such as exploitation, invasion, destruction, expropriation, theft, and genocide.

But how much logic is there to this narrative of racially motivated genocide via capitalism, and how well does it stand up to historical scrutiny? The first red flag goes up as soon as one realizes that it is difficult to look up terms such as settler colonialism or primitive accumulation without running into a bevy of openly Marxist critics. The theories are steeped in radicalism of a kind that, until about 2010, had long been discredited in serious historical circles. For example, on the first page of the 2010 book *Settler Colonialism: A Theoretical Overview*, author Lorenzo Veracini tells us that a "theoretical analysis of what is here defined as the settler colonial situation could perhaps start with Karl Marx and Friedrich Engels' remark that the 'need of a constantly expanding market for its product chases the bourgeoisie over the whole surface of the globe,' which 'must nestle everywhere, settle everywhere, establish connections everywhere.'"

As we shall see, most of the concepts associated with settler colonialism collapse into a rubble of illogic once one identifies and removes the Marxist theory that props them up.

Let us begin with the theory itself. Ironically, a vein of "Western exceptionalism" lies at the core of much settler colonialist theory. Western exceptionalism is the conscious or unconscious idea that Western civilization is fundamentally "different" from all other civilizations—an idea that Edward Said was at pains to refute.

Settler colonialism is "Western exceptionalism" because, even though it is rabidly anti-Western, it nonetheless assumes that Western civilization is exceptional. It assumes that Western colonies and colonists were worse than others, that Western ideologies were more cruel than others, and that Western economies were more brutal than others. Much of this can be traced back to anti-Western theories that were prominent on Western college campuses in the 1960s, '70s, and '80s, and ultimately to Marx's own western exceptionalism.

As for the historical facts behind New World settlement, we have already shown that European colonialism was not genocidal in any meaningful sense, since this was not the intention of any colonial government, nor did Europeans succeed in displacing the major population clusters of the New World. We have seen how many anglophone academics treat the situation in the United States—home to less than 10 percent of the

New World population in 1491—as though it was emblematic of the entire New World. This is a form of "imperialist thinking" if ever there was one. As in Mexico and Peru, so it was in almost all of Africa, Asia, and the Pacific Islands: wherever there were large Indigenous populations prior to European expansion, there remain large Indigenous populations today.

Where then is this supposedly unstoppable machinery of settler colonialism? To suggest that European "capitalism" was founded on a racist desire to displace non-Europeans, backed up by an inexorable logic of genocidal capitalist destruction—is to ignore the situation in the vast majority of territories controlled by Europeans over the last five hundred years. The only reason parts of the New World, such as the present-day US and Canada and also Australia and New Zealand, are majority non-Indigenous is because the Indigenous population of these lands was so truly sparse—1 percent or less as dense as most of Europe at the time. And that the land was, as contemporary sources frequently describe it, virtually empty and more or less there for the taking. Few of us realize that before European contact, for example, all of Australia was home to about three hundred thousand Aboriginal people. That's one person for every twenty-five square kilometers, and yields a population density of 0.04 people per square kilometer. Even doubling this long-standing figure—as modern activist-archaeologists attempt on the basis of little evidence—yields a density of less than one person per ten square kilometers.

This simple demographic logic means that no grand conspiracy theory is needed to explain the fate of various regions around the globe. Given two facts—population density and agricultural fertility—one could have predicted in the year 1600 which parts of the globe would be majority European by the year 2000. Fertile and temperate places that had less than one person per square kilometer in the year 1600 had a much greater chance of becoming majority European, while regions with higher population density are today majority mixed-race or Indigenous.

The timing of settler colonialism has also been greatly exaggerated. Accounts such as Chomsky's *Year 501* suggest that Europeans have been continuously moving against Indigenous North Americans throughout five hundred years of relentless conquest. But as we shall see, most Indigenous people, during most of these long centuries, had little or no direct contact with outsiders. And it is indisputable that the majority of those who were forced from their homes during those centuries were victims of Indigenous raids and attacks, rather than European pressure.

For the first two and a half centuries after Columbus, Europeans remained confined to limited enclaves in the New World. Large parts of Mexico and Latin America remained in the hands of Indigenous people throughout the colonial period and beyond. As recently chronicled by Pekka Hämäläinen, most of the actual "dispossession" of Indigenous people in North America occurred quite rapidly, during the nineteenth century, due to a combination of natural population increase and European immigration.[65] This land grab happened only after the Indigenous population was outnumbered by a factor approaching one hundred to one.

In the realm of policy, the settler colonialist ideologues have searched in vain for any statement by governments that wished to displace or do away with Indigenous populations of the New World. The Spanish and the French actually sought to bolster Indian and mestizo populations, and we will see how the English and the early American presidents repeatedly sought to limit contact between Indians and settlers, with the express purpose of protecting the Indians from depredation. The few cases of enforced migration that academics point to, such as the Trail of Tears, have long been infamous and do not carry much demographic weight. The Trail of Tears came very late in the European colonialist game, and as we will see it met with enormous resistance from Americans themselves both at the time and afterwards.

The idea that there was some grand colonial policy orchestrated by the great powers of Europe or its leading business interests can be dis-

---

[65] More will be said on this in chapter 13. The book referred to is *Indigenous Continent: The Epic Contest for North America* (Liveright, 2022).

patched in two strokes. First, while "capitalist interests" sometimes had a say in early modern European governmental policy, their influence was often quite limited. Royalty, nobility, and church were notoriously opposed to business logic in fundamental ways. In major land powers such as France and Spain, business interests continually struggled to maintain an influence on governmental policy, while in smaller states they were somewhat more successful.

The second consideration is just how small, disorganized, and improvisational most European governments were throughout the early modern period. Anti-European writers seem to imagine a boardroom where European leaders gathered to discuss long-term strategies for maintaining white supremacy through the exploitation and displacement of brown people. Yet well into the twentieth century, national governments had a difficult time maintaining a coherent policy or strategy on *anything* for more than a few years, and their efforts were invariably underfunded. For most of the colonial era, European countries were too broke, distracted, and disorganized to affect large populations in such a grandiose way.

Finally, there is the fact that humanitarian and anti-racist sentiments were common in Europe throughout the early modern period. This was the era of the Enlightenment, which saw Europe quite literally invent the modern discourse on human rights. When McGill professor of religious studies Arvind Sharma posed the question *Are Human Rights Western?* in his 2006 book, his conclusion was "yes." The global discourse of human rights as we know it today is fundamentally European in its pedigree. Thus, for every ten freebooters bullying their way into a fortune, there was always a Las Casas, a Queen Isabella, a William Wilberforce, or simply a humble local pastor ready to call such ruffians out for their cruelty. We simply do not find such a plethora of humanitarian sentiment in most traditional cultures, where individual human rights are normally subsumed under the rights of powerful men, institutions, and family honor.

The bourgeoning language of human rights was one of the European humanitarians' principal tools, and it was a very effective one.[66] The cultural climate ensured that their arguments held weight in the court of European public opinion. This helped to keep a check on policies that were seen as inhumane—as a deliberate policy of enslavement, genocide, or mass displacement certainly would have been. From the time of Cortes through that of Thomas Jefferson and beyond, Europeans were continually searching their souls over the issue of slavery and Indigenous rights. Thousands of pages of letters, pamphlets, and other writings attest to this fact.

In the end, simple inertia, tempered by this influential public discourse of human rights, helped ensure that the great majority of Indigenous populations under European rule stayed more or less intact over the long haul. The demographic facts of this claim are a Google search away for anyone who cares to see the truth.

DID "CAPITALISM" DISPOSSESS THE INDIANS?

A major component of the settler colonialism argument is that a system of "capitalism" drove it by a relentless logic of acquisition and exploitation. Such arguments are often traced back to Eric Williams's 1944 book *Capitalism and Slavery*, in which the author attempts to prove that transatlantic slavery jump-started European capitalism. In Williams's eyes, capitalism then perpetuated a demand for further slave labor. The appeal of this argument for Marxists such as Williams is that it indicts the hated system of capitalism not only with exploiting the working class—a charge that in recent decades has become cliché and decidedly ho-hum—but also with being a major cause of transatlantic slavery.

---

[66] The effectiveness of European ministers' humanitarian concerns has been amply documented, at different times and places around the globe, in Nigel Biggar's *Colonialism: A Moral Reckoning* (William Collins, 2023).

In today's environment, this latter charge is much more exciting, and Indigenous activists have made sure to hitch their wagon to the myth that capitalism is racist and relentlessly exploits non-European people. They have coined the awkward acronym BIPOC (Black, Indigenous, and People of Color) in an attempt to suggest that the European "system" has been primed to make white people into oppressors and non-white people into a sort of homogenous oppressed.

Arguments about systems of exploitation have a visceral appeal, but they remain notoriously difficult to pin down. Even a concept as seemingly concrete as "capitalism" has proven elusive.

If economic historians agree on anything, it is that capitalism never actually existed. The very notion is based on Marx's nineteenth-century understanding of European history, which is itself based on the theories of the German philosopher G. W. F. Hegel. For Marx and Hegel, European history had moved through a series of stages. These included ancient slavery, feudalism, and capitalism. Every stage of history brought with it a distinct set of economic laws based on exploitation of one "class" by another. This "stage theory" is why Marx believed that capitalism could be overthrown and replaced. Marx thought that if we could only replace the laws of capitalism with some other economic law, then—voilà!—we would have a new and improved economic and social order entirely different from the previous one.

The USSR learned the hard way that it is impossible to change the fundamental laws of economics, any more than it is possible to change the laws of physics. By the early 1920s, after only a few months of "pure socialism," Lenin began to advocate a New Economic Policy that sought to restore capitalism to Russia until such time as true socialism could be figured out. (Hint: it never was.)

Today we realize that there have never been major shifts in the fundamentals of economics, at any stage of history. Every economy, whether based on cowrie shells or crypto, has been subject to the same basic laws of supply, demand, and market forces. That's why we can say that there is no such thing as capitalism per se—because there is no such thing as not-capitalism either. All economies are fundamentally the same; the only difference is how you organize them.

Before the later nineteenth century with its factories, railroads, telegraphs, joint-stock companies, and stock markets, it's difficult to find serious evidence of what we would call "capitalism" anywhere in the New World. By this time, most of the damage that was going to be done to Indigenous populations in the US and Canada was a fait accompli. So blaming the decline of Indian populations on capitalism seems misguided at best.

It is true that from the seventeenth century, the Dutch and the British organized their Caribbean slave plantations in such a way that investors could buy shares in them, but this in itself is barely capitalistic. Plantation systems were simply a variety of the "great estate" system that had been in use in the Old World for thousands of years. In Egypt, in Sumer, in Rome, and in medieval Europe, great estates were set up by elites as a way of maximizing their profits from the agricultural productivity of a given region. To pretend that there was something fundamentally different in New World plantations is to confuse kind with degree.

We will discuss Indigenous notions of property in a later chapter; what is surprising is how quickly both Indigenous and European peoples settled on mutually intelligible economic conventions in a myriad of local situations across the centuries of their encounter. As for the role of capitalism in the New World, we can turn to Alan Greer, who is probably the greatest living expert on Native American property. A major theme of his book *Property and Dispossession* was "the very limited role of developments associated with capitalism, property and modernity in the early colonization of North America." Greer adds that "the establishment of settler tenures revolved more around the requirements of residence and subsistence than of profit," finally concluding that "colonial property formation had devastating consequences for Indigenous America, but that is not to say that it was the work of greedy and rapacious colonizers. Wealth and profit could accrue to some proprietors, though that was not actually a major factor impelling colonization in New France or New England through most of our period."

Greer's inescapable conclusion is that there was no world system of capitalism, or even of individual profit motives, that drove settler dispossession of Indian land in North America. Nothing akin to a "capitalist system" made North American land markets nastier—let alone more racist—than they otherwise would have been, and any assertion to the contrary is based on theory and emotion rather than fact.

DID COLONIALISM AND SLAVERY MAKE EUROPE RICH?

Other critics level a related charge: that it was only colonialist exploitation of nonwhite peoples that made modern Westerners rich. Ibram Kendi, for one, is fond of quoting Eric Williams's argument in *Capitalism and Slavery* that the transatlantic slave trade was the main source of modern European wealth. In Kendi's eyes, every European with a Gucci bag only has it because one of his African ancestors worked for them, directly or indirectly, as a slave sometime in the past. As Noam Chomsky put it in *Year 501*:

> the colonies of the New World offered enormous riches. The Acts and wars expanded the trading areas dominated by English merchants, who were able to enrich themselves through the slave trade and their "plunder-trade with America, Africa and Asia" (Hill), assisted by "state-sponsored colonial wars" and the various devices of economic management by which state power has forged the way to private wealth and a particular form of development shaped by its requirements.

The public intellectual Ta-Nehisi Coates likewise testified to Congress in the summer of 2020 to the effect that in the nineteenth century, half of all American wealth was derived from or was reliant upon slave labor. Presumably for Coates, the other half would have been derived from land appropriated from Native Americans.

Figure 5.1. Chambord Castle, Built 1516. (No Indigenous Person Was Harmed in the Construction of this Edifice).

This tale has all the ingredients to stoke a rage born of injustice. It paints a picture where in the year 1500, BIPOCs across the globe were on an economic par with Europe, poised to create a harmonious and prosperous future for themselves. But European rapaciousness, driven by the alienating logic of capitalism and a thirst for conquest, not only stole this bright future but also rendered BIPOCs desperate and subservient, while white people used colored capital to create a glittering civilization for themselves. In this view, Europeans have been little more than schoolyard bullies for the better part of a millennium.

One response to this argument would be to direct Kendi and Coates's attention to Chambord Castle in France's Loire valley. Chambord was built in 1516. It was started only twenty years after Columbus founded the town of Santo Domingo on Hispaniola and before Jacques Cartier staked France's first claim to the New World. In all, thousands of grandiose palaces like Chambord Castle, together with soaring cathedrals such as Notre Dame, and magnificent cities like Venice and Bruges were built across Western Europe during the long centuries before transatlantic slavery began. These grand monuments attest to a single indisputable fact: Western Europe was already rich—the richest region in the world—before the New World was discovered and before Europeans had more than the foggiest notion of what a nonwhite person was.

Indeed, researchers repeatedly show that transatlantic slavery contributed only a modest sum to total European GDP. At the very height of the slave trade, between 1750 and 1800, this amounted to somewhere in the neighborhood of 5 to 10 percent. Before and after that period, the numbers become even more inconvenient for anyone trying to make this argument.[67] According to the global GDP figures published by Angus Maddison in his seminal *The World Economy: A Millennial Perspective*, European per capita wealth in the year 1000 was at about the same level as the rest of the globe—that is to say, about $400 to $500 per person, measured in 1990 international dollars. Maddison's 2010 figures are freely available online and in various printed formats.[68]

Between the years 1000 and 1500—long before Europeans could be accused of exploiting more than a tiny handful of nonwhite people—a remarkable thing happened. The per person GDP of Western Europe steadily grew to nearly double the global average, while the GDP of every other region stagnated or grew by a modest amount. Maddison's dataset shows European per capita GDP in 1500 at nearly $800, while Mexico, Peru, and Africa still stood where they were five hundred years earlier—at about $400. Nor did the per capita GDP of Mexico, Peru, or Africa plummet after the arrival of the Europeans—it simply remained on the same slow-growth trajectory that it had been on for centuries. So much for the notion that European arrival constituted an economic disaster for the majority of Indigenous inhabitants.

---

[67] Pepijn Brandon and Ulbe Bosma, "Slavery and the Dutch Economy, 1750–1800," *Slavery & Abolition* 42, no. 1 (2021), 43–76, https://www.tandfonline.com/doi/full/10.1080/0144039X.2021.1860464.

[68] Maddison's dataset is available at the University of Groningen website: "Maddison Database 2010," Groningen Growth and Development Centre, University of Groningen, https://www.rug.nl/ggdc/historicaldevelopment/maddison/releases/maddison-database-2010.

Meanwhile, the richest non-European areas in the year 1500 were China and India, whose GDP has been estimated at $600 and $500. This was a modest increase on the $450 per person these societies had produced in the year 1000. In five centuries during which they were unmolested by European colonialism, then, China and India only managed to grow their economies at a few percent per century. After 1500, the European economy continued to grow at the same strong pace that it had done in the preceding five centuries. It did not suddenly grow at a faster pace, even as it forged Wallerstein's "World System." Over the eight hundred years between the year 1000 and 1800—both before and after colonization—Europe's GDP experienced a remarkably consistent growth rate of about 10 to 15 percent per century. European per capita GDP went from $800 in 1500 to $900 in 1600 to $1,000 in 1700 to $1,200 in 1820.

This suggests that the European economy was already set on its growth trajectory prior to its colonial adventure and that the discovery of New World colonies—while very helpful for some regions at certain times—did not significantly alter the growth trajectory of the West European economy as a whole. All of Maddison's data thus points to the conclusion that the relatively small amount of wealth generated by New World trade—including both slavery and land appropriations from the Natives—was mere icing on the economic cake of long-term European growth.

Stronger evidence against Ibram Kendi's wishful thinking would be difficult to find.

As for Ta-Nehisi Coates's idea that, centuries after Columbus, a significant portion of American wealth was derived from slave labor in the South, this notion has also been debunked time and again, most recently by Phillip W. Magness in chapter 1 of his critique of the 1619 Project. By most estimates the GDP of the US North was several times—probably about four to five—as large as the GDP of the US South during the Civil War. The pretense that the Northern economy was shackled to slavery in a meaningful way is belied by the Civil War itself, which saw the

North switch to other sources of cotton and manufacturing. The North experienced an enormous economic boom in the aftermath of the war, while the economy of the South collapsed. According to recent research presented in the *American Economic Review*, slave-generated capital did not as a rule survive the Civil War.[69]

In sum, all the evidence points to the conclusion that the wealth of modern Europe and America was categorically *not* built on the backs of African slaves. Anyone who makes this misleading argument is likely beginning from a place of anti-European prejudice, rather than an acquaintance with the facts. Nor is it correct or useful to suggest that American and European wealth was built on the backs of Indigenous people. American real estate taken from the Indians did not begin to turn a profit until the later nineteenth century, and the great majority of American wealth from that period came from the marshaling of natural resources unknown to Indigenous people such as oil, coal, and steel.

The real dynamos of modern American wealth were factories, which require very little land. These became increasingly dominant in American wealth creation during and after the Civil War. Most of them were located in the Northeast, and most workers were European immigrants. The factory system, in turn, depended on the long evolution of trade, manufacture, and financial institutions in Europe, which had been ongoing since the Middle Ages, long before the Age of Exploration began.

***

In Part I of this book, we debunked a number of popular myths about early European colonization of the New World. We can summarize our findings as follows:

Christopher Columbus was not a mass murderer, and he did not start the African slave trade. The Spanish did not commit genocide in

---

[69] Philipp Ager, Leah Boustan, and Katherine Eriksson, "The Intergenerational Effects of a Large Wealth Shock: White Southerners after the Civil War," *American Economic Review* 111, no. 11 (November 2021), 3767–94, https://www.aeaweb.org/articles?id=10.1257/aer.20191422.

the New World. Claims that Europeans killed one hundred million Indigenous people in the New World are gross exaggerations with no basis in reality. The real population of the New World in 1491 was closer to twenty-five million people, and Hispaniola likely had two hundred and fifty thousand people rather than three or eight million as is usually claimed.

Sensationalists want us to believe that over 90 percent of these people died by fire and sword at the hands of bloodthirsty racist Europeans, but much of the population decline was a simple failure of Indigenous societies to maintain replacement birthrates. The remainder was largely caused by the natural spread of disease.

The majority of the people who died during the conquests of the Aztec and Incan Empires were killed by Indigenous people, not Spaniards. The Spanish conquest of the Aztec Empire saved at least thirty thousand people per year by ending the barbaric practice of mass enslavement, human sacrifice, and the cannibalism associated with it.

All the major pre-Columbian population centers are still home to large populations of Indigenous and mixed-race people: they may have been conquered but were not dispossessed or exterminated en masse.

Compared with Mexico and Peru, North America was a mere fringe territory with only a few percent of the total New World population.

Credible experts have calculated that the total number of North American Indians who were massacred during the entire five-hundred-year history of European colonization is less than ten thousand individuals, maximally twenty thousand if one accepts Benjamin Madley's figures for California after 1848 (as we will discuss in a later chapter). This is out of a population initially numbered at more than one million. Very likely, more Europeans were massacred by Indians during the settlement period than the other way around. As of this writing, Wikipedia agrees.[70] Certainly far more than ten thousand Indians were massacred by other

---

[70] "List of Indian Massacres in North America," Wikipedia, https://en.wikipedia.org/wiki/List_of_Indian_massacres_in_North_America.

Indians in North America during this same time period, though next to no attention is paid to this fact by modern historians.

Today's Latino people are the result of one of the most successful experiments in mass racial mixing to occur anywhere in the world over the past one thousand years, with North Africa being a close second. The races mixed readily throughout Latin America and Canada because early Europeans were not racist against Amerindians in any demonstrable fashion, at least until hundreds of years after they arrived. Even then, the nineteenth-century high point of European racism was also the high point of the European and American abolitionist movements, and these two facts must always be weighed against one another for a true picture of "European racism" to emerge.

There is no such thing as a system of settler colonialism that served as a dynamo of historical development. The theory of settler colonialism is a mishmash of pseudo-Marxist misreadings of economic history, which relies on outdated nineteenth-century concepts such as "primitive accumulation." Reality can seldom be pigeonholed into a system, and many of the academics who vocally promote such faddism are not historians or economists but literature professors and others with little grasp of how human societies evolve in their baroque glory.

For hundreds of years after the Europeans arrived in America, they harbored no plan to displace the majority of Indigenous people. In most places, the goal was to maintain coastal trading forts rather than to exclude or evict Indians from vast areas. The theory of settler colonialism is given the lie by the simple fact that in 95 percent of the places where Europeans landed around the globe, they never displaced Indigenous populations. Rather than obey some inexorable capitalist logic, Europeans merely took advantage of places where there were few or no Indigenous people able to make a viable land claim. This included only the most thinly populated places such as Australia (which had about one hundred thousand Indigenous people before Europeans arrived, and nearly eight hundred thousand today), and North America (which likewise had a negligible population density in most of its territory).

In Mexico, which was thickly populated then and now by Indigenous and mixed-race people, the Indians were granted extensive tracts to govern where it was illegal for non-Indians to purchase land. Indian villages were accorded the same political institutions as enjoyed by Spaniards. These arrangements lasted for several centuries until independence. Farther north, almost 90 percent of North America remained in Indigenous hands for the first three hundred years of European presence in the New World.

In Part II we turn our attention from the early European explorers to the Amerindians themselves. The American Left has saddled our popular conception of Amerindian societies with a number of politically charged concepts that obscure the reality of New World civilization and its people. We will begin by gauging the actual technological achievements of the Aztecs and Incas, challenging some of the wilder claims that have been made in influential books over the last decade or two. We will then turn to the idea that Native Americans were more peaceful and benevolent than people elsewhere on the globe. Next we turn to the misconceptions that Native Americans were enlightened stewards of the environment and that they lived under some quasi-mystical form of communist, feminist government that was more equal than European forms of government. Finally, we debunk the myth—spread by a pair of academic quacks—that the American Founding Fathers stole democracy from the Iroquois.

II

THE NATIVE
PEOPLES

CHAPTER 6

WERE NEW WORLD CIVILIZATIONS EQUAL OR SUPERIOR TO EUROPE?

[The Indians one encounters in parts of Latin America today are but] the persecuted survivors of a recently shattered culture. It is like coming across refugees from a Nazi concentration camp, and concluding that they belonged to a culture that had always been barefoot and starving.

—Charles C. Mann, *1491*

C harles C. Mann's *1491: The Americas Before Columbus*, published in 2005, is arguably the most influential book ever published on Mesoamerican civilization. Mann began his career as a science writer but later turned his hand toward a description of the New World civilizations. The main goal of Mann's book is to bust the "myth" that Amerindians lived Stone Age lives in sparsely populated villages; instead, Mann describes the New World as teeming with large, technologically wonderous cities, many of which were larger than any European city. Mann goes to great lengths to "prove" that Amerindian peoples had a large impact on their environments, and he asserts that Amerindians were just as advanced as Europeans not only in metallurgy but also in philosophy and mathematics.[71]

In the book's opening pages, Mann recounts the adventures of an anthropologist named Allan R. Holmberg, who visited remote parts of the Andes in the 1940s in order to collect data on the Indians living there. Holmberg described them as "among the most culturally backward people in the world." They lived in constant want and hunger; they had no clothes, no domestic animals, no musical instruments, no art or design, and almost no religion. They could not count above three, and they could not make fire but had to carry it from camp to camp. Holmberg assumed that these Indians had lived this way since time immemorial.

Mann argues that Holmberg's assumption could not be more wrong. According to Mann's provocative thesis, the Indians Holmberg encountered were the equivalent of "Holocaust survivors," and the people who had inflicted this holocaust were European colonists. Mann assures his readers—more by implication than explicit assertion—that prior to colonization the Indians of Mesoamerica and the Andes had been living in civilizational splendor equal to that of Europe. Then the conquistadors came and reduced the Indians of the Andes to abject nakedness and poverty.

Mann plays up every possible bit of evidence to conjure a portrait of the New World as thickly urbanized, opulent, and culturally world-leading. In his portrayal, the Americas were "immeasurably busier, more diverse, and more populous than researchers previously imagined." He further asserts that his "revelations" about the Americas are new and revolutionary and that he is reporting things no specialist has realized in the past. He implies that the real reason no one has reported on the splendor of the New World in 1491 is because lingering Eurocentrism in academia has caused specialists to suppress the true opulence of Amerindian culture, out of shame for the crimes of their ancestors.

---

[71] For example, for his take on metallurgy, see Charles C. Mann, *1491: New Revelations of the Americas Before Columbus* (New York: Alfred A. Knopf, 2005), 83.

Mann's book has done tremendous harm. First, he pretends that he is conveying "new revelations of the Americas before Columbus," while specialists who review his book assert that Mann has, in fact, said nothing they had not already known for many years. His fervent claims are insulting and frustrating to serious specialists who have spent decades amassing data and drawing careful, measured conclusions.

But the real problem is that Mann slyly disguises his book as history when its primary aim is polemical. He therefore represents one of the worst aspects of our new culture of misinformation, one that deliberately distorts history to generate attention (and book sales) while bolstering a political narrative.

In order to "prove" that the Americas were just as advanced, urbanized, and civilized as Europe in 1491, Mann employs a judicious combination of cherry-picking and insinuation. By using Holmberg's Indians of the Beni in Bolivia as a stand-in for all Amerindians, Mann deliberately chose some of the most impoverished Indians in the entire Andes, as they appeared over eighty years ago. The image of them "naked, starving, and cold" implies that European colonialism had inflicted a similar level of destruction on every Indigenous group across the New World.

Of course, most Bolivian Indians in the 1940s were far better off than the Beni, and most Bolivians today are much better off than they were in 1940. Mann's imagery is a sophisticated rhetorical trick, one few readers would pick up on. And Mann employs such tricks masterfully throughout his book.

He plays similar trick when he compares Aztec and Greek philosophy; for example, he asserts that the corpus of surviving Aztec philosophy is greater than that of the Greeks. By which he means that the number of texts we have in Nahuatl, the Aztec language, exceeds the number that have survived from ancient Greece. (Most of these were in fact written after the Spanish arrived, often under the guidance of Nahuatl-speaking missionaries; the majority were administrative records kept by the Republicas de los Indios.) But the way Mann words his sentence, he implies that the *quality* of Greek philosophy was also lower than the Nahuatl, leaving countless readers with the impression that the philosophy of the Aztec Empire was as detailed and consequential as that of Socrates, Plato, and Aristotle.

The demographer and critic Thomas M. Whitmore has noted how Mann's approach "highlights controversy" among scholars, implying that certain issues are contested, and hence open to reinterpretation, when in fact they are not. For example, Mann repeatedly emphasizes the highest estimates for Mesoamerican population, while ignoring the majority of solid scholarship that points to much lower figures. Whitmore drily concludes that Mann's "tactic may be used effectively for narrative impact, but it does not represent adequately the extant literature." He therefore recommends that readers move beyond Mann and look at more serious scholarship before drawing conclusions about Mesoamerican reality.[72]

In popular culture, Mann's portrait has trickled down into the now common belief that the Aztecs were at least culturally and technologically equal to European civilization when Columbus arrived in the Caribbean—and that if left alone they would have evolved into a superior civilization, like some version of the African nation of Wakanda as portrayed in the movie *Black Panther*. (In fact, this theme of a technologically advanced Mesoamerican civilization has since been mainstreamed in *Black Panther: Wakanda Forever*.)

THE AZTEC TECHNOLOGY LEVEL: CIRCA 3000 BC

Mann's book has led to a lot of sensational claims about the state of New World civilization. Nonetheless, specialists continue to agree that the technology level of the Aztec and Incan societies was comparable to the

---

[72] Thomas M. Whitmore, "Many Died, but Many Lived: Mann's Revelations about an American Tragedy," *Geographical Review* 96, no. 3 (2006), 502–505, https://www.tandfonline.com/doi/abs/10.1111/j.1931-0846.2006.tb00273.x. In the same volume see also a discussion of the specialist's response to Mann as "we already knew all of this," W. George Lovell, "A Year by Many Other Names," *Geographical Review* 96, no. 3 (2006), 478–480.

dawn of civilization in ancient Mesopotamia. That is to say, the most advanced New World societies were roughly 4,500 years behind the Old World civilizations of China, Islam, India, and Europe when Columbus stumbled into the Caribbean.

Comparisons between the Aztecs of AD 1500 and the ancient Sumerians of circa 3000 BC began as early as 1966, when the anthropologist Robert McCormick Adams published *The Evolution of Urban Society: Early Mesopotamia and Prehispanic Mexico*. Adams's work continues to be influential and was commemorated in a volume as recently as 2018. Major scholars such as Bruce Trigger, whose *Understanding Early Civilizations* appeared in 2003, assert similar figures; the Aztec fiscal historian Michael E. Smith recently asserted the same thing in a 2015 paper.

The fact that there was a gap of nearly five thousand years between the technological levels of the Old World and the New will come as a revelation to many people and upset many more, but it is based on a wealth of information and scholarly consensus, meaning that it is more or less indisputable.

Before laying out the proof, it is worth pointing out that Mann is correct insofar as the Aztec and Incan civilizations were truly remarkable in world history, especially considering their isolation from the rest of the world. If the Aztecs had not been in the grip of the biggest cult of human sacrifice the world has ever seen at the time the Spanish landed, they would be remembered much more fondly by academics and popular culture alike. Despite this gruesome flaw, the Aztec civilization was far more complex and sophisticated than most people recognize. Mesoamerican civilization had been capable of constructing great cities for over a thousand years before Cortes arrived, and the city-state was long established as a fixture in the political, economic, and cultural landscape. Dozens of cities around Mesoamerica contained tens of thousands of people; buildings in their centers were elaborately constructed of stone and decorated with sculpture. Cortes himself described the Aztec capital in the following terms:

This city has many squares where trading is done
and markets are held continuously. There is also
one square twice as big as that of Salamanca, with
arcades all around, where more than sixty thousand
people come each day to buy and sell, and where
every kind of merchandise produced in these lands
is found; provisions as well as ornaments of gold and
silver, lead, brass, copper, tin, stones, shells, bones,
and feathers. They also sell lime, hewn and unhewn
stone, adobe bricks, tiles, and cut and uncut woods
of various kinds. There is a street where they sell
game and birds of every species found in this land:
chickens, partridges, and quails, wild ducks, fly-
catchers, widgeons, turtledoves, pigeons, cane birds,
parrots, eagles and eagle owls, falcons, sparrow
hawks and kestrels, and they sell the skins of some
of these birds of prey with their feathers, heads and
claws. They sell rabbits and hares, and stags and
small gelded dogs which they breed for eating....

Like the ancient Sumerians, the Aztecs had an elaborate class system, military and priestly castes, elaborate fiscal systems of regular and
recorded taxation, pictographic writing that could be used for various
administrative purposes, and they were capable of producing finely made
gold and copper items and high-quality pottery. They also engaged in
intensive farming, which included terraced hillsides and, in some regions,
highly productive floating gardens.

Cortes and other conquistadors sent back several accounts of
the Mesoamerican cities that described them as being "greater than"
this or that European city, and superficially they were correct. Some
Mesoamerican cities had more people than most European cities of the
time, and some of them boasted impressive buildings, temples, squares,

and markets that seemed equal or greater in size. Ornaments and clothing could be elaborate and of high artistic quality.

With all this opulence on display, it becomes easy for the nonspecialist to assume that the New World civilization was, as Mann asserts, just as technologically advanced as those of Eurasia and Northern Africa. Look a little more closely, however, and we are forced to turn back the dial. Had he stumbled upon the Sumerian city of Ur as it was in circa 3000 BC in the middle of a Mesoamerican jungle, Cortes would have found similar wonders to report.

TECHNOLOGICAL AND CULTURAL COMPARISONS

Much has been made of the pyramid-building techniques of the Mayans and the Aztecs, which compare to the ziggurat-builders of ancient Mesopotamia and the pyramid-builders of ancient Egypt. The similarities between these civilizations' prestige buildings are so clear that more than one conspiracy theorist has concluded that their builders must have been taught by benevolent aliens.

The real explanation is fascinating, if not quite so exotic. All these societies built pyramids first, because pyramids are the simplest monumental buildings that can be constructed out of stone. They are incredibly stable, because they have no vertical surfaces that might bow and collapse. They are easy to build, because they provide natural ramps, up which material can be carried to the highest levels. They require no columns, and they can be filled up with rubble and earth. Their lack of all but a tiny interior space means that they require no sophisticated understanding of support structures and material strength. At the same time, they are visually very impressive, because of their height and regular geometry.

Like the early Egyptians, the Aztecs had also learned how to use basic stone columns to create colonnades along the front of their buildings. A few millennia later, however, the Egyptians went on to create huge colonnaded structures such as the temple of Luxor, which was built in 1400 BC. The interior of Luxor presents a veritable forest of very tall, regularly proportioned columns that fan out in all directions; this was clearly beyond the means of even the most advanced Aztec builders three thousand years later.

Meanwhile, the Greeks borrowed from the Egyptians and improved upon their techniques. They perfected the column, the lintel, and the tympanum, meaning they could create wider, airier, and column-free interior spaces by about 500 BC. A few centuries after this, the Romans hit upon the idea of stacking rows of columns on top of each other. This enabled them to build much taller structures than the Greeks had been able to do, leading to the construction of works such as the Colosseum in Rome and great aqueducts such as the Pont du Gard in southern France.

The Aztecs or their successors probably would have hit upon these innovations had their civilization continued unaltered. But as impressive as the Aztec cities were, Sumerian cities of the fourth millennium BC showed virtually analogous levels of architectural sophistication.

Mesoamerican writing tells a similar story. Mesopotamian writing began from a desire to keep records of how many taxes had been paid and by whom. This incentivized authorities to make marks in clay tablets, which showed both numbers and pictures of the types of goods that had been turned in. After several thousand years, scribes had invented elaborate pictorial systems that rulers used to issue proclamations, and which priests employed to record or illustrate religious doctrines. In this intermediate phase, writing was a combination of pictures and alphabetic signs. The classic Egyptian hieroglyphs evolved into a similar form, until they were eventually superseded by much more efficient alphabet forms invented by Phoenician merchants. The earliest Mesopotamian cuneiform writing appeared in about 3500 BC, while fully fledged alphabets did not appear until about 1000 BC. Meanwhile the earliest major work of Old World literature that we have, the *Epic of Gilgamesh*, dates from about 2100 BC.

Aztec writing at the time of Columbus was still in what we would consider an early phase of pictorial symbolism. Aztec tax records showed standardized pictures of the types and quantity of goods that were to be paid for and might include symbols representing the month in which they were due. The Mayans had been slightly more advanced in their writing skills, but the collapse of their civilization led to a regression in Mesoamerican writing levels. Like early Egyptian hieroglyphs, Aztec writing contained some syllabic elements, while others remained purely pictorial.

As with their architecture, the Aztecs' writing built upon traditions that had been developed by the Olmecs and Maya hundreds of years before. We have to assume that had Aztec writing been allowed to go on for another thousand years or two, their writing would have developed into a more fully fledged alphabetic or syllabic system and that production of literature, laws, and religious texts would have continued apace.

Even abstract political institutions like kingship and priesthood equate with the Old World circa 3000 BC. In Mesopotamia and Egypt, the concept of a strong king (such as Gilgamesh or Ramses) did not come naturally. Strong kingship was an invention that these civilizations had to discover. In earlier societies, the concept of leadership had been fluid. Chiefs might have authority in some matters but not in others. They might share some powers with a council, while retaining other powers for themselves. Often, they held authority at certain times (such as when the community was under attack) and were expected to relinquish this authority when the emergency passed.

The "invention" of kingship in Mesopotamia changed everything. Archaeologists believe that the Sumerians developed this institution in the third millennium BC. Over the course of this millennium, kings increasingly acted as major focusers of the community's resources. While we may lament that Sumerian kings used a great deal of exploited slave labor, often for projects that served little purpose other than to satisfy their vanity, it remains true that only an extremely centralized, universally recognized authority could direct so much labor to a single purpose.

It is the gradual emergence of kingship, then, that is believed to be responsible for the massive boost in civilizational achievement that we see in the Old World circa 3000 BC. Kings directed the building of the great pyramids at Ur and Giza, the construction of massive city walls, the creation of huge armies of conquest, the requisition and stockpiling of enormous grain reserves, and ensured that new cities were built according to a rigorous geometrical street plan.

Both the Incas and the Aztecs were in the process of building up similar traditions of kingship when the Spanish arrived and arrested their progress. The Incas had been preceded by the Tiwanaku and the Wari, both of whom had been organizing states over several centuries, beginning roughly a thousand years before Pizarro. The Aztecs likewise built their political traditions on the foundations of the Olmecs, Toltecs, Maya, and other organized peoples.

But traditions of Incan and Aztec kingship were still in a fragile, nascent state when the Spanish arrived. Scholars have described Mesoamerica in 1518 as a "city-state culture," where people's loyalties and conception of society revolved around their city-state rather than the kingdom writ large. There were as yet no established traditions of kingship, no ancient lines of dynastic rulers, upon which Aztec or Inca kings could draw for support. Both the Incan and Aztec empires were quite new—less than two hundred years old at the time.

The same goes with technical innovations such as the wheel and astronomy. The Mayan and Aztec astronomical innovations, including an elaborate calendar and a system for predicting eclipses, were certainly impressive—but they were still on a par with those of the early Sumerians. To this day, we continue to use a "base 60" system for keeping time, and for compass directions. Astronomers continue to divide the sky into 360 degrees of longitude (right ascension), and 180 degrees of celestial latitude (declination). We inherited this base 60 system from the ancient Babylonians, who themselves inherited it from earlier Mesopotamian peoples such as the Sumerians.

In other words, the Babylonians were so advanced in astronomy, and their systems for measuring the sky, the earth, and time were so practical, that even in the modern world of supercomputers and space-based telescopes we continue to use their innovations as the basis of our own computations.

In about 3000 BC, Mesopotamian people were just beginning to employ the wheel for use in transportation. They started out using it as a potter's wheel, which made the production of uniform pots more efficient. It took them about one thousand years before the use of wheels on chariots became commonplace. The Aztecs also had the wheel in 1491, but at the point of the Spanish conquest, they were only employing it for children's toys. We are left to assume that had the Aztec culture continued uninterrupted, they would have begun employing it for pottery creation, and/or for wheeled carts (drawn by humans in the absence of appropriate draft animals).

Meanwhile, the Europeans arriving with Columbus and Cortes were the beneficiaries of thousands of years of advancements made across the Old World. Europeans inherited numerous ancient advances in iron smelting, Roman law, the Greek invention of coined money, the medieval invention of the codex (book), the Arab invention of the bill of exchange, the Chinese invention of gunpowder, the European development of cannon, millennia of experience with building oceangoing vessels, lenses for eyeglasses, and innumerable other advances.

A combination of all these factors, including early kingship, nascent bureaucratization, fragile state building, and vulnerable food supplies, as well as the more obvious technological disadvantages, is what caused the Aztec and Incan Empires to dissolve so completely under the influence of Spanish adventurism. Had these civilizations been at, say, Roman or Han Chinese levels of administration, they would have proven more resilient, and more elements of New World imperial culture would have survived.

WHY DID THE NEW WORLD LAG BEHIND?

Jared Diamond's 1997 bestseller *Guns, Germs, and Steel* has been accused of geographical determinism, and his methodology does downplay too much the role of human culture and institutions. Nonetheless, Diamond's logic does come into play in the grand scheme of human civilization, because geography sets basic parameters such as resource bases and how many people a given area can support at a given technological level.

We have seen how the New World offered a lamentably small area for civilization to take root. The growth of civilization requires fertile, largely frost-free areas that are not overgrown by thick jungle; the existence of large rivers to boost agricultural fertility, facilitate trade, and speed communication also helps immeasurably. This is why the New World had only one-tenth of the world's total population in 1491. In the relatively small areas of central Mexico and the Andes that ticked off many of these boxes, the lack of suitable rivers severely hampered the growth of civilization. Farther north, the Mississippi River system was subject to harsher climatic conditions and lower fertility levels, meaning that its population densities remained much lower, and its advance toward civilization consequently lagged behind Mesoamerica and the Andes.

The advance of civilization is dependent on the presence of large population nuclei. Large numbers of people living in close quarters are forced to organize their societies, and innovations such as writing and specialized craftsmanship tend to follow. Such population nuclei are fostered by the adoption of intensive forms of agriculture, which forces people to stay put in the same place, year after year. Gradually, people learn to build more permanent settlements. Often there are false starts, where quasi-permanent settlements are abandoned after a few centuries. Only after millennia of settlement do people become so habituated to life in cities that they come to regard their settlements as truly permanent. Early descriptions of Ur describe the walls and temples with a sort of braggadocio that suggests an expectation of permanence. The Mississippian culture had not yet gotten to this point, while the Mesoamericans, and to some extent the Incas, were further along this scale.

The Mississippi and southwestern US areas were in a state of advanced civilization similar to that of the Fertile Crescent in about 10,000 to 7000 BC. Early Fertile Crescent "mound builders" created proto-cities and artifacts similar to what we find in the southwest and the Mississippi Indian cultures. They were in turn thousands of years behind the Aztecs, and contact between the two areas was minor and indirect. Nonetheless, they were in the process of making significant advances over the Paleolithic habits carried by their ancestors across the Siberian land bridge.

These advances might have primed them to develop more rapidly, perhaps borrowing from Mesoamerican civilization as this continued to innovate. Had the Americas been left to develop in isolation, they might have boasted at least four separate civilizational nuclei by our year AD 2500. As it was, the Old World made contact and introduced them to thousands of years of technological and cultural advancements, all in the space of a few generations. The results were bound to be completely transformative on New World ways of life. This is a tragedy in many regards, but we must not lose sight of the fact that it was a blessing in many others—including for the hundreds of millions of descendants of Indigenous people across the Americas who are alive and well in the modern world. It is disturbing how many academics, including non-historians who fetishize Charles Mann, breezily teach their students to regard human progress as a terrible mistake, or to suggest that it caused people to go to war with one another—as if tribal people never knew war before Europeans brought it to their shores.

While researching the popular influence of Charles Mann and Jared Diamond, I came across a blog post by a PhD student in biology entitled "The Worst Mistake in the History of the Human Race." The "mistake," it turned out, was the invention of agriculture—the very invention that enabled cities to take root and civilization to be born. This student reported how her environmental studies professor taught that human "progress" had caused more harm than good. The professor explained that had agriculture never been invented

> the environmental problems that exist in our world would never have appeared. Also, without agriculture it is likely that many human health issues such as cancer, diabetes, and heart disease would not exist. Finally, if agriculture had never existed, human populations and culture that have been exterminated would never have disappeared to begin with.

Progress is always a two-edged sword. Joseph Schumpeter famously observed that economies engage in a continuous process of "creative destruction." The same thing can be said for human society. Every change brings loss, and humans are continually changing. The modern environmentalist Left has become so mired in despair, so worried about what climate change might do in the future, that many have given up hope. Rather than work toward realistic solutions (such as nuclear power or carbon-scrubbing machines), these despondent people, like the Steward Denethor in the *Lord of the Rings*, have begun to pray for the death of civilization itself. How else can one explain their wish that agriculture had never been invented, or that cities, writing, technology, culture, medicine, bath tubs, human rights, and equality had never become possible?

When the Europeans arrived in the New World, they introduced New World peoples to five thousand years of advancements in the space of a few generations. This was bound to cause upheaval and spell the end of many Native American ways. All the same, we must recognize that New World people began to use metal tools, firearms, and various European food-production techniques not because they were forced to but because these things made their lives easier. After the Europeans arrived in Mexico, large-scale conflict among tribes ceased for the first time in recorded history, and peace descended across the land to an unprecedented extent. People should be talking about the Pax Hispanica, which was brought to the peoples of Mexico and South America in the wake of the conquest—a peace that saved hundreds of thousands of people from capture, torture, slavery, human sacrifice, and refugee status. The encomienda system in Latin America and the silver mines gave scope for large-scale rights abuses, but whoever tries to weigh these against the value of the peace that was imposed? Meanwhile, roads were constructed, the quality of buildings improved, literacy increased, iron tools introduced, and the quality of life for most Mesoamerican people increased dramatically.

So, while it is fair to lament the passing of so many New World customs, it is important to remember that the lifestyle the Europeans had to offer was in most ways far superior to the late Stone Age society of 1491. While the New World would probably have gone on to develop Roman-era levels of technology if left undisturbed by Europeans, this might well have taken them until about AD 4500. Looking at the big picture, most Latin Americans alive today would probably prefer a world in which Columbus discovered America.

CHAPTER 7

WERE NATIVE AMERICANS NATURALLY PEACEFUL AND BENEVOLENT?

A prevailing characteristic of the savages on the eastern coast was the barbarous cruelties which they inflicted upon their [Indigenous] prisoners of war. Having kindled a fire, they selected a victim, and proceeded to excoriate his back with red-hot burning brands, and to apply live coals to the ends of his fingers, where they would give the most exquisite pain.

—Samuel de Champlain, *Voyages*

U ntil the 1960s, the American popular mind saw Indians as warriors: proud, skilled, and noble. Boy Scout manuals were filled with "Indian woods lore," and instructions on how to imitate the elite skill set of the Apache scout. Such Indians might be trusted allies, like the Lone Ranger's sidekick Tonto, or dangerous antagonists. Sports teams and US Army units were named after them, invoking their traditions of honor, dignity, and courage in battle.

Beginning in the 1970s, however, the academic Left began to appropriate the popular image of the Indian for their own ends. Rejecting the earlier "brave warrior" stereotype, they replaced it with a new flower-child image of Native Americans as wise ecologists, a people close to the Earth who understood better than the white man how to maintain a balance between nature and human societies. We will address this image of the nature-loving "ecological Indian" in a subsequent chapter.

Meanwhile, the peace movement sought to downplay the element of violence in Native American culture. They portrayed Indians as naturally disposed toward peace, seeking agreement and consensus, and only resorting to war as a last option. Even in wartime, their culture was supposedly moderated by the same wise tendency toward balance and restraint that they showed toward nature.

In his *People's History of the United States*, Howard Zinn introduces the Arawaks of the Caribbean as a "mostly peaceful" people who were "remarkable for their hospitality and their belief in sharing." Zinn implies that people who shared their homes and food were not tainted by "greed," a vice that he and other anti-capitalists naively imagine to be a leading cause of war. This (false) stereotype of the "peaceful Arawaks," by the way, is based on a single line from Columbus's journal, which we have already encountered.

Early in her *Indigenous Peoples' History*, Dunbar-Ortiz emphasizes the Iroquois Great Law of Peace as though it were the founding principle of all Indigenous governments. (She also falsely claims it was the basis of the US Constitution—more on that in another chapter.) On the Great Law, Dunbar-Ortiz quotes a modern-day chief who explains: "The first principle [of our law] is peace. The second principle, equity, justice for the people. And third, the power of the good minds, of the collective powers to be of one mind: unity. And health. All of these were involved in the basic principles. And the process of discussion, putting aside warfare as a method of reaching decisions, and now using intellect."

While these are indeed noble sentiments, they represent a distinctly modern, distinctly Americanized interpretation of these traditions. A seventeenth-century chief would not have put them in quite the same way. The ideas so approvingly quoted by Dunbar-Ortiz have been borrowed wholesale from the British and American Enlightenment. (The chief she quotes also inherits the benefits of a monopoly of violence long maintained by the overwhelming power of the American state. In the seventeenth century, no Indigenous chief enjoyed anything close to this level of external security, and therefore warfare was a fact of life that could not be wished away by platitudes about peace and equality.)

The idea that New World Indigenous societies were inherently peace-loving has carried over into mainstream portrayals of United States history. *The Brave New World*, a textbook by Peter Charles Hoffer, paints European society in 1500 in a uniformly negative light. In his judgment, European society was hierarchical, oppressive, exploitative, greedy, misguided, superstitious, and arrogant. By contrast, Native society was moderate, egalitarian, and harmonious; a society that only resorted to violence on rare occasions. Hoffer explains that "when war erupted between villages or peoples, tradition and religious beliefs controlled the use of violence," and he reminds us that "tradition and traditionalism in Indian life kept a balance between aggressiveness and aggrandizement on the one hand, and reciprocity and hospitality, on the other."

Hoffer ends his encomium with the ominous warning that "this balance, along with the traditions sustaining it, would be destroyed when Europeans arrived." As if the minute Columbus set foot on Hispaniola, every Indian society from Alaska to Tierra del Fuego immediately lurched from enlightened bliss into a *Lord of the Flies* scenario unlike anything it had known before.

This sounds absurd and yet the belief is widespread among academics and laymen alike. It is the dominant picture of Indians and Europeans that is now being taught to children around the world. In this way, the Left maintains its fiction that "colonialism" changed Indigenous society immediately, completely, and entirely for the worse. This enables the anti-colonialists to pretend that any "bad" or violent habits encountered by Europeans were merely the result of Europe's own corrupting influence.

A SOCIETY BUILT FOR WAR

There is one small problem with this image of peace-loving Native American societies: it is completely untrue. Before the Spanish imposed peace on Amerindian tribes from California to Tierra del Fuego, the unrelenting reality of their lives was a Hobbesian war of all against all. (The parallel with Rome, which imposed a similar peace through violence on the Gauls and other tribal peoples of Western Europe, is striking in this regard.) Outside of a tiny area of city-states in Mesoamerica and the Andes, Native American societies were uniformly tribal chiefdoms. Wherever in the world such city-states and chiefdoms have arisen, warfare has been a continuous part of life. As a rule, the majority of males in chiefdoms are trained in the art of war; in city-state areas, elite males train in war while the rest of the males participate in agriculture or crafts that support the warrior elite.

There are very few general truths in the history of global civilization, but one of the most reliable is that in areas where rulers monopolize violence on a small scale, warfare, raiding, and slavery will be endemic. Steven Pinker calls this "the inescapable logic of anarchy." Only modern-day first-world anarchists for whom war remains an abstraction—e.g., people such as Dave Graeber (whom we met in chapter 2)—would argue otherwise. General peace is only possible when strong rulers monopolize violence on a large scale; this is the only thing that has historically protected people from a near-continuous threat of localized raiding.

The prevalence of violence in tribal society was summarized in a recent interview with Korsai, one of the last Indigenous inhabitants of Papua New Guinea to give up his traditional ways of life. The interviewer noted that the village next to Korsai's had been enticed by American missionaries to go and live in an apartment building in town. When asked whether he felt he was missing out on modern amenities by not going along with them, Korsai responded:

'Not for long! Off our neighbours went, and we were left alone on the mountain. And we loved the missionaries—because they'd taken those neighbours away! We didn't need to worry about being attacked anymore. Also, we didn't have to get up in the night to attack them!' Now the Yaifo women could go off to tend the gardens without fear; the gardens were expanded and no one ever went hungry; health dramatically improved.[73]

The same dynamic of continuous raiding, fear, and want framed the earliest experience of the ex-slave Olaudah Equiano, who was born and raised in Benin during the eighteenth century. Among his first memories was the time when he and his sister were kidnapped from his village by neighboring tribespeople and sold to a distant chieftain. Equiano describes the situation as follows:

My father, besides many slaves, had a numerous family.... I was trained up from my earliest years in the art of war; my daily exercise was shooting and throwing javelins; and my mother adorned me with emblems, after the manner of our greatest warriors. In this way I grew up till I was turned the age of eleven, when an end was put to my happiness in the following manner.

Generally when the grown people in the neighbour-hood were gone far in the fields to labour, the children assembled together in some of the neighbours' premises to play; and commonly some of us used to get up a tree to look out for any assailant, or kidnapper, that might come upon us; for they sometimes took those opportunities of our

---

[73] As related by Benedict Allen in "What the World's Most Isolated Tribe Can Teach Us about Happiness," *Telegraph*, November 23, 2021, https://www.telegraph.co.uk/travel/destinations/oceania/papua-new-guinea/worlds-last-happily-isolated-tribe-can-teach-us-ignoring-rest/.

parents absence to attack and carry off as many as they could seize.

One day, when all our people were gone out to their works as usual, and only I and my dear sister were left to mind the house, two men and a woman got over our walls and in a moment seized us both, and, without giving us time to cry out, or make resistance, they stopped our mouths, and ran off with us into the nearest wood. At length, after many days travelling, during which I had often changed masters I got into the hands of a chieftain, in a very pleasant country.

The political structure of New World societies ensured that they would experience similarly endemic raiding, warfare, slavery, and the extermination of rival tribes.

A glance at the history of the major civilizations of South and Central America shows the same dreary tale of the rise and destruction of cities and civilizations that one can find in Mesopotamia, the ancient Mediterranean, sub-Saharan Africa, or anywhere else where similar forms of government prevailed.

One of the first major cities of Mesoamerica, Teotihuacan, attained a population of over one hundred thousand people just as the Western Roman empire was in decline. The rulers of this city later overthrew the rival Mayan city of Tikal and established a puppet dynasty there. Tikal in turn engaged in a centuries-long bloody rivalry with its neighboring Mayan city-state Caracol. Meanwhile, Teotihuacan was destroyed by violence; its central districts were burned, and the city went into decline after AD 600. Tikal met a similar fate about the same time at the hands of Caracol. That city went on to become a major power in the region, winning hegemony over many neighboring cities, and putting down many armed rebellions.

By AD 900, internecine warfare led to a general collapse of the Mayan civilization, and the cities were abandoned. A few centuries later, the future Aztec capital of Tenochtitlan allied with the neighboring city of Texcoco for the purpose of destroying the rival city of Azcapotzalco. The victors later united with another city called Tlacopan to form a triple alliance; and their highly trained armies went on to conquer dozens of formerly independent city states. They imposed heavy taxes on the subject peoples and sometimes displaced or exterminated entire city-states as a result of conquest or rebellion. Aztec elites also regularly conducted "Flower Wars" for the purpose of gaining sacrificial victims for their religious rites; credible sources suggest that at Tenochtitlan alone, tens of thousands of people were sacrificed every year.

The picture of Andean civilization farther south is also one of nearly continuous warfare stretching as far back as the archaeological record allows us to see. The Moche civilization arose around the same time as Teotihuacan and the Mayan city-states; the Moche were imperialists who spread their influence for hundreds of miles via a policy of continuous warfare. Like the Aztecs and Maya, the Moche culturally fetishized success in warfare; they were also in the habit of sacrificing captured warriors in religious rituals.

Later on, the Andean Tiwanaku and Wari people spread imperialist states via warfare and intimidation; these eventually collapsed and were replaced by the coastal Kingdom of Chimor, whose capital was Chan Chan. Various Chimorese leaders conquered people of the neighboring valleys such as Sana, Pacasmayo, Chicama, Viru, Chao, and Santa; they then imposed their own religious rituals there, in an action that—to be fair—should be counted as "cultural genocide" by any modern Leftist. The Chimor people were eventually surrounded by and then conquered by the Incans in a war that lasted several decades. After the defeat of Chimor, its capital Chan Chan was forcibly depopulated, and many of its people were carried off to be sacrificed or enslaved at the Incan capital of Cuzco. Such acts of genocide, forced immigration, and imperialist warfare were commonplace during the building of the Aztec and Incan Empires fetishized by Charles C. Mann and his disciples.

In North America, the history of Indian tribes shows a similar pattern of warfare with little evident "moderation." On the contrary, victorious tribes often found it expedient to exterminate enemy tribes altogether, so as to avoid the problem of retributive attacks. Women and children of defeated tribes were carted off and enslaved to ensure no continuation of enemy bloodlines and traditions.

Iroquois history begins with the tale of Hiawatha, a semi-mythical leader who was remarkable insofar as he was a peacemaker—the implication being that most other tribal leaders were not. The archaeology of the period before Hiawatha has revealed many warrior skeletons riddled with arrows and/or hacked into pieces, indicating that violent warfare was normative in these regions before contact with Europeans.

The seventeenth century, the first for which we have written records, shows the Iroquois Confederacy maintaining an uneasy truce among its own membership, but only insofar as this enabled them to intensify warfare against their traditional enemies the Huron and the Algonquin. These so-called Beaver Wars lasted for many decades; they witnessed the destruction of the Wendat people, the Neutral Indians, the fabled Mohicans, and many other tribes.

Faced with the threat of what the modern Left should acknowledge as genocidal warfare, many of the Iroquois' enemies were forced to flee to French, Dutch, and English settlements for protection, where their descendants eventually took up farming, converted to Christianity, or otherwise assimilated into the dominant culture. They gave up their vaunted "traditional" lifestyle because they preferred a peaceful life as a farmer to the omnipresent threat of death by tomahawk. Later in the eighteenth century, a few thousand Iroquois were to visit similar grisly fates on dozens of other neighbors, until only a handful of Native Americans remained in the entire territory circling the Great Lakes.

EATING YOUR ENEMIES

It is a well-established fact among anthropologists and historians that many tribal groups around the world have engaged in cannibalism; this was far more common than squeamish first-world academics want to allow. Cannibalism was common for a very simple reason. In hunter-gatherer societies, protein is always at a premium, and eating one's enemies might well make the difference between survival and extinction. Other reasons for cannibalism include intimidation, the building of a reputation for fierceness in battle, and also a sort of ritual in which one dominates one's enemies utterly, while appeasing some sort of divine command.

Compared with groups like the Aztecs, many North American Indians engaged in cannibalism only sporadically, out of necessity rather than as a matter of course. Still, such things are known to have happened; for example, the French writer Chateaubriand tells the story of a certain Captain Wells, whose heart was supposedly eaten in the vicinity of Chicago during the War of 1812.

For many years, Left-leaning academics attempted to deny the mounting evidence that Indians of the southwestern United States—including the oft-fetishized Hopi—were, in fact, cannibals. In recent decades, however, our ability to forensically analyze human feces at the molecular level has provided the smoking gun, if you will. As reported in the *Seattle Times* in the year 2000:

> As many as 40 sites scattered around the Southwest contain human bones that show distinctive evidence of having been butchered and cooked—signs consistent with cannibalism. Until now, however, most archaeologists have shied away from conceding the evidence proves cannibalism—favoring explanations such as ritual burial or the execution of people believed to be witches.

The new, conclusive evidence comes from preserved pieces of human excrement that were found at the site. The pieces contain human proteins that could be there only if the subjects had eaten human flesh. Researchers believe that if cannibalism has been definitively proven at this one Southwestern site, it is overwhelmingly likely that cannibalism was common enough to have taken place at the other sites where butchered bones have been found.

The report in *Nature* is certain to add fuel to a bitter argument among scholars and Native Americans over cannibalism among the Anasazi, regarded as the ancestors of the modern Hopi, Zuni and other Puebloan peoples in the North American Southwest.[74]

It is now hypothesized that the cliff-dwelling Anasazi people of the American southwest built their homes in such out-of-the-way places because they were being actively hunted by cannibalistic groups who had moved into the neighboring lowlands.

The Aztecs engaged in cannibalism on a far grander scale. This was on account of the sheer number of excess human corpses that their culture created on an annual basis. The very first group of Spaniards captured by Mexican Indians in 1520 were ritually slaughtered and cannibalized along with their Indigenous allies. As reported by the *Guardian* in 2015, a group of fifteen Spaniards, forty-five colonial soldiers, fifty women, ten children, and "hundreds of their Indigenous allies" were captured and put in cages. Like a scene out of a particularly disturbing movie, one or two per day of the Europeans and captured Indians were chosen at random and sacrificed in a gruesome manner, within earshot

---

[74] Thomas H. Maugh II, "Conclusive Evidence of American Indian Cannibalism Found," *Los Angeles Times*, printed in *Seattle Times*, September 7, 2000, https://archive. seattletimes.com/archive/?date=20000907&slug=4041058.

of the other prisoners. The bodies were then dismembered and cooked, and the flesh distributed to the people of the town.

The slow, steady pace of human sacrifice, which occurred over the course of many months, shows a desire to propitiate different gods on their feast days—for example, rain gods preferred children. But archaeologists also speculate that it served to provide an ongoing source of protein for the people of the town. The Aztecs were notoriously short of large domesticable animals to use for food, so this steady ritual of human sacrifice met a social need for protein. The town where this occurred was previously named Zultapec—but after this windfall of sacrificial victims, its name was changed to "Tecoaque," which meant "the place where they ate them."

MURDER IN THE NAME OF GOD

Human sacrifice has been practiced all over the world: in ancient China, among the ancient Celts and the pre-Christian Scandinavians, and in West Africa before the Europeans arrived. The New World was no exception.

The practice of human sacrifice developed in South and Mesoamerica over the course of many centuries. During the classic Maya period (before AD 900), human sacrifice was common, but it was apparently done on a modest scale. Religious beliefs suggested that blood ensured renewal, and sacrifice was required in order for the gods to continue to perpetuate creation.

With the rise of the Aztecs, cities became larger, and the ritual apparatus of the state became larger still. Accordingly, the number of sacrifices ramped up significantly, and this has been proven by archaeologists examining the size of the skull walls (*tzompantli*) that displayed the skulls of sacrificial victims in the center of Mesoamerican settlements. Credible authorities believe that the number of human sacrifices at the Aztec capital topped twenty thousand *per year*, with satellite cities sacrificing smaller yet still significant numbers. If the Aztec capital of Tenochtitlan contained some two hundred thousand people in 1491, this suggests that a number of captives and slaves equal to fully 10 percent of the population of the city was sacrificed each year. Most of their corpses were dismembered and distributed as food to members of the population, often depending on their social status.

The main skull wall in the Aztec capital has recently been revisited by archaeologists and its dimensions measured. It was over 110 feet long, 40 feet wide, and 15 feet high when the Spanish arrived. Skulls of victims were impaled through the temples and displayed in a side-by-side fashion. Since the skulls tended to disintegrate after a few years, this means that the tens of thousands of skulls displayed in this wall were relatively fresh. A single row of skulls, 110 feet long, would have contained about two hundred skulls, meaning that the wall would easily accommodate one hundred and twenty thousand. Meanwhile, analysis of the victims' bones shows that most were males of prime age—between twenty and thirty-five, while another 20 percent were young women and children. Many of these will have been captured in the Aztec Flower War raids whose purpose was to subdue and capture as many people alive as possible, so that they could be sacrificed (and eaten) later.

Human sacrifice was also practiced by Indians living in the continental United States. In the Mississippian culture, where centers such as Cahokia reached their apogee around 1200 CE, human sacrifice was probably a central facet of the community's religious life. Some of the few artifacts that come to us from this culture depict priests holding the heads of sacrificial victims. Mass graves have been found, including one that interred fifty women—perhaps the brides of a deceased chief—who had all been sacrificed at the same time.

In the larger cities, the Mississippian culture was socially stratified, meaning that the priests' and nobles' lands were worked by slaves and forced labor. Prisoners captured in war were likely to end up either as slaves or sacrificial victims for the community's religious festivals.

Early Spanish explorers did find some evidence of the Mesoamerican skull cult in the southern US but not of the large-scale ritual slaughter that went along with it. However, human sacrifice was practiced by many Indian groups well into the historical period. One article from 1931 published in a French journal by the renowned Amerindian scholar William Christie MacLeod describes eyewitness accounts from several North American tribes, wherein humans, particularly infants, were ritually slaughtered in order to appease some perceived affront to a deity or the natural order. Among the Natchez Indians of Mississippi, the following ritual had been reported:

> If the kings of the Natchez fell ill, infants were usually immolated to appease the spirit…and babes were sacrificed at the death of a king or one of his close relatives among royalty. If at the time of death of a king any commoner has a child at the breast, or at any rate one of very tender years, he repairs with his wife and his child to the cabin where his chief (king) is laid out. As soon as they have arrived there the father and mother wring the neck of their infant, which they throw at the feet of the body as a victim whom they immolate to the spirit of their chief. After this barbarous sacrifice they roll between their hands some twists of Spanish moss which they put under their feet, as if they would signify by that that they are not worthy to walk on the Earth; and in this condition they both remain standing before the corpse of the great chief without changing their positions or taking nourishment all day. Finally when the sun has set the man and the woman come out of the cabin and receive the compliments of all the warriors and Honored Men, to the number of whom they have been added by this strange and cruel ceremony. Being raised now to the rank of the Honored Class the father and mother now

both acquire the right to tattoo themselves and so distinguish themselves from the Commoners.[75]

It is difficult to avoid the conclusion that this ritual represents the exploitation of one social class by another. Chiefs utilized the incentive of increased social status, in return for the sacrifice of a child, in the hope that its death might help a chief recover from an illness. Knowing that one might be asked to sacrifice one's child whenever the chief fell ill must have filled lower-status commoners in many tribes with dread.

NATIVE AMERICAN SLAVERY

Many accolades, including the coveted Bancroft Prize, have recently been heaped on a book called *The Other Slavery*, which catalogues the Amerindians who had been enslaved by Europeans over the course of the colonial era.[76] This despite the general prohibition by most European governments against the enslavement of Indians.

What these self-congratulatory academics obstinately ignore is the *other* slavery—the simple, incontestable fact that Indians enslaved far more Indians than Europeans ever did. It is likely that more Africans were enslaved by Indians in the New World, than Indians by Europeans. Next to no academics are brave enough to do research on important topics such as this for the simple reason that their colleagues do not want to hear the whole truth about Indigenous slavery.

Partly in order to supply the huge markets for sacrificial victims, Mesoamerica was home to a huge and well-documented network of slave markets in the years prior to the Spanish conquest. We have seen how Cortes' partner Marina had been captured, trafficked, and traded from chief to chief before she was given to Cortes as a prize. *The idea*

---

[75] William Christie MacLeod, "Child Sacrifice in North America, with a Note on Suttee," *Journal de la Société des Américanistes* 23, no. 1 (1931), 127–38, _https://www.persee.fr/doc/jsa_0037-9174_1931_num_23_1_1088.

[76] Andrés Reséndez, *The Other Slavery: The Uncovered Story of Indian Enslavement in America* (Boston: Houghton Mifflin, 2016).

that the Spanish or the English imported slavery to the New World is therefore utterly ridiculous. Slavery was widespread not only in Mesoamerica but also throughout the Indian tribes of the New World. Even far to the north, in present-day Canada, Native Americans routinely enslaved one another. The French were able to take advantage of this preexisting practice, buying slaves from the Indians and sometimes selling them in Caribbean markets—despite the fact that French authorities had made such trade illegal. During their ascendancy in the eighteenth and early nineteenth centuries, the imperialist Comanche made slave raiding and trading a staple of their economy, until they became the terror of rival tribes for hundreds of miles around.

Modern people tend to forget the fact that slavery was a feature of almost every premodern culture. But slavery was ubiquitous in the New World for the same reason that it was common in the Old. Humans were continuously at war with one another, and when one is at war, a victory leaves few ways to dispose of the vanquished. One can either kill them (with the option to eat them for protein), enslave them, ransom them, or let them go. Letting them go seems like a poor return for risking one's life in war, and so this was uncommon. Demanding ransom was an option, but only if one could be sure that the defeated people would continue to pay. Often, as soon as they were freed, conquered people would refuse to pay, and things would return to the status quo ante. Killing one's enemies might satisfy bloodlust, and it certainly guaranteed that they would not be able to retaliate, but slavery often provided the most attractive and beneficial option.

In the Americas, many groups opted for a mixed solution based on gender. Since most men were warriors with a sense of honor, they tended to escape, rebel, or even try and kill their captors when given a chance. Accordingly, many tribes developed a habit of killing captured males as a matter of course. Women and children proved more docile, so they were usually enslaved, with the added benefit that they could increase the population of the conquering tribe (whether they wanted to or not).

In a premodern society, almost every task required a good deal of human labor, and any such slaves were extremely valuable.

The historian Brett Rushforth has written the following about a Native American slave halter that can be found in the Colonial Williamsburg Foundation:

> No honor was more important to a young man than capturing slaves. His success was celebrated in public ceremonies, etched into his war clubs, and displayed on his body with tattoos representing each enemy he had captured. Although the enslaved probably found little beauty in the halters that bound them, they would have understood that the physical and cultural work that produced their restraints also created a network of interest in their subordination. Their capture and domestication had been the shared purpose of the women who crafted their halters, the warriors who led them home like pets, and the community celebrating their capture. As an object revealing both the intent of the slavers and the earliest experiences of the enslaved, the halter is a fitting emblem of indigenous North American slavery.[77]

Because they already practiced slavery among themselves before the Europeans arrived, Native American tribes adapted readily to the idea of owning African slaves once these were introduced.

Indians began to purchase African slaves in the seventeenth century, and they continued to own African slaves until after the US Civil War. Many modern articles attempt to spin Indian slavery as though it was adopted from Southern Americans, but, again, Amerindians had

---

[77] Brett Rushforth. *Bonds of Alliance: Indigenous and Atlantic Slaveries in New France*. (UNC Press, 2012).

already been enslaving one another for centuries before the Southern Americans adopted African slavery in earnest.[78] At most, then, the adoption of African slavery by the Five Civilized Tribes was merely an adaptation of preexisting practice. During the Trail of Tears marches of the 1830s, thousands of African slaves were moved westward, along with their Indian masters. In the lead-up to the Civil War, some tribes were split into pro- and anti-slavery factions; others, such as the Chickasaw Indians, remained committed to African slavery and sided with the Confederacy.

CRUELTY AND INHUMANE TREATMENT

One of the chief delights for successful warriors was the torment and torture of prisoners of war before they were killed. This behavior attested not only toward white prisoners but also toward Amerindian prisoners from rival tribes.

The main way for a male prisoner to be spared torture was either to be killed on the spot or claimed as a slave. Those who were not were often subjected to the most exquisite tortures. An early account of how capturing parties amused themselves after a successful raid is described by the French explorer Samuel de Champlain.

> Having kindled a fire, they selected a victim, and proceeded to excoriate his back with red-hot burning brands, and to apply live coals to the ends of his fingers, where they would give the most exquisite pain. They tore out his finger-nails, and, with sharp

---

[78] One of the researchers peddling this plainly false "Indians never had slavery until white people taught them" narrative is the University of Pittsburgh historian Alaina E. Roberts. Her specialty in the intersection of Native American and black history has helped to accord her a media presence out of proportion to her academic contributions. Typical of her writing is "How Native Americans Adopted Slavery from White Settlers," Aljazeera, December 27, 2018, https://www.aljazeera.com/opinions/2018/12/27/how-native-americans-adopted-slavery-from-white-settlers.

slivers of wood, pierced his wrists and rudely forced out the quivering sinews. They flayed off the skin from the top of his head, and poured upon the bleeding wound a stream of boiling melted gum. Champlain remonstrated in vain. The piteous cries of the poor, tormented victim excited his unavailing compassion, and he turned away in anger and disgust. At length, when these inhuman tortures had been carried as far as they desired, Champlain was permitted, at his earnest request, with a musket-shot to put an end to his sufferings. But this was not the termination of the horrid performance. The dead victim was hacked in pieces, his heart severed into parts, and the surviving prisoners were ordered to eat it.[79]

Champlain's description of warriors as eager for war as "enraged tigers" who spent the entire night boasting and belittling one another, and who then delighted in torturing their victims afterwards, sounds all too realistic; in addition to Champlain, countless chroniclers and letter writers attest that such behavior was indeed not exceptional but normative.

Finally, some activists have made hay out of the fact that on two occasions in North American history, British commanders (in 1747 and 1749) passed laws that paid money for Indian scalps. This made headlines in Canada around the year 2000 when some Indian groups argued that these laws were still on the books: lawyers later found that they had long since been superseded. What the purveyors of outrage ignore is that this was done mostly to compensate Indian allies—not colonial soldiers—for a practice that was already common with them and to encourage them to fight enthusiastically for the British. These skirmishes were so small-scale that it is unlikely that more than a few dozen scalps were

---

[79] Champlain, *Voyages*.

turned in. In any event, during the American Revolution, at least one British commander was suspected of paying his Indian allies for colonial scalps. To argue that this was some gruesome form of racism, then, is once again to ignore the historical context.

FEMALE SEX SLAVES

When Native American women were captured in war, they were often added to the capturing warrior's wives. This was not voluntary; if Europeans had done this, it would be decried by the Left as forced reproduction and sex slavery. Often, however, the captured women became used to this life (a form of Stockholm syndrome) and chose to remain with their captors and the children they had by them.

Most of the women captured and forced into sex slavery by Native American men during the colonial period were Indigenous. But a few European women also got caught up in this facet of Indian culture.

Mary Jemison was a Scots-Irish girl captured by Indians during the French and Indian War. She was subsequently adopted into the Seneca tribe, where she was married to and had children with a Delaware man and later a Seneca man. She lived until the 1830s, but even after her tribe was contacted by missionaries in the 1820s, she was so accustomed to a Native American lifestyle that she chose to remain among the Seneca. One of the missionaries wrote down the story of her life, which was published in 1824. In her narrative, she describes how she was captured along with her family and a few other settlers many years before, when she was twelve years old. When this passage begins, Mary, her family, and a few other people had already been captured by Indians:

> After a hard day's march we encamped in a thicket, where the Indians made a shelter of boughs, and then built a good fire to warm and dry our benumbed limbs and clothing, for it had rained some through the day. Here we were again fed as before. When

the Indians had finished their supper, they took from their baggage a number of scalps and went about preparing them for the market, or to keep without spoiling, by straining them over small hoops which they prepared for that purpose, and then drying and scraping them by the fire. Having put the scalps, yet wet and bloody, upon the hoops, and stretched them to their full extent, they held them to the fire till they were partly dried, and then with their knives, commenced scraping off the flesh; and in that way they continued to work, alternately drying and scraping them, till they were dry and clean. That being done, they combed the hair in the neatest manner, and then painted it and the edges of the scalps yet on the hoops, red. Those scalps I knew at the time must have been taken from our family by the color of the hair. My mother's hair was red, and I could easily distinguish my father's and the children's from each other. That sight was most appalling, yet I was obliged to endure it without complaining.[80]

These and other sources paint a picture of what life and warfare were actually like in Indian society. Most societies raised all males to be warriors; this was seen as their primary occupation and purpose in life. As in Viking-age Europe, the life expectancy of Indian males was accordingly low, and the likelihood of being killed in battle was high. Political power was highly fragmented, ergo war and the threat of enemy raids were seldom far away. The fate of anyone captured was slavery at best, though it might often mean torture and/or the prospect of serving as a feast for one's enemies.

---

[80] James E. Seaver, *A Narrative of the Life of Mary Jemison*, 1824.

The Left-wing fantasy of Amerindians as peaceful, or even as "moderate and reasonable" in warfare, is a product of the 1960s and 70s peace movement, and it simply does not square with the majority of evidence coming from all parts of the Americas for the better part of the past two thousand years. Nor indeed does it square with the view that both Native and non-Native Americans had of Indian civilization, right up to the 1970s.

CHAPTER 8

WERE NATIVE AMERICANS NATURAL ENVIRONMENTALISTS?

In addition to building roads, causeways, canals, dikes, reservoirs, mounds, [and] raised agricultural fields...the Indians before Columbus trapped fish in the seasonally flooded grassland. The Indians maintained and expanded the grasslands by regularly setting huge areas on fire. Their current descendants still burn [the grasslands].... When we flew over the region, the dry season had just begun, but mile-long lines of flame were already on the march. In the charred areas behind the fires were the blackened spikes of trees, many of them of species that activists fight to save....

—Charles C. Mann, *1491*

Another of the many stereotypes about Native Americans favored by the modern Left is that Indians were "wise stewards" of the land. Many believe that left to their own devices, groups of Indigenous people would create a sustainable, eco-friendly "cottagecore" society of the kind fashionable in hipster circles in recent years. The flipside of this theory holds that Europeans have been so tainted by capitalism that a European's only possible relationship to nature is exploitative and destructive. This is a longstanding viewpoint that has once again been around since the 1960s. As one academic recently put it: "The market system, with its need for constant growth and its inability to see the natural world as anything other than an exploitable resource, is in direct and inherent antagonism to the preservation of nature. Consequently, there is no solution to the problem of climate change without an end to capitalism, a fact that becomes very clear when we examine Karl Marx's writings on nature."[81]

Faced with this preexisting belief that capitalism and the Europeans who invented it are environmentally destructive by nature, it was all too easy for Leftists to argue that "primitive" peoples must have some sort of special relationship with nature, a conclusion that many modern Indigenous leaders are happy to adopt for their own ends.

In his 2020 book *The Dawn of Everything*, anthropologist Dave Graeber dismisses reams of scientific data that show modern people to be happier and healthier than ever; he also dismisses data showing how environmentalist movements are strongest in those countries where capitalism has been most successful. Instead, he argues that most people would reject modernity if they could; that our human instincts would be best served if we ran off into the woods to live like an idealized Indigenous person. To make his case, he provides examples of people who, when abducted by Indigenous tribes, chose to remain with them rather than rejoining "civilization." In his utopian vision these Stone Age societies were the real "civilization"—they lived off the land in peace and prosperity, gardening, farming, and raising animals in a humane and sustainable fashion. Modernity—the main product of European culture and society—meanwhile stands for drudgery, exploitation, and environmental destruction.

---

[81] Elizabeth Terzakis, "Marx and Nature: Why We Need Marx Now More Than Ever," *International Socialist Review* 109 (2018), https://mronline.org/2018/06/06/marx-and-nature/. Terzakis is yet another English literature professor who writes sweeping generalizations about market economies and environmentalism based on bits of nineteenth-century Marxist theory that she has picked up.

One of the founders of Greenpeace was a (white) Canadian named Bob Hunter. Like many other youths growing up during the golden age of "cowboys and Indians" in the 1940s and '50s, Hunter became obsessed with Amerindian culture. Being a writer and visionary rather than an historian, Hunter accepted many apocryphal stories that were circulating about Indians during the '60s, without much concern for whether or not they were true. So Hunter propagated a "Cree Myth of the Rainbow Warrior," which supposedly runs something like this: "When the earth is sick, the animals will begin to disappear. When that happens, The Warriors of the Rainbow will come to save them." Hunter used this myth to inspire his fellow activists to consider themselves the new Rainbow Warriors who would fight to fulfill the Cree prophecy. (Today this would ironically be considered "cultural appropriation.")

Modern history textbooks continue to pander to this environmentalist Indian stereotype. A typical passage can be found in Hoffer's textbook on American history (introduced in the previous chapter). In soothing prose, Hoffer assures us that Indian culture was adapted to the "deep rhythms of nature" that "gave life its strength and shape." He asserts that the "landscape itself reminded Indians of their obligations to the old ways," arguing that Indians were influenced by the landscape in a way Europeans were not. Because of this, Indians respected nature and wildlife in ways that were supposedly antithetical to the capitalistic European way of looking at the world as a source of natural resources.

This idea achieved its ultimate expression in Disney's animated movie *Pocahontas*, in which the beautiful Indian maiden invites the English colonial invader John Smith, who is blind to the wonders of nature, to appreciate the forest and the "colors of the wind." The same timeworn trope appears, transposed to outer space, in the blockbuster film *Avatar*.

But the influence of this stereotype is not limited to popular culture; in the United States, Canada, Australia, and New Zealand, it is being actively exploited at the public's expense. For example, a handful of Hawaiian activists halted the construction of the ultra-advanced Thirty-Meter Telescope by claiming religious and environmental affinity with the building site—despite the fact that several other telescopes already exist in the same area. The modern Left has deemed it "racist" to question the motives of these activists, making it virtually impossible for any non-Native to question the motives or benefits of the interested parties. This has resulted in an intractable political gridlock and the ongoing loss of priceless scientific data.

In 2021, the *Yale Environment 360* newsletter published a piece praising the transfer of more and more US public land to Amerindian tribes, on the grounds that these tribes have a special knack for stewardship. As the (non-Indigenous) reporter Jim Robbins, who has been writing on environmentalism since the 1970s, assures us:

> It is hard for outsiders to fathom how differently Indigenous cultures perceive the landscape and wild creatures.
>
> The use of Indigenous management styles that evolved over many centuries of cultures immersed in nature—formally called "Traditional Ecological Knowledge (TEK)"—is increasingly seen by conservationists as synergistic with the global campaign to protect biodiversity and to manage nature in a way that hedges against climate change.
>
> "If you look at it from a land justice perspective, we need to support a strengthening and healing of that relationship," said Erin Myers Madeira, director of Indigenous Peoples and Local Communities program for the Nature Conservancy. "If you look at it practically, Indigenous people are the original stewards of all the lands and waters in North America, and there's an extensive knowledge and management practices that date back millennia."

Such logic would justify virtually unlimited claims to public resources in any country previously inhabited by Indigenous people.

And these arguments are having real-world effects. In Sonoma County, California, seven hundred acres of wine country land were recently transferred to the local Kashia Band in perpetuity. As the *Guardian* breathlessly reports in an article titled "This is all Stolen Land":

> "The day we took ownership was one of the most emotional experiences of my life," said the tribe's chairman, Reno Keoni Franklin, adding that California should now support similar efforts throughout the state. "Kashia created a blueprint to follow…a process that protects our sovereign rights and at the same time gives us back precious sites."[82]

In Northern California, the Yurok tribe is using this blueprint in the hopes of having over one million acres returned in perpetuity to their band of 5,500 people. This would amount to about 180 acres per person—if only the rest of us could be so lucky.

There is good reason for cynicism about these activists' true motives in promoting the "Ecological Indian" stereotype. Until quite recently, it was a view commonly held among environmentalists that modern-day Indigenous groups were among the biggest *obstacles* to the preservation of natural resources. As reported in the landmark 1999 book *The Ecological Indian*, Wisconsin sport fishermen had become so fed up with Chippewa Indians fishing an unsustainable number of walleye game fish in the 1980s that they coined the slogan, "Save a Walleye, Spear an Indian." Its author reports how whale preservation groups, anti-seal hunting groups, and many others have likewise found themselves on opposite sides of the table from Indigenous people when it comes to preserving and sustaining endangered animal populations.

---

[82] https://www.theguardian.com/us-news/2019/jun/20/california-native-americans-governor-apology-reparations

The Ecological Indian presents hundreds of pages of damning criticism of the idea that Indians had any right to claim environmentalist superiority over non-Native Americans. The book's author, Brown University anthropologist Shepard Krech III, opens with a reference to the famous 1980s US public service commercial known as the "Crying Indian," the famously kitschy advertorial that was the cornerstone of the national "Keep America Beautiful" campaign. It played on prime-time television for the better part of ten years and featured a craggy-looking (Italian-American) actor dressed as an Indian, shedding a woeful tear as he contemplates the pollution unleashed by modern factories.

> Through the Crying Indian, "Keep America Beautiful" cleverly manipulated ideas deeply engrained in the [American] national consciousness. "Pollution: it's a crying shame" expressed the widely held perception, then and now, that there are fundamental differences between the way Americans of European descent and Indians think about and relate to land and resources. In what amounted to a powerful indictment of white Americans, the Crying Indian unequivocally implicated white polluters; they, not Indians, were the people who start pollution. He shed a tear for land and resources, which, by implication, he and other Indians treated kindly and prudently (as conservators might), and understood ecologically. But after arriving in North America, Europeans and their descendants ruined its pristine, unspoilt nature.[83]

In fact, Indian responses to the environment have been complicated and multifaceted; they have been both environmentalist and anti-environmentalist. As Krech puts it:

---

[83] Shepard Krech III. *The Ecological Indian: Myth and History.* (WW Norton, 1999).

Native people have often favored the extraction of resources, storage of waste, and other development projects—even those with a serious potential environmental impact—if they can gain control over them. They have debated these issues heatedly. In the 1970s to 1980s, the arguments unfolded many times in the context of coal and energy development. For example, Crow Indians sought to gain control over the lease of their lands for strip-mining—not because they were opposed to stripping coal but because the leases negotiated for them by the Bureau of Indian Affairs (BIA) shortchanged them. The Northern Cheyenne sued to break BIA-negotiated leases. Like the Crow, they wanted to develop coal reserves themselves—but they were also interested in controlling the ravages of strip-mining and energy production on their lands. Their strong interest in halting environmental degradation put them on a collision course with the Crow.[84]

This account reflects what common sense would obviously predict—different groups of Indians will display a wide spectrum of attitudes, behaviors, and beliefs, just as different groups of Europeans have done. To imagine that a racial or cultural group will be uniquely "good" or "bad" on environmental issues due to the "system" that drives their culture is ahistorical and reductive.

THE PLEISTOCENE EXTINCTIONS

One of the oldest debates concerning the impact of Native Americans on their environment involves what are known as the Pleistocene Extinctions.

---

[84] Ibid.

Geologists tell us that North and South America separated from the rest of the global landmass about 150 million years ago. Long afterwards, early humans began to appear in Africa. African animals evolved alongside humans over millions of years, meaning that they were able to adapt to increased human predation over a long period. The reason Africa contains the majority of the world's megafauna today is because they figured out how to live alongside these early humans, with their stone tools and javelins. It was not until the spread of modern rifles in the later nineteenth century that the animal populations of Africa came under serious threat.

Animal populations in other parts of the world fared less well—and this is because Paleolithic humans were able to hunt them successfully, after they developed stone-tipped weapons such as the spear and the bow and arrow. As humans fanned out across Europe and Asia beginning around 40,000 BC, they hunted large game that was less adapted to cope with their new hunting techniques. The result was the eventual extinction of many large animals from Europe, Asia, and Australia, including mammoths, cave bears, saber-toothed tigers, and the like.

On smaller islands, the coming of humans was usually catastrophic to Indigenous animal populations. For example, as the Polynesians spread across the Pacific, Krech notes:

> [In Hawaii they] cleared land with fire, introduced animals, diverted streams for irrigation, and transformed forested coastal areas into farms and grasslands, and mudflats into fishponds. The result: over one-half of all endemic bird species became extinct. The Hawaiians ate some and killed others for their feathers to ornament clothing. Some birds vanished with their habitats. In New Zealand, early Polynesian colonizers hunted thirteen species of moas—ostrich-like flightless birds, one of which towered over men and women—to extinction and

turned their attention to what remained—shellfish, fish, seals, and small birds.[85]

New World megafauna had also evolved in complete isolation from humans until recent times. This is why many scholars believe that the irruption of human hunters into the New World, sometime between fifteen thousand and twenty thousand years ago, was the cause of the catastrophic "New World Pleistocene Extinction Event," which paleontologists have detected in the fossil record.

Shortly after the first "Paleo-Indians" arrived in the New World, no fewer than thirty-eight genera of large mammals disappeared. In North America this included giant sloths, short-faced bears, tapirs, peccaries, giant tortoises, American cheetahs, the American lion, saber-toothed cats, dire wolves, various species of camel including llamas, several now-extinct species of bison, the stag-moose, the shrub-ox, horses, mammoths, mastodons, the giant armadillo, giant beavers, giant condors, and thirteen out of fourteen species of American antelope.

Meanwhile, in South America, mass extinctions were concentrated in the time period after 8000 BC, which coincides with the first arrival of large numbers of human hunters in that region. South America at the time had large populations of bears, capybaras, llamas, saber-tooth cats, giant sloths, armadillos the size of a hippopotamus, camels, and rhinoceroses. Every single one of these species was gone by about 6000 BC. In all, every South American species larger than one hundred kilograms disappeared forever.

There are those who claim that the "overkill hypothesis"—the idea that humans were responsible for these extinctions by killing them faster than they could reproduce—is wrong. Most shrill are those who believe for political reasons that it is wicked to attribute anything un-environmental to early Indians. Such people hope to pin the Pleistocene extinctions on changes in the Earth's climate.

---

[85] http://nationalhumanitiescenter.org/tserve/nattrans/ntecoindian/essays/pleistocene.htm

The obvious critique of this theory is that the environment had been changing dramatically for many millions of years, and yet these animal species had been evolving continuously since the time of the dinosaurs. This is why most scientists continue to favor the "overkill hypothesis." The correlation with the arrival of human hunters is simply too strong to leave much room for any other interpretation.

It is therefore very likely that Paleo-Indians were responsible for the mass extinction of almost all the large animals in the Americas—and this is why Europeans found the Americas so poor in megafauna when they arrived after 1492.

But does it matter what Paleo-Indians did five thousand or ten thousand years ago? Does this have any impact on how we should interpret the more recent history of European-Indian interactions? In fact, it does have several important implications.

The first is that the extinctions left the New World people with precious few animals they could use for riding, work, or food. It is unfortunate that the people who arrived from Siberia were still following Paleolithic patterns of migrating after herds of large game animals. These people did not have any domesticated animals, except perhaps dogs, and they neither used animals for work (such as ploughing) nor kept herds of grazing animals for milk, wool, or meat. Instead they simply killed and ate them all.

In the Old World, certain groups of humans hit upon the idea of domesticating oxen and other farm animals in the years after 8000 BC, and they learned to use some of them for ploughing around 6000 BC. In the New World, however, by the time human society became sophisticated enough to need plough and farm animals, the available resources had already been plundered. The near absence of suitable animals contributed to the fact that even the most advanced Mesoamerican groups had domesticated only dogs, turkeys, and ducks, and the latter two were only kept in a few regions, notably by the Aztecs.

Old World agriculture was in turn driven by the use of plough animals; so, by Roman times Old World ploughing civilizations (which grew staples such as wheat and rice) were able to produce far more calories per acre than societies that did not use an animal-drawn plough. This is a big part of why the Old World was so much more populous than the New by 1491.

The lack of riding animals in the New World also helped to make the playing field unequal when the two cultures finally met. When the Aztecs and Incas first saw the Spanish on their horses, they at first believed them to be a sort of centaur—an impressive super-human monster standing ten feet tall. Even as they became acquainted with the Spaniards, this initial impression of Spanish invincibility continued to weaken Indigenous American resolve against the Europeans.

More to our purposes, the fact that Indigenous Americans are probably responsible for the greatest ecological catastrophe to befall the Americas since the demise of the dinosaurs provides a badly needed dash of cold water for everyone involved in this debate.

While Paleo-Indians hunted many magnificent species to extinction, no one seriously "blames" them for their actions. They had no way of understanding or even assessing the total impact of their actions. They were hunters; they were following game. They made choices that made sense at the time. They did not have the benefit of knowing how vast North America was, or was not. They had no idea what the total populations of their prey species were or whether they would be able to reproduce themselves fast enough to sustain their need for food.

Assuming that Indians did cause these extinctions, this provides evidence of a simple truth about how history and ecology work. As one reviewer of Krech's Ecological Indian put it:

> Whether or not a particular person or population behaves in an ecologically responsible manner is a value judgment, one typically made by an outside observer. Outside observers who credit themselves with the wisdom to make such judgments sometimes do so with more formidable scientific skills, or

(perhaps more often) just the enviable benefit of hindsight.

People make ecological choices all the time, and they are typically constrained by resource availability and the immediacy of need. Modern individuals, those of us who have the leisure to write or read commentaries like this one, are typically so far removed from critical choices that they (we) cannot accurately assess the effects of specific choices...

One can detect in [various historical examples] the basic anthropological principle that no matter what people do it seems like a good idea at the time. It is a principle often overwhelmed by the politics of blame placing.[86]

If only today's academics and activists would recognize that just as the Paleo-Indians had little means of assessing their impact on the megafauna of the New World, so too Europeans for most of the colonial period had no way of assessing their impact on the Indian populations and societies they found here. And by the later eighteenth century, when the problem of Indian population decline became more obvious, we will see that many European policymakers went to great lengths to protect these populations from further harm.

WERE HISTORICAL INDIANS ECOLOGICAL?

In 2019, a study from the University of London claimed that the death of millions of Native Americans in the wake of the Spanish conquest caused massive reforestation in the New World. This study was widely reported in the media, since it appeared to "prove" that fifty million

---

[86] Snow, D. R. "The Ecological Indian: Myth and History, by Shepard Krech III." *Human Ecology Review* 8.1 (2001): 73-75.

Indians had died from European colonialism.[87] The authors, who turned out to be a group of social-media-savvy graduate students in environmental science, further claimed that these new trees soaked up so much CO_2 that global temperatures decreased by 0.15 degree Celsius. Being environmental science majors with no expertise in researching past societies, they based a lot of their historical assumptions on the authority of none other than Charles C. Mann, who greatly exaggerates—in his attempt to demonstrate the grandeur of New World civilization—the impact that Indigenous Americans had on their environment.

The students' article has been roundly debunked on numerous grounds, including the fact that the Indians in question had never cleared substantial areas of forest. Indigenous Americans did not as a rule clear forests except by the controlled burning of underbrush. Many groups did not farm at all, and permanent fields were virtually unknown. Because they only had stone (and in a few cases copper) axes, the felling of large areas of forest was beyond their capability. Even in Europe, massive deforestation did not take place until the invention of the iron axe, which was orders of magnitude more efficient for chopping down trees.

If Indians seemed to have a relatively small impact on nature and the natural world, this is partly because their ancestors had already done enormous damage to the ecosystem thousands of years before when they hunted the native megafauna to extinction. Indian populations stayed mobile, because their activities tended to deplete or scare off game after a few years. From the perspective of local and regional ecosystems, pre-Columbian Indian groups were regionally devastating enough.

The adoption of European firearms by Indians was another major blow to the North American ecosystem. Both Indians and Europeans used firearms in their hunting from the 1500s onwards; the dramatically improved effectiveness of firearms over the bow and arrow meant that animal populations began to spiral downwards. How much of this was

---

[87] Oliver Milman, "European Colonization of Americas Killed So Many It Cooled Earth's Climate," *Guardian*, January 31, 2019, https://www.theguardian.com/environment/2019/jan/31/european-colonization-of-americas-helped-cause-climate-change.

due to Indigenous hunting and how much to European hunting will have differed in every area. But there is little evidence to suggest that Indian hunters were careful to preserve the numbers of game or that they were any more attentive to this issue than Europeans; both groups learned to harvest furs for market sale to the extent possible. There was little difference in the behavior of the two groups, even during the great slaughters of buffalo and other creatures that took place after the invention of modern firearms in the later nineteenth century.

In sum, historical Indians were just as beguiled by the advance of technology and evolving markets as everyone else. Like people everywhere, when they discovered a labor-saving technology, they used it, and they tended to do so despite any negative impact on the natural world. Then and now, when there was a market for animal furs or other natural resources, they proved more than willing to exploit that market to the best of their ability, even if it meant harvesting furs at unsustainable levels. Many Indian tribes moved farther west in the eighteenth century after their firearms depleted their old hunting grounds. Generally speaking, early modern Indians were not much prone to abstract theorizing. When every day is a question of survival, philosophical questions such as the long-term ecological outlook take a back seat. As Shepard Krech rightly observed, such questions are luxuries that only modern people with our abundance of technology, leisure, and hindsight can afford to address.

There is also little truth to the assertion that "capitalism" has an inherently negative relationship with nature. This too is mere bluster, bandied about by academics with little understanding of economic history. If we have any chance of solving the global warming crisis, for example, it will be due to proper incentivization of the market by governments. It will also require raw geopolitical power, as long as semi-capitalist dictatorships such as Russia and China remain some of the worst polluters on Earth, with no sign of stopping for any reason short of economic or military duress.

CHAPTER 9

WERE NATIVE AMERICANS NATURAL COMMUNISTS?

*The American Indians were Communists. They
were. Every anthropologist will tell you they were
Communists. No rich, no poor. If somebody
needed something the community chipped in.*

—Pete Seeger, folksinger and
Communist Party USA member

At the Perimeter Institute for Theoretical Physics in Waterloo, Canada, every public lecture is preceded by the following statement:

In the spirit of respect and reconciliation, we acknowledge that Perimeter Institute is located upon the lands that have been inhabited by Indigenous peoples from the beginning. In particular we acknowledge the Haldimand Tract. We thank the Anishinaabe, Haudenosaunee, and Neutral peoples for hosting us on their land.

This statement of guilt serves both as political theater and as a sort of religious liturgy, asking for the forgiveness of sins committed by one's ancestors. Only after this ritual cleansing of guilt has been performed is the process of modern-day theoretical physics allowed to proceed. Such a statement of faith should strike one as creepy or even outrageous—as though the Inquisition had taken over the halls of modern higher education. And yet due to the sensitive nature of the material, administrators kowtow to the new dogma with nary a peep. Few signs of the quasi-religious, anti-rational nature of modern identity politics could be more clear.

In this chapter, we will address the issue of how Amerindians actually acquired and held their land, and more importantly what political ends the story of Amerindian land tenure has been made to serve.

For example, the confessional statement appended to Perimeter Institute lectures relies on the assumption that the land on which the Institute now stands was owned *in perpetuity* by three specific tribes—as though the moment at which the land changed hands from Indian to European was somehow the most important moment in the history of that land.

One of the many factors this statement of guilt ignores is whether, for example, these three tribes had held that land for more than a generation prior to the arrival of the white settlers or government officials purchased or squatted on it. It is perfectly possible, in other words, that the Perimeter Institute land had changed tribal ownership a dozen times in the century prior to the arrival of the white people, often due to massacre. Genocidal wars against rival tribes were common in the centuries preceding the arrival of the French and British in that area; archaeological finds of young warriors riddled with arrows complement oral histories on this score. Why then should we fetishize the moment of transfer to European hands while ignoring the often violent transfer of this land from tribe to tribe, or—later—the sale of this land under Canadian law?

The assumption of modern American and Canadian guilt for ancient land transactions lies behind the popular mobile phone app called Native Land Digital. This app has been featured on CNN and distributed to thousands of US college students across the country. It encourages students to type in their home address so that the app can tell them from which tribe their land has been stolen. While the most stridently anti-European claims of the app and its users were carefully scrubbed from the web after it received negative media attention, its purpose remains obvious. This is to teach students that their country and society are fundamentally illegitimate, along with all of Western civilization and modernity itself. It teaches them that their family home and school sit on stolen ground, and implies that this was done via murder, military occupation, or some other violent means—with the further implication that Native American violence was categorically okay, in a way that European violence was not.

Any institution could, if it so chose, make a statement of apology for wrongs that had been committed on its land in the centuries before the present. Indeed, thousands of American and Canadian institutions have adopted a liturgy similar to the Perimeter Institute, in a fad that has become known as a "land acknowledgment." But such public performances are nothing more than a power play designed to showcase the politics of an ascendant group, even as they seek to shut down debate on the topic at hand.

Why has the idea of Indian land tenure suddenly become a hot topic, after more than a century in which people were willing to let the past stay in the past? The main reason is that Indian land tenure has become an important part of the postcolonial story the modern Left is trying to sell to the global public. A secondary reason is that individual tribes stand to benefit a great deal from stories about how they used to own this or that important (and valuable) piece of real estate. Small groups of (often mostly white) "Indians" with tribal affiliations stand to reap enormous financial gains should this or that valuable piece of land be ceded to them on the modern real estate market. In an age when a small family farm can be worth several million dollars, any such transaction is bound to be lucrative. The years-long holdup of the Thirty-Meter Telescope on

Mauna Kea, which has enriched a number of key Indigenous players, is only the most visible of thousands of under-the-radar transactions going on every day.

Like many politically convenient interpretations of history, the Leftist story of Indian land tenure has been forced to adopt mutually contradictory positions, depending on the main thrust of the argument. For example, when someone argues that Amerindians didn't own property and it was therefore okay for European settlers to move in and start farming abandoned areas, other writers hasten to assert that Amerindians had longstanding traditions of individual property rights that were highly specific and based on well-established legal principles.

But most writers who generalize about Indian land tenure focus on the notion that Indians were communistic. This idea took hold in the mid-twentieth century when actual communism was in vogue with Hollywood and various elements of the American cultural establishment. Intellectuals who saw American society as corrupted by capitalism found it useful to portray the Indians as communistic underdogs who offered an idealized model of how a pristine, natural life of communistic bliss might still be our lot today if only we would give up our capitalistic propensity to overconsume and so on.

A related reason to portray Indians as communistic is to portray them as morally superior to Europeans. According to this view, holding property in common instilled Indian culture with the values of caring, sharing, economic and social equality, sustainability, moderation, and humility. Oxford historian Pekka Hämäläinen claims that due to the nature of Amerindian farming, a "sweeping retreat from hierarchies, elite dominance, and large-scale urbanization may have turned North America... into the world's most egalitarian continent..."[88] Meanwhile European property systems supposedly encouraged acquisitiveness, exploitation, hierarchy, violence, overproduction, and the destruction of the natural world.

---

[88] Pekka Hämäläinen, *Indigenous Continent: The Epic Contest for North America* (Washington, DC, National Geographic Boooks, 2022), Chapter 2.

Some activists are still motivated by the orthodox Marxist idea that property ownership is wrong per se. In this view, Native Americans were morally superior either because they did not own property or because their property regimes are deemed egalitarian, a la Hämäläinen above. (A "property regime" is an economic historian's term for a system of property holding, including both the property itself and the ways in which this property is legally transferred and recognized by political authorities.)

The scholar M. A. Jaimes Guerrero asserts that all Native American governance was done by deliberative councils, an arrangement that flowed naturally from their communist notions of property.[89] In *The State of Native America: Genocide, Colonization, and Resistance*, contributor Glenn T. Morris emphasizes that European property rights were based on the Roman legal principle *territorium res nullius*, which the Spanish interpreted as empowering Christian authorities to legally occupy territory inhabited by "infidels." But for Morris and similar authors, Roman law is morally suspect because Roman property ownership was exclusive; it conveyed a sense of dominium, or the right to dispose of a possession as one wished. According to Jaimes, "It was Aristotle who first wrote that all women—as well as all children, slaves/servants, and animals—were to be the property of male heads of patriarchal households." In this rather flimsy way, Left-leaning scholars attempt to portray Western property regimes as morally tainted and exploitative from the beginning.

Patrick Wolfe, the inventor of settler colonialism, went further, asserting that the essence of being an Indian was "collectivity," or holding property in common. He writes that "tribal land was tribally owned—tribes and private property did not mix. Indians were the original communist menace." [90]

---

[89] M. A. Jaimes Guerrero, "'Patriarchal Colonialism' and Indigenism: Implications for Native Feminist Spirituality and Native Womanism," *Hypatia* 18, no. 2 (2003), 58–69, https://www.jstor.org/stable/3811011.

[90] Patrick Wolfe's article "Settler Colonialism and the Elimination of the Native" (*Journal of Genocide Research* 8, no. 4 [2006], 387–409, https://www.tandfonline.com/doi/pdf/10.1080/14623520601056240) has as of this writing been cited over 5,000 times—an astonishing number in comparison with similar articles.

In this jocular aside Wolfe also implies a threat: Indian society was seen as threatening to European capitalism because it offered a viable alternative. Wolfe goes on to explain that Indians who accepted (the common and widespread) US government offers to become a homesteader became individual proprietors, each to his own, of separately allotted fragments of what had previously been the tribal estate, theirs to sell to white people if they chose to. Without the tribe, though, for all practical purposes they were no longer Indians. Here in essence is assimilation's Faustian bargain—have our settler world but lose your Indigenous soul. Beyond any doubt, this is a kind of death. Assimilationists recognized this very clearly.

According to Wolfe, then, the only way for an Indigenous American to react to the presence of Europeans was to cling tightly to "Indigenous ways"—especially to the supposed custom of holding their property in common; for Wolfe, anything else was a betrayal of some set-in-stone ideal of Indian culture. This view is ironically Eurocentric in that it assumes that Indian life never evolved in the absence of contact with Europeans.

Other scholars focus on the environmental aspects of the two property systems, asserting that the Native system was "balanced" while the European system was inherently "unbalanced." As James Swaney put it back in 1990:

> The conversion of North America to private property also contained a strong commercial element...such commercial invasions were repeated countless times during the European settlement of North America, usually with the same outcome: "production" for the market overran an indigenous culture and overexploited a renewable resource. Yet [some commentators] view this commercial invasion—this invasion that in fact wreaked ecological havoc—as

the spontaneous development of efficient private property!"[91]

One does not have to be a gung-ho free marketeer to recognize that there are multiple sides to the story: farming fertile land makes it far more productive than using it as hunting grounds; when it is farmed as part of a larger global market, the value of the agricultural produce increases even more. One can lament the passing of pristine Indian land regimes and be in favor of sustainable land development while still recognizing this fact.

The idea that European land ownership was tied to "patriarchy" has impelled some feminist scholars to assert that Indian property holding systems were "matriarchal" while European property systems were "patriarchal." According to Suzanne M. Spencer-Wood: "Post-colonial feminist theories and research have shown how the social institution of patriarchy, including sexual relationships, was fundamental to European military conquest, colonization, economic exploitation of indigenous people, and cultural entanglements."[92]

Behind all this talk of Indian communism is an implied critique classical liberalism, including its major thinkers such as John Locke, whose ideas underlie the US Constitution. Fundamental to Locke's worldview is the idea that people are free individuals first and foremost. Locke argues that rights to property are sacrosanct because they are the basis of both life and liberty—the fundamental "good things" that make life worth living. Patrick Wolfe recognized this fact when he accused Indian schools of "teaching individualism." For Wolfe and other promoters of the myth of the communist Indian, liberal individualism lies at the heart of all that is wrong with modern society. By portraying the liber-

---

[91] James A. Swaney, "Common Property, Reciprocity, and Community," *Journal of Economic Issues* 24, no. 2 (1990), 451–462, https://www.tandfonline.com/doi/abs/10.1080/00213 624.1990.11505044.

[92] Suzanne M. Spencer-Wood, "Feminist Theorizing of Patriarchal Colonialism, Power Dynamics, and Social Agency Materialized in Colonial Institutions," *International Journal of Historical Archaeology* 20, no. 3 (2016), 477–491, https://www.jstor.org/stable/26174303.

al-individualistic culture of the United States as a perpetrator of mass theft, slavery, and genocide, these commentators seek to undermine the Lockean foundations of the United States, in the hope of bringing about some version of socialist collectivism. One important reason to debunk this myth is thus to deprive anti-liberal thinkers of one of the weapons in their ongoing war against capitalism, a war in which actual Indians typically want no part.

Let us therefore proceed with a look at what Indian property ownership was like in historical reality.

DID INDIANS OWN LAND?

We can begin with some basic questions: Did Native Americans own property, or did they hold all their goods in common? If the latter, how precisely did this work? Was land distributed by tribe? By family group? Did women own property? Was it inherited through the female line, as is often alleged? Did Indians steal from one another? Did "traditions and deep wisdom" keep the worst parts of human nature from marring their system of ownership? Did they keep the same land for generations? Was their property system "better" or more moral than that of the Europeans?

Questions of historical property holding by Indians quickly run into the problem of sources. Because nearly all New World peoples were pre-literate when the Europeans arrived, there are virtually no sources that provide firsthand accounts of what property holding was like among Amerindians. Oral traditions that have come down to us have been "corrupted" by centuries of contact with Europeans before they were written down. However, a look at the economic history of indigenous peoples reveals a complex picture, in which ideas of property changed and adapted over time, particularly in response to the advent of Western economic systems.

For example, a strong statement of Native American property holding was made by D. W. Bushyhead, principal chief of the Cherokee Nation in his letter to Congress in 1881:

Our own systems of law and land tenure are admirably suited to our people. The statements made to you that we, or any of the Indians, are communists and hold property in common are entirely erroneous. No people are more jealous of the personal right to property than Indians. The improvements on farms may be, and often are, sold; they may descend in families for generations, and so long as occupied cannot be invaded, nor for two years after abandonment. These farms and lots are practically just as much the property of the individuals as yours are. He who does not wish to keep can sell to all lawful citizens. The only difference between your land systems and ours is that the unoccupied surface of the earth is not a chattel to be sold and speculated in by men who do not use it.[93]

Bushyhead's letter was written for the political purpose of dissuading the US Congress from allotting specific farms to individual Cherokee householders. On a deeper level, the letter reflects his beliefs in 1881, by which time property holding among the Cherokee had changed enormously from what it had been two or three centuries earlier. For example, one does not imagine a Cherokee leader of the 1600s discussing the ability of Cherokee warriors to "sell improvements on farms" on some sort of secondary market.

A major debate in Amerindian studies raged throughout the twentieth century on just how much and how quickly Amerindian property systems adapted to strong colonial systems of property holding; the general conclusion being that exposure to lucrative markets, especially the

---

[93] Quoted in Kenneth H. Bobroff, "Retelling Allotment: Indian Property Rights and the Myth of Common Ownership," *Vanderbilt Law Review* 54, no. 4 (2001), https://scholarship.law.vanderbilt.edu/vlr/vol54/iss4/2/.

market for furs, encouraged Indian groups within hundreds of miles of a marketplace to intensify their own property systems for the purpose of increasing productivity.

If we attempt to go further back to find a "real" pre-contact Indigenous property system, we must rely on archaeology in the absence of written records. But archaeology gives us few clues, because property markers were not a common feature of Amerindian property regimes. And archaeology can tell us almost nothing about who held land and how it was transferred. For this reason, we have to rely almost entirely on later European accounts and anthropological theories, augmented by as many "authentic" Amerindian voices as have survived in those accounts.

One basic truth is clear: the nature of an Indian group's economic activity was the main determinant of their property regimes. A few groups such as the Aztecs and Incas lived in permanent cities, and their property holdings were therefore more definite and more elaborate. These groups are sometimes called "state societies," because their societies had a relatively well-developed concept of the state or, more precisely, of the city-state. Other groups of Indians lived in what we call "semi-sedentary villages," and, finally, many groups were hunter-gatherers.

The main thing that distinguished these groups is the extent to which they relied on agriculture. Agriculture makes specific plots of ground far more valuable than they otherwise would be, with the result that they take on far more importance in a property regime. The "state society" Indians relied mostly on agriculture; the "semi-sedentary villagers" relied on a mix of hunting, gathering, and hoe farming performed in clearings; while hunter-gatherers made little to no use of agriculture.

In state societies such as the Aztec Empire, land was organized similarly to ancient Mesopotamia. That is to say, there were lands that belonged to the major temples and the king, and there were lands that were reserved to the nobility. Each of these estates was worked either by slaves or conscripted labor. Conscription means that individuals in the surrounding area were forced to work on a lord's or priest's land for a certain number of days per twenty-day month. The system was therefore based on exploitation of slave or serf labor, in a manner every bit as "oppressive" as that of ancient Rome or medieval Europe.

This is the obvious way to maintain elite castes of priests and nobles. But we are not really concerned with these relatively rare societies since most American scholars are too timid (read, too fearful of appearing to be anti-Latinx) to accuse Mexico and its people of genocide and land theft in the way they do in the US and Canada. And as we have seen, the majority of people who farm ancient Aztec land today are the direct descendants of the Aztecs themselves.

In New England aboriginal societies, people lived in what are called "semipermanent" villages. They cleared fields by burning the underbrush and then farmed these for several years until the land and the hunting grounds around it became exhausted. After a generation or so, these people would move on to another area, where they would clear new fields and begin the process all over again. They usually roamed in the region of their settlement every season to maximize their hunting yield; they therefore combined hunting expeditions and life in temporary shelters with their more permanent residence. Semipermanent villages in such regions might number fewer than one hundred people, or they might attain a population of up to one thousand or even two thousand in exceptional cases. However, this also explains why individual Indian groups encountered by the English seldom numbered more than a few hundred.

This generalization does not encapsulate the many ways in which people made a living in pre-European New England and the Appalachian Mountains. Corn farming had come to the region quite recently—only some two hundred years before Europeans began to appear along the coast. This means that many groups had not yet adopted it. Some farmed only squash, while others farmed a combination of squash, corn, and beans. Other groups, especially those who inhabited rockier or more mountainous regions, continued to eschew agriculture altogether. Part of the difficulty New England Indians faced was finding vegetable varieties that could survive in the relatively short summers and whose seeds could survive the hard winter freezes.

In the areas occupied by the so-called Five Civilized Tribes of the South, Mississippian traditions of city-dwelling were combined with occasional mound- or midden-building in low-lying regions. These areas therefore featured somewhat larger, more permanent villages, though only in a few cases was an individual site occupied for more than a generation or two.

Nearly all the farming activity on the East Coast and in the Southeast was conducted by women. As a rule, Indian men viewed this work as inferior "women's work." While feminist scholars such as Spencer-Wood or Jaimes Guerrero want to believe that Indian society was matriarchal, countless sources prove that it was nonetheless thoroughly "sexist" by modern standards, with women's work being marginalized at least as much as in contemporary European society. This strong bias against agricultural work is a major reason why Indian males continued to resist lucrative offers of farmland during the nineteenth century to the detriment of their families' well-being. In nearly every Indian society, the higher-status occupations of hunting, soldiering, and political leadership were dominated by men. Feminism was an alien concept in nearly every society on Earth until the legal concept of women's rights began to be discussed during the European Enlightenment.

Semi-permanent village societies tended to define landholdings in terms of a tribe or "people"; groups claimed a certain amount of territory, and the territory would be defined in terms of central places such as mountains and waterways where applicable. On the Atlantic coast, the adoption of corn planting caused people to stay in the same place for a longer time. This increased the value of the land and provided opportunities for individual chiefs to dominate smaller tribes. By the time the English arrived, most local groups had been subjected to a ruler, or sachem, who demanded payment. While each tribe might have a sachem, some sachems were more powerful than others. They might demand tribute from lesser sachems. Sachems were expected to consult with the village elite of their particular group, but they were generally considered to be above all others. Tribute was typically demanded in the form of food, animal products, beads, tools, clothing, and the like. Sachems had to be careful not to demand too much from a given group, and tributary arrangements were subject to continual change, as the power of individual chiefs and groups waxed and waned.

Sometimes, tribal groups came to arrangements about common resources such as hunting grounds, clamming beaches, and the like; but people who hunted without permission in other tribes' hunting grounds could be attacked, and this might start a feud. Every year, hunting grounds were assigned by the sachem or village elite to individual hunters; these would be doled out according to status. Status for males was usually determined by a combination of birth, age, number of wives and children, success in warfare, and the possession of special talents such as being a priest or medicine man. Fishing areas might be similarly allotted to individuals or else to groups who wished to work together. Meanwhile, specific mounds of corn, squash, and beans were allotted to individual women, who were expected to care for these. During the growing season, children were assigned to protect the plants and produce from birds and other pests.

Whether in camp or in semipermanent villages, individual houses were likewise allotted by the chief or council. Homes were often given to specific males, who would then keep one or more wives and family members in their household. Usually, women would carry materials for building a home along with them while the group migrated. Contrary to most matriarchal fantasies about Indian society, women on the hunt were expected to carry cooking pots, fuel, and blankets, and generally to act as beasts of burden, while men carried only their weapons. Other sources describe Indian women as being treated as "continual slaves" in the household, though they were usually "cheerful and obedient" about their servile status.[94]

---

[94]   This from a nice series of excerpts prepared by the National Humanities Center, all of which make interesting reading: "Becoming American: The British Atlantic Colonies, 1690–1763," National Humanities Center Resource Toolbox, http://nationalhumanitiescenter. org/pds/becomingamer/peoples/text3/indianscolonists.pdf.

Semipermanent village societies therefore had a quasi-communistic way of holding land. The land belonged to the tribe; it was allotted to individuals every season or so, and the use of a given house might change regularly. Since groups migrated often, even seasonally, no one got attached to a particular area or house for very long. Some people have called this form of landholding an "indigenous commons."

When the Europeans arrived, the sachems were already fairly powerful along the Atlantic coast. European commentators had found strong kingship in most places around the globe, including the Islamic World, India, and China. They therefore described tribal lands as belonging to the sachem, whom early Europeans described as a "king." It was after all the sachem who had the power to distribute the land and also to give gifts from the tribute he (or in some cases she) received from the tenants. Likewise, Europeans interpreted the sachems as having the right to trade and sell lands, if they so desired. In most cases, sachems (in consultation with their leading counselors) acted as though they did.

As the English arrived in the decades around 1600, the vast majority of North America belonged to nomadic societies. These generally smaller groups required much more land than semipermanent village societies and followed the age-old Paleolithic method of following herds in order to provide sustenance. They often vacated their seasonal hunting grounds for half the year or more and might not return to an area for several years. Ranging as they did over enormous territories, nomadic tribes understood boundaries in a very general sense, and they might come into conflict if they wandered into a valley or area that another group claimed as their own. Nomadic Indian bands claimed to have "power" or "control" over a given area, meaning that they were entitled to extract resources from it. This was often the extent of their notion of property.

Usually in these nomadic societies land did not belong to an individual but to a band. Most tribes appointed "hunting bosses," who would be chosen from the males with a claim to leadership status. Like sachems in village societies, hunting bosses were seen as being in charge of the resources in their area and were expected to distribute them to dependents according to custom, with the expectation that everyone would be provided for to the extent possible.

The answer to the question of whether Indians owned property, then, depends on the tribe and region. In permanently settled areas such as the Nahua-speaking area of central Mexico, individual households and noble families did make claims to specific houses and particular plots of land. Spanish authorities often went to surprising lengths to respect these claims in subsequent decades. By law, Indian land rights were honored by Spanish officials, and lawsuits and other arrangements surrounding the Republicas de los Indios often involved claims of ownership.

Ownership under Spanish colonial law was sometimes understood to be common to a particular Indian community or pueblo, but bands could assign houses and plots to particular individuals. Within the Indian pueblo and its territory, Indians were allowed to sell land to other Indians. But if land was located within an Indian pueblo, then it was not allowed to be sold to Europeans or mestizos, because this would alienate the land from the community.

In Northeast Indian village societies, bands likewise laid claims to large areas of land; however, such claims were often vaguely defined, especially when it came to the extent of hunting grounds. Unlike in central Mexico, there were no permanent structures such as stone walls or dug foundations for individual Indian families to claim, making it more difficult for Europeans to take land claims seriously. Villages and corn mounds were more clearly defined but constituted only a tiny percentage of the lands claimed by any given tribe. All these claims tended to shift quite rapidly along with the power of individual chiefs, alliances, and the fortunes of war. Early colonial settlers differed, however, on how much of this tribal territory should count as actual property, and it is easy to see why this should cause genuine debate.

The main problem is that the hunting grounds that made up the majority of land claims were by nature huge tracts of land that were virtually empty and devoid of any human habitation. For this reason, some commentators argued that hunting grounds should not be considered Indian property, since next to nothing was done with this land, except for annual hunting forays. They argued instead that only actively cultivated agricultural ground should be counted as tribal property. This was in line with the labor theory of value (ironically in this context favored by Karl Marx), which argued that something only belonged to a person when they "mixed their labor" with it. Others took a more expansive view, suggesting that hunting grounds also had to be purchased from individual sachems in order for colonists to have a rightful claim to them. But the idea that Northeast Indian societies had property systems where certain individuals held the same land for long periods is wide of the mark.

In hunter-gatherer societies, which ranged over at least three-fourths of New World land north of Panama, property ownership was always tenuous in the extreme. Property in these vast empty regions was claimed by small bands, who might visit it only every few years. Population density was well below one person per ten acres; often, it was much lower than this.

To claim that hunter-gatherer bands had sophisticated notions of property is to misunderstand how hunting and gathering economies worked. Such people followed rivers, and knew the lay of the land, but primarily they followed animals and sought out regions where game was plentiful. As early modern Europeans plainly realized, such groups had no need for 99 percent of the land they claimed, as soon as they gave up hunting and gathering, since a single small farm would provide more reliable calories than one hundred square miles of hunting and gathering territory every year.

As soon as agriculture and firearms were introduced to North America by Europeans, human populations shot upwards and game populations plunged. Firearms rapidly spread to Indian communities hundreds of miles from the frontier. Under such conditions hunting and gathering became unsustainable within the course of a few generations. As this happened, ancient claims to territories the size of some US states by a few thousand individuals became increasingly unjustifiable—even though modern activists seem to have no grasp of how absurd such land claims are in any economy except that of a Paleolithic hunter-gatherer.

Almost all the modern hubbub about land claims and land redistribution is therefore strongly anachronistic. It attempts to apply a modern agriculturalist's logic (of high population density and extreme value for small plots of land due to high productivity of said land) to a hunter-gatherer society where populations were miniscule and land was next to valueless due to its extreme unproductivity. However you slice it, it's an apple-and-orange comparison that does not make sense.

DID INDIANS STEAL EACH OTHER'S LAND?

The "stolen land" acknowledgments noted earlier imply that the first white people who acquired Indian lands in a particular region were manifestly guilty of some heinous crime, worse than any Indigenous person had ever committed.

What this assumption neglects to consider is the ubiquity of intertribal Indigenous violence. This is a violence that incidentally, many European groups including the English, French, and Spanish went to great lengths to curtail over the centuries, saving hundreds of thousands of Indian lives in the process. Any map of New World Indian tribes prior to 1789—and even afterwards—should therefore come with the caveat that this pattern was continually fluid; the logic of tribal anarchy means that no one group held a specific territory for more than a few generations before migration, food scarcity, warfare, or other upheavals changed the boundaries.

The idea that these lands permanently belonged to any of these groups is thus a Eurocentric fiction colored by our own familiarity with European property norms. To find a good European analogy of the landholding situation in the New World during the early modern period, one would have to reference the Germanic migrations in Northern Europe after the fall of Rome. During these centuries, seminomadic tribal groups were continually at war; chiefs gathered war bands and conquered or dislocated neighboring populations as strength and luck permitted. Early English kingdoms such as Mercia, Wessex, Sussex, Kent, and East Anglia were likewise characterized by highly fluid borders; and many kingdoms were extant for less than a century.

The speed with which Indian land changed hands from one tribe to another seems astonishing to those unfamiliar with this type of political system. We have already outlined the Indigenous political history of Latin America, which is a fifteen-hundred-year archaeological record of conquest, forced migration, mass murder, dispossession, and sometimes the enslavement or extermination of entire ethnic groups. Meanwhile in early Virginia, the Jamestown settlers arrived to find that Chief Powhatan had subjugated no fewer than two dozen tribes during his own lifetime via a combination of warfare, intimidation, and intrigue. In Massachusetts, the Mohawks, Narragansetts, and Wampanoag had all displaced one another, or were threatening to do so, within a generation of the foundation of the Plymouth Colony.

The same process occurred farther west in the Great Lakes region, where the Five Nations territory proved to be continuously in flux. The Five Nations group is thought to have been formed only a generation or two before French explorers contacted them, and the early years of French settlement in the region witnessed a number of horrific (dare I say "genocidal") encounters. In 1649, the Iroquois took advantage of the weakened position of the Huron people to practically wipe them off the North American map.

> "About twelve hundred Iroquois came," a Huron remembered. "They took their anger out on the Fathers: they stripped them naked; they tore their fingernails off. They rained blows on their shoulders with sticks, on their kidneys and stomach and legs and face, and no part of their body was spared this torment."

In the process of the Beaver Wars, the Iroquois "stole" land from the Hurons and other tribes equal in size to their original territory in New York State. Later on, the Iroquois continued their imperialist campaigns, ranging far to the south and west of their original territories. They destroyed the Erie Indians and the famed Mohicans, and conquered several other tribes. In the years around 1700, they ousted the Sioux Indians from West Virginia and Kentucky, who were forced by Iroquois aggression to vacate the land forever and to settle farther west on more marginal ground. The Iroquois thereafter claimed the Sioux hunting grounds for their own.

By 1780, the Iroquois Nation had stolen the equivalent of at least six times their original territory, all from neighboring tribes. From their original base in New York State, they had emptied much of Pennsylvania, West Virginia, Ohio, Indiana, and much of southern Ontario of its former inhabitants. Whether or not one ascribes the Iroquois success to the presence of European firearms, the fact is the Iroquois, when given enough power, proved more than willing to permanently extinguish every Indian tribe they could get their hands on—this despite the efforts of the French and English to protect many of the Iroquois' victims.

If anyone in seventeenth-century America can be considered genocidal, it should be the Iroquois, rather than the French or English. It is believed that the intra-Indian wars of attrition, which resulted in the expulsion of many tribes from the Great Lakes region, so fatally weakened Native populations in the area, that they had little choice but to abandon most of this land to American settler expansion in subsequent decades.

Farther west, groups such as the Apache are famous for displacing and dispossessing dozens of tribes from their ancestral lands within living memory of the whites' arrival. The Apache are thought by archaeologists to have originated in Alaska and then rampaged southwards. Conquering and intimidating as they went, like a group of New World Huns or Vandals, the Apache finally reached the region of Texas by the time the first Spanish arrived in the early sixteenth century. From the Spanish, the Apaches received horses and guns, which enticed them to give up their semi-agricultural lifestyles and start hunting buffalo full time. The irony is that many of these Indians only began hunting riding horses and buffalo because contact with Europeans enabled them to do so.

Meanwhile, shortly after 1700, a push by the Comanches displaced many Apache Indians, who in turn put pressure on the Pueblo Indians, raiding them and despoiling them of their own food supplies. The fierce Comanche went on to displace, assimilate, and/or annihilate dozens of other tribes and smaller groups in a series of well-documented attacks. Neighboring tribes feared them as a merciless scourge, and rightly so: like most other Native American tribes they routinely killed babies, tortured men, raped women, and enslaved children as they conquered.

In short, the nomadic and semi-nomadic peoples of the future US held their land in a manner similar to that of other nomadic and semi-nomadic peoples across the globe. A tribe's relationship with property depended on how much farming they did. Hunter-gatherers had only the lightest notion of tribal ownership. The vast majority of semi-permanent village peoples' land was hunting ground and scrub. These people held some lands in common, while key tracts were allotted to individuals. Control of land and resources depended very strongly on an individual's status. The idea that Native Americans were "communistic" is therefore not particularly helpful. Tribes claimed certain territories for a while, but they might equally migrate to a new area, or else lose their current lands to the aggression of neighboring tribes. They were constantly engaged in an ages-old game of displacement, conquest, and territorial fluidity, where no one tribe inhabited a certain area of land for more than a few generations. Because of their economic practices, the land was extremely thinly settled to the eyes of anyone who grew up in a farming society. To imagine that European colonization interrupted a natural process of tribal confederation and ultimate state formation is implausible at best. Lacking the military and economic technologies to bring an end to this fluid, anarchic system, there is no prospect that Indian land claims would have become more permanent for many centuries to come.

Such was the state of Native property holding before and after the arrival of Europeans in the New World. We will leave the question of how and when Europeans ended up in control of most of this land for another chapter.

CHAPTER 10

DID THE FOUNDERS STEAL DEMOCRACY FROM NATIVE AMERICANS?

We, the people, to form a union, to
establish peace, equity and order....

—Attributed to the Iroquois Treaty
of the Five Nations, 1520

N early every myth about Indians and Europeans debunked in
this book has its origins in stereotypes circulated by New Left
academics and students during the 1960s and '70s. The current myth is no exception.

In recent years, news outlets have been promoting the idea that
American Founding Fathers not only stole our modern form of democracy from the Indians, but stole the credit for inventing democracy as well.
Rather than trying to undermine the Lockean principles that underlie the
US Constitution by attacking the liberal basis of private property, as we
saw in the last chapter, this argument attempts to undermine those principles by framing American democracy as yet another theft perpetrated
against the Indians by a morally inferior people.

According to Cody Cottier of *Discover* magazine in an article dated July 4, 2021, democracy was already "old news in the New World" when Thomas Jefferson proclaimed certain truths to be self-evident. In this telling, the achievements of the Founding Fathers should count as naught compared with the Amerindian statesmen (and women!) whose system of democracy had been perfected many centuries before 1776. As Cottier puts it:

> As the founding fathers began crafting a more perfect union from scratch, the Haudenosaunee Confederacy of what is now upstate New York carried on with the one it had been perfecting for centuries, grounded in an oral constitution known as the Great Law of Peace. Dating to perhaps as early as 1142, this charter is based on notions of unity, liberty and equality. It even provides for the separation of powers and outlines impeachment procedures. Is it a coincidence that American democracy emerged in a land so long imbued with such principles?

Some versions of this rumor even hold that the US Constitution is a derivative document based on an Amerindian original—specifically, the constitution of the Iroquois confederation. The main source of this rumor is a 1940s biography of the Founding Father and second chief justice of the United States John Rutledge. According to Rutledge's biographer John Barry:

> At the first meeting of the Drafting Committee [of the US Constitution], on the morning of July 27 1787, in Independence Hall, Rutledge, as chairman, drew from his pocket a parchment, which had never been referred to in the Convention or by any of the delegates outside, and read it aloud.

> It was a replica of the constitution of the Treaty of the Five Nations (the Iroquois) of 1520. Rutledge read what the Indians had written more than two and a half centuries before: "We, the people, to form a union, to establish peace, equity and order...."
>
> The chairman made no speech. He merely read the dry, quaint, and archaic words of the Indian parchment.

As the Black Lives Matter movement gained momentum in 2014, an internet meme crediting the Indians with writing the US Constitution went viral, though it was later debunked by PolitiFact as "mostly false." Nonetheless the story and this line of supposed Indian text has made it into an increasing number of popular articles and books.

Personally, I would find it kind of cool if the US Founding Fathers had borrowed some of their political ideas from the Native Americans. Why not? This could lend support to one of our main arguments here, which is that settlers and Indians interacted in many positive ways, with more extensive two-way cultural exchange than most people realize. It would be wonderful, in fact, if Native governments had contributed in a substantial way to the success of the American democratic experiment: this is something of which both Indian and non-Indian Americans could be proud.[95]

The major problem with this idea is the way it has been spread, and the motives of the people who spread it. A historically neutral fact such as Indian influence on the Constitution—if it were true—should not ruffle anyone's feathers. The problem is that the people pushing this idea do so as part of a more generalized attack on the West and its institutions. The goal of their rhetorical exercise is to make the supreme achievement of a lasting democracy look less obnoxiously amazing, and less

---

[95]   For example, I agree with much of what Charles Riley Cloud says about the positive points of Indian and American democracies in his foreword to Bruce Johansen's *Encyclopedia of Native American Legal Tradition* (1998).

obnoxiously Western, in the minds of those who have a preexisting beef against European civilization. For ideological authors like Dave Graeber, Western civilization itself is a poison, its greatest achievements are stolen from other cultures, and anything that makes its triumphs appear hollow is one more point to score in his attempt to tear it down.

Against all this flimflam, the historical record stands clear and unequivocal. The Founding Fathers were steeped in British and European political theory and also in the Greco-Roman classics. They were influenced most especially by the English political philosopher John Locke but also by French Enlightenment thinkers such as Voltaire, Montesquieu, and Rousseau. They were also familiar with the strengths and weaknesses of classical and modern republics, including Athens, and the Swiss cantons.

Meanwhile, the idea that the Iroquois provided the blueprint for the US Constitution only gained currency during the 1980s and has since become known as the "influence theory." As early as 1995, an article in the highly esteemed *William and Mary Quarterly* debunked this theory as the willful misreading of a few scraps of the historical record by a handful of quacks.[96] The fact that influence theorists have not to this point managed to publish a book with a major university press or land a spot in a major historical journal shows that the historical profession has long held the idea in contempt: there is just not enough evidence to challenge the standard reading.

It might seem at first as though the influence theory is just an organic part of American historical folklore, an idea as old as the hills. Scratch the surface, however, and you will find that the lion's share of books, articles, and web pages promoting this theory over the past four decades have been the brainchild of a single pair of academics.

The main source of this idea is a communications professor named Bruce E. Johansen. Born in 1950 in San Diego, he worked as a reporter

---

[96] Philip A. Levy, "Exemplars of Taking Liberties: The Iroquois Influence Thesis and the Problem of Evidence," *William and Mary Quarterly* 53, no. 3 (1996), 588–604, https://www.jstor.org/stable/2947206.

for the *Seattle Times* and got a PhD from the University of Washington in 1979. His doctoral thesis was about the influence of Amerindians on the US Constitution, and he published a version of this as a book called *Forgotten Founders: How the American Indian Helped Shape Democracy.* He later found an academic job in communications (not history) at the University of Nebraska. Johansen continues to publish books with titles like *Environmental Racism in the United States* and *Canada: Seeking Justice and Sustainability* (2020). He has also worked with the other major proponent of this theory, University of Buffalo Africana and American studies professor Donald Grinde. Together, the pair produced such stereotype-exploiting works as 1995's *Ecocide of Native America: Environmental Destruction of Indian Lands and Peoples.*

Despite the fact that most academics regard Johansen and Grinde as a pair of snake oil salesmen, the influence of their theory on American culture has not been negligible.[97] In the 1980s, Grinde was called by then-Senator Daniel Inouye (D-HI) to testify before the US Senate that the influence of Iroquois institutions on the US Constitution had been profound. Inouye used their testimony to prompt Congress to pass a resolution acknowledging this influence. In such a way, politics can elevate the wishful thinking of a handful of discredited experts into a rumor that kicks around the popular mind for many decades.

THE IROQUOIS CONSTITUTION

Who were the Iroquois, and did they actually invent concepts such as democratic government, federalism, constitutionalism, and separation of powers? This question has proved fascinating to countless investigators. The major problem, once again, is that we have no written records about Iroquois government dating from before European contact. Indeed, the

---

[97] William A. Starna and George R. Hamell, "History and the Burden of Proof: The Case of Iroquois Influence on the U.S. Constitution," *New York History* 77, no. 4 (1996), 427–452, https://www.jstor.org/stable/23182553.

mobile nature of Iroquois society meant that we possess very few physical artifacts from the precontact period at all.

The Iroquois had no system of writing; Richard Barry's notion that the Iroquois constitution had been "written down" on "parchment" in 1520 is therefore completely fallacious. There is no chance that John Rutledge had any parchment with Indian writing on it, let alone any words similar to the Declaration of Independence. Nor is there any evidence that Thomas Jefferson, who wrote the Declaration, was aware of the workings of Iroquois government in more than a general fashion. Indeed, the fact that John Adams could write an enormous, three-volume account of hundreds of historical republics ancient and modern, without listing the Iroquois among them, suggests that the Founding Fathers had only foggy reports about how the Iroquois constitution worked at the time the US Constitution was being written.[98]

According to Iroquois oral tradition, their Confederacy was born when a chief known as the Great Peacemaker convinced a number of other tribes to lay down their weapons and create a council in which each of the tribes would gain representation. Another supposed participant in this first council was Hiawatha, a legendary Onondaga chief. As we've seen, some writers attempt to put the origins of the confederacy back as early as the year 1100, claiming that it is "the oldest continuously functioning participatory democracy in the world." Serious scholars, however, place its origin in a far later period, merely a generation or two before the Dutch and the French began to interact with the Iroquois and their eastern neighbors.

If this consensus is correct, it gives us grounds for taking any claim for extreme longevity of the Iroquois constitution with a large grain of

---

[98] Adams's massive work was published in 1787–88. It does mention the Iroquois but only in passing rather than with a proper chapter—which is unfortunate. His study is misleadingly titled *A Defense of the Constitutions of Government of the United States of America*, even though the Constitution was in the process of being drafted as he wrote it. The main purpose of the work was to show skeptical Europeans how many successful republics had existed in the world up to Adams's day, with the implication that if these republics had been successful, then the United States could also be successful. (Adams was right.)

salt. It may be true that certain basic institutional arrangements persisted for a century or more. But in societies without written laws, political institutions are necessarily fluid, shifting from generation to generation as individual leaders rise and fall. We see a similar set of political arrangements in Dark Age Europe, where even fundamental institutions such as kingship and nobility remained in a continuous state of flux. Kingship in fifth-century Denmark meant something rather different from kingship in sixth-century England, and so forth. It is arguable that in a preliterate society, this is the only possibility, since the inability to write laws down means that they must be kept orally and will inevitably be subject to change.

According to its proponents, the Iroquois constitution was originally recorded on wampum belts; however, in reality these belts could only convey pictures and patterns. They were not textual, and they were not terribly precise. They were meant as a mnemonic device to enable lore keepers to remember the order of the laws and their main subjects. While this is undeniably ingenious, it still means that every time the laws were recited, they would be recited in a different pattern. This is why so many versions of the Iroquois constitution, which vary from tribe to tribe, are extant today.

Furthermore, the Iroquois constitution was not actually published in any known format until the 1880s, when American ethnographers like Lewis Henry Morgan first began to take a serious interest in surviving Amerindian cultures. By this point, of course, Indian contact with the West had been so extensive that Western values such as equality, liberty, and self-determination worked their way into versions of the text dictated to ethnographers. For this reason, extant versions tend to contain a mishmash of original Indian political conceptions, such as viewing people as either brothers or children, in a soup of Western political rhetoric. Many modern authors—such as Dunbar-Ortiz—then make the mistake of thinking this is proof of Indian influence on the settlers.

The classic Iroquois Confederacy was an alliance of six tribes—the Seneca, Cayuga, Onondaga, Oneida, Mohawk, and later the Tuscarora.

By the time Europeans made contact with them, each of their chiefs was hereditary rather than elected. Indeed, the French commentator Chateaubriand described the Iroquois and Hurons as having a number of "aristocratic republics," where noble families held power, while consulting a number of interlocking and overlapping elected councils.[99] Chateaubriand described the system as "extremely complicated," though he does praise the system for making full use of the rhetorical and intellectual talents of women—something he regretted that European political schemes had not yet managed to do. Chateaubriand, like many earlier commentators, likewise praised the Huron and Iroquois for high degrees of eloquence at their meetings.

So while Europeans had a sense that the Amerindians governed partly by councils, they realized that many elements remained hereditary and aristocratic. Not all votes were equal. The more powerful tribes such as the Mohawk and Seneca were regarded as "older brothers," meaning that their votes might sometimes be more equal than others. In rather a long stretch, some advocates have argued that the older-brotherhood of the Mohawk and Seneca provided a model for the bicameral system of the US Congress, where the older brothers played a role similar to the US Senate.

Among the most famous bits of evidence cited by influence theorists is a line by Benjamin Franklin, who in a letter of 1751 to James Parker, wrote the following:

> It would be a very strange Thing, if six Nations of ignorant Savages should be capable of forming a Scheme for such an Union, and be able to execute it in such a Manner, as that it has subsisted Ages, and appears indissoluble; and yet that a like Union should be impracticable for ten or a Dozen English Colonies, to whom it is more necessary, and must be

---

[99] François-René de Chateaubriand, *Travels in America and Italy*, *Volume 2* (1828, facsimile published by Applewood Books, Carlisle, MA, 2018), 76–77.

more advantageous; and who cannot be supposed
to want [i.e., lack] an equal Understanding of their
Interests.

This sentence can and should be read as an acknowledgment by
Franklin that the Iroquois constitution was venerable, durable, and func-
tional. But it does not at all need to be read, as influence theorists would
have us do, that Franklin therefore believed that the Iroquois were a
major reason why the Founding Fathers decided to create a democracy
in the United States.

THE ACTUAL ORIGINS OF
THE US CONSTITUTION

Most framers of the US Constitution were steeped in the "classical" literature of the Greeks and Romans. The classics remained the foundation
of European education between the Middle Ages and the early twentieth century. The standard form of education for men such as Jefferson,
Hamilton, and Madison was to be tutored from an early age until they
were fluent not only in modern languages such as French but also in
Latin and Greek. Alexander Hamilton is regarded as a founder of the
Philolexian Society at Columbia University—the elaborate-sounding
Greek name means "lovers of words." Even the famously self-educated
Franklin spent two years of his youth at a Latin school. For such men,
the idea of eloquence was tied to Greco-Roman ideals embodied by the
likes of Cato and Cicero.

The Greeks and Romans were very fond of their republics and wrote
about them often. But the Founding Fathers did not have to look back
two thousand years to find a blueprint for democracy. Dozens of colonial
legislatures, assemblies, governing bodies, commissions, and charters
already existed in the British colonial empire. The British had no formal
constitution, but the Magna Carta of 1215 guaranteed such freedoms
as the right to habeas corpus and trial by jury, and they had proclaimed

a Bill of Rights in 1689. Government by committee was critical to the British parliamentary model in the eighteenth century, and this system was "democratic" in many senses of the word. It was rules-based, subject to written public codes of law, and many bodies and commissions functioned through the medium of public debate and votes by delegates or members. Town governments throughout England and Western Europe elected councilors and mayors, and in Protestant countries church governance functioned in the same democratic way through voting by synods and councils.

As John Adams pointed out, Western Europe provided any number of examples of modern-day republics during the 1770s and '80s. Italian republics such as Genoa, Milan, Florence, Siena, and Venice contributed to the European political landscape for hundreds of years, and the Republic of Venice was not disbanded until Napoleon conquered it in 1797. Meanwhile, the Dutch state was a constitutional monarchy, in which parliaments and assemblies at the local, regional, and national levels often had ultimate authority. The Dutch had colonized New York and the Hudson River valley, thereby spreading their republican ideas to the New World. In fact, the Pilgrim fathers set out on their journey to Plymouth Rock from the Dutch city of Leiden, where they had sheltered for several years from English religious prejudice. Even more influential was the ancient Swiss Republic of Helvetia, which included the Calvinist Republic of Geneva together with other democratically run provinces or cantons.

For all their bluster about England being governed by a cruel tyrant, the American founders were aware that the true power in England since 1688 was not the British monarch, but the Parliament. Monarchs such as George III ruled on the understanding that if they angered Parliament too much, they would be replaced. The England of Thomas Jefferson's day was not only a constitutional monarchy—it was de facto a parliamentary state.

Europe in the eighteenth century was a breeding ground for ideas about how to limit the excesses of absolute monarchy and create lasting governments by the people. The Scientific Revolution of the seventeenth century had laid the groundwork for the eighteenth-century fixation on restructuring society along more "rational" lines. If Isaac Newton had discovered the laws of physics, surely someone else should be able to discover the invisible laws governing human societies. Unfortunately, societies proved to be much more chaotic, and subject to fewer absolutes, than the building blocks of nature. But that did not stop intellectuals and citizens across Europe from becoming inspired by the possibility of creating new, scientifically designed modern republics that would be responsive to the needs of their citizens. Thomas Hobbes argued that anarchy was the only possible outcome of any attempt to do away with a strong king. Jean-Jacques Rousseau seemed to argue that people would be best off with a participatory democracy. Even Rousseau, however, who famously promoted the idea of the unspoiled and innocent Noble Savage, did not advocate the adoption of an Iroquois constitution by European societies.

If evidence does come to light that the Iroquois influence on the US government was more extensive than is currently believed, this should be welcomed as an interesting development. The Iroquois leaders of the sixteenth and seventeenth centuries were remarkably successful at creating a large-scale, stable government that maintained peace between previously fractious tribes. Their system, though it contained strong elements of class stratification, nonetheless provided an admirable amount of agency for large sections of the population, including many women. This is a remarkable achievement deserving study and recognition.

But the Iroquois and European achievements can both be celebrated without partisanship or downplaying the extremely important innovations made by constitutional framers in Europe and America. Enlightenment Europe gave rise to some of the most astonishing, innovative, and influential social experiments in all recorded history. Many Europeans of the eighteenth century sought to create stable, large-scale governments of the people, by the people, and for the people. Some of them desired governments in which hereditary distinctions based on nobility could be abolished and a new citizenry of equals could be established.

Many American framers realized that the abolition of nobility was only the first step. Many spoke openly and repeatedly against slavery and sometimes even the subjugation of women to men. They saw their constitutional experiments as a practical and momentous first step in the liberation of all people—a liberation that we, their descendants, have fulfilled to a remarkable degree.

History has proven the Founding Fathers prescient. To obfuscate the story of this improbable triumph, based on a few conspiracy theorists' personal hobbyhorses, would be a serious injustice to our understanding of how democracy has developed over time—and how best to safeguard it in the future.

***

In Part II we have looked at some general myths and misconceptions about Amerindian societies. We can briefly summarize our findings as follows.

The peoples of the New World were not primitive or backward; they had advanced considerably in technology and culture since their Paleolithic ancestors crossed the Alaska land bridge before 10,000 BC. The most advanced areas of New World culture were the population centers of greater central Mexico and greater Peru. These areas witnessed several waves of cultural advancement, culminating in such achievements as proto-writing, record keeping, elaborate religious rituals, and advanced stone architecture.

By 1491, they had attained technological levels similar to Old World civilizations in 3000 BC. This was a remarkable achievement considering the much smaller population base of the New World, whose geography was less civilization-friendly than that of the Old World.

Nevertheless, they were considerably behind the curve of technological development of Old World civilizations. The claim advanced by some popular writers that the Incas and the Aztecs were equal to European (or

Asian or Islamic) civilization in AD 1500 is patently absurd and has never been advocated by any serious historian of New World society. This claim has only been put forward for the political purpose of making Europeans look bad; their goal is to be able to blame Europeans for causing even more civilizational damage than they actually did.

Meanwhile, nearly all the stereotypes about American Indians that the Left holds dear are traceable to the naivete of the 1970s progressive movement. Almost all these stereotypes arose in white, middle-class American households; they generally reflect liberal talking points such as environmentalism, anti-capitalism, and the peace movement. As such they are anachronistic projections not firmly grounded in real historical analysis.

Native American society was far from peaceful and benevolent—it was as brutal as any other of its day, and frequently more so. The history of the Mayan, Aztec, and Incan Empires, such as we can reconstruct it from archaeological sources, is a dreary litany of occupation, depopulation, mass enslavement, and mass sacrifice. The Aztecs ruled by maintaining a reign of terror over subject populations, to the point of routinely harvesting subject populations as sacrificial victims. The fact that this reality is not acknowledged by modern activist historians is for all practical purposes a deliberate coverup borne of embarrassment.

The idea that Native Americans were peace-loving environmentalists and natural communists has been roundly debunked as another 1970s stereotype. As demonstrated in books such as *The Ecological Indian*, today's Native Americans' track records on environmentalism are often inferior to environmentalist groups such as the Sierra Club. The idea that Native American government was particularly egalitarian, democratic, or matriarchal has likewise never been advanced by serious specialists. The ahistorical idea that the Founding Fathers "stole" their form of democratic governance from the Iroquois is the brainchild of a single pair of professors, who have been relentlessly pushing the same message since the 1970s.

In Part III we turn to the American story, beginning with an analysis of how settlers and Indians interacted in early New England and Virginia. We then face head-on the question of whether, and to what extent, the United States was "stolen" from Native peoples. We also look at the charges of anti-Indianism levelled against the Founding Fathers, tackle the thorny question of the Trail of Tears, and look at the Plains conflicts and the massacres that took place after gold was discovered in California.

III

AMERICAN DISPLACEMENT

CHAPTER 11

IS THANKSGIVING RACIST?

*Trudging through the Wampanoag's summer villages
and burial grounds, [the Pilgrims] rummaged houses,
unearthed graves, and picked through funerary offerings.
Their next move was to loot the Wampanoag's stockpiles
of food. The English credited "God's good providence"
for this supposed discovery, explaining that because
they had nothing to plant the next year, "they might
have starved" if they had not taken this measure. Just
days into their American venture, the English had
already established themselves as rotten guests.*

—David Silverman, *This Land Is Their Land*

I n the past several decades, a small but determined faction of kill-joys have made it their business to eviscerate the American holiday calendar. The so-called "war on holidays" has put increasing pressure on school boards to end school-sponsored festivities that do not "include" everyone.

Even Valentine's Day is now under attack—on February 13, Hillary Clinton sent around a "Happy Galentines Day" message to her millions of followers. Thinking this was a typo, I looked it up, only to find that some radical feminists found Valentine's Day too "heteronormative" for their taste. They preferred to celebrate a separate holiday that excludes males altogether. So much for inclusivity.

The war on holidays originates with similarly fringe segments of the population: people who would rather see old traditions scrapped than adapt them to modern sensibilities. Such impulses are selfish and novel—a symptom of our historically myopic "me first" culture, whose instinct is to fragment social cohesion rather than promote it. For centuries, immigrant communities made it their business to adapt to the customs of their new homelands with a minimum of fuss. They did this in the understanding that community, and the rituals that hold it together, is at least as important as individual sensibilities.

Not so long ago, Thanksgiving was mostly just "Turkey Day"—an excuse to set a grand feast, watch parades on TV, and savor the only four-day weekend sanctioned by American law. The myths around it were mostly concocted for elementary school children, and the goal was to teach something edifying about the American project as a whole. Today, Thanksgiving has become a political battlefield, like everything else in our collective culture. Fabricated as it was during the nineteenth century, the Thanksgiving story we've inherited is a minefield of potential multicultural offense.

The historical basis for Thanksgiving rests on a handful of sentences scribbled by the Plymouth colonist Edward Winslow. He notes that in 1621, Governor William Bradford invited the Wampanoag chief Massasoit and his people to a three-day harvest festival. Winslow notes how "[with] many of the Indians coming among us...we [engaged in] recreations...[and] entertained and feasted with them." He further describes how the Indians "went out and killed five Deer, which they brought to the Plantation and bestowed on our Governor, and upon the Captain (Miles Standish), and others." The celebration was held partly in gratitude to friendly Indians such as Squanto, who helped teach the settlers how to grow crops in their new environment. Such harvest festivals were a feature both of Indian and settler life, and so both groups chose this method as a show of cultural unity and political alliance.

The historical first Thanksgiving resulted in a peace treaty between the Pilgrims and the Wampanoag that lasted more than two generations, until the outbreak of King Philip's War in the 1670s. As historical achievements go, two generations of peace are not terribly shabby. Until recently, Thanksgiving was accepted as a festival of togetherness: a recognition that despite differences and a history of violence, even people of wildly varied backgrounds could overcome their differences. Previous generations understood that violence was normative among both Indians and Europeans, and that Europeans were at least somewhat guilty of destroying the Indians' way of life. Still, Americans took Thanksgiving as a symbol of hope, a sense that striving for peace and unity was a noble goal on which all people could agree. Underneath, it reinforced the important idea of *e pluribus unum*—that despite our many differences, it is still better if we strive to live as one people, under a single set of democratic institutions. Our ancestors realized better than we do just how open-minded and tolerant our immigrant society has made us, in stark contrast to many Old World societies where people have been living in the same place for centuries. Though these ideas flew under the radar of most "Turkey Day" celebrants, there was always, at base, a pro-democracy and pro-tolerance message at the root of it. This is part of why Thanksgiving and its story were more than "just a holiday."

Unfortunately, today's internet has become overburdened with anti-Thanksgiving articles and messages that portray it as an attempt to airbrush atrocities committed against Indigenous peoples. Any lingering messages of hope, reconciliation, social cohesion, and democratic renewal have been jettisoned in favor of a scramble to paint the American founders as fundamentally wicked.

For better or worse, the internet is where most teachers and journalists now turn for information on historical events. A Google search on "the story of Thanksgiving" returns a depressing litany of self-perpetuating clickbait. Of the top articles, only a single piece by parents.com attempts to bring out any positive aspects of the story, and the website takes care to justify this on the grounds that children might be upset by the "real truth" of Thanksgiving. The rest unanimously paint Thanksgiving in a negative light.

Today.com tells us that "members from numerous Indigenous communities as well as non-Natives will [not celebrate Thanksgiving but] instead come together for the annual National Day of Mourning to mark the historical atrocities against Native Americans that often get lost in the traditional telling of Thanksgiving." History.com tells us "the traditional narrative paints a deceptively sunny portrait of relations between the Pilgrims and the Wampanoag people, masking the long and bloody history of conflict between Native Americans and European settlers that resulted in the deaths of tens of thousands." (As we have seen, the total Indian death toll from massacre for the entire 250 years of English and French colonization in America before 1848 was less than eight thousand. Such flippant sensationalism, such a willingness to bamboozle the reader boggles the mind, but it's everywhere.)

The year 2020 marked the four hundredth anniversary of the sailing of the *Mayflower*, and yet few American news outlets bothered to run a story on the Pilgrims' landfall at Plymouth. News editors felt any mention of Thanksgiving would be insensitive at best and probably "racist" to boot. One of the few major outlets that did was the BBC, and predictably their slant was overwhelmingly negative.

According to BBC journalist Nick Bryant, the Puritans should not be celebrated; instead they should be called out for a long list of sins, including slavery, racism, classism, and attempting to "erase Native Americans from history." On the issue of slavery, Bryant says: "Not only did the colonists import African slaves, they exported Native Americans. By the 1660s, half of the ships in Boston Harbor were involved in the slave trade. At least hundreds of indigenous Americans were enslaved." Bryant claims that "the Pilgrim Fathers asserted the dominance of the white race, often with murderous force," continuing: "those first white settlers marked out the color line in the blood of Native Americans. To this day, however, the Pilgrim Fathers continue to be portrayed primarily as the victims themselves of persecution, the original asylum seekers who fled the religious intolerance of their homeland." Bryant further argues that the "Pilgrim Fathers were the originators of the American class system," going so far as to suggest that ongoing classism in New York City is what caused Donald Trump to become a megalomaniac.

The more serious internet articles base their stories on a new wave of anti-European works by academic historians. Bryant's article follows the Princeton-educated historian David J. Silverman in turning the Plymouth narrative completely on its head. Silverman's idea, laid out in his book *This Land Is Their Land: The Wampanoag Indians, Plymouth Colony, and the Troubled History of Thanksgiving*, is to look at the Pilgrims' landing from the Indigenous point of view. This is not a bad idea in theory. The problem lies in the execution. Silverman's book is rife with rhetorical sleights of hand that score cheap points with CRT-influenced audiences. Many of his duplicities are laughably transparent.

In Silverman's telling, the Pilgrim fathers brought with them a "trail of blood and mourning." He claims that "nearly every European voyage to Wampanoag country (in Massachusetts) ended in violence." While he admits that some Indians did, in fact, welcome the Pilgrims in the early decades, he claims they only did so because they were desperate—"reeling from their losses to an unforgiving epidemic" and "under relentless pressure from neighboring tribes." According to Silverman, "Only such conditions would lead them to look for help from English strangers whose nation had a lengthy track record of attacking and enslaving the people."

Silverman's introduction provides a key to his perspective. In it he devotes a fair amount of space to the life of 1970s Indian-rights activist Frank James. In Silverman's telling, James is presented as a sort of folk hero whose ideas are beyond reproach. Not least because James holds the sacred identity card of "Native American," an identity that in liberal circles gives certain people a monopoly on truth as "lived experience," no matter how irrational their ideas might be. A firebrand who served as president of the Federated Eastern Indian League, James drew inspiration from the radical arm of the black civil rights movement and eventually joined the "Red Power" movement. The dual symbolism of red for "Indian" and "communist" was deliberate. James's politics were Marxist and revolutionary, and ultimately aimed at regaining Indian sovereignty from the "imperialist" US government. One of his major goals, in other words, was to fragment the United States and its democratic institutions into anarchic cells as much as possible. To this end, James organized the first "National Day of Mourning" at Plymouth on Thanksgiving Day 1970. The activist's aim was to associate Thanksgiving and the entire Plymouth Colony with white guilt, and some fifty years later—with the complicity of goodhousekeeping.com and similar outlets—Frank James has succeeded beyond his wildest dreams.

HOW FREQUENT WAS
SETTLER-INDIAN WARFARE?

In the popular mind, as in Silverman's telling, the history of New England–Indian relations was one of nearly continuous, racially motivated slaughter. A Wikipedia page of "Indian Massacres of North America" provides details for most of the violent incidents that took place between settlers and Indians, defining a "massacre" as an event in which five or more disarmed combatants or noncombatants were slaughtered. Among the most egregious slaughters of seventeenth-century New England were the Pequot or Mystic Massacre of 1637 and the Great Swamp Massacre of 1675.

The Mystic Massacre took place in the context of the Pequot War. It saw a group of Connecticut colonists under Captain John Mason besiege a Pequot village containing between four hundred and seven hundred civilians. They shot anyone who tried to escape. In the end, the Connecticut colonists and their Indian allies stormed the fort, slaughtering all inhabitants including men, women, and children.

Some thirty-eight years later, the Great Swamp Massacre saw a group of Connecticut colonists and their Pequot allies slaughter hundreds of Narragansett women and children. They had been staying in a fortified village with a natural moat, but winter temperatures froze the moat, enabling the colonists and Pequots to storm the Narragansett settlement. In this case, however, the massacre was not entirely one-sided; the colonists lost some 70 killed and 150 wounded, in a struggle whose alternate name is "the Great Swamp Fight."

Despite the relative rarity of such massacres in New England history, they feature prominently in popular articles on Thanksgiving. Such portrayals are distorted from multiple angles. First, they are spun to represent one-sided instances of colonist-on-Indian aggression. Secondly, they are spun to appear unprovoked. Third, they are spun as though they were motivated by racial hatred and a desire for ethnic cleansing above all else, based on an underlying greed for land. And finally, they are spun as though this sort of thing was happening all the time—as though they were typical of and "stand for" early New England history. All four of these interpretations are false, or at least misleading.

The charge of continuous warfare is a highly embellished view of colonial New England history. According to William M. Osborn, who incidentally is cited on the "Indian Massacres" page referenced above, the total casualties of Indian-settler massacres between 1511 and 1890 were about 7,193 Natives who died at the hands of Europeans, and about 9,156 Europeans who died at the hands of Native Americans.[100] Osborn's account might well be undercounting the number of Natives who died in the California Gold Rush era, as we will discuss in a later chapter. But it's important to remember that for all this talk of massacre, the numbers involved were surprisingly small. Not only this, but Osborn's numbers make plain that Europeans were at least as much victims as perpetrators in the grand scheme of things. When you remember that we are discussing a period of some four centuries of conflict, then approximately ten thousand victims over four hundred years gives us an average of twenty-five massacred Indians per year, across an entire conti-

---

[100] William M. Osborn, *The Wild Frontier: Atrocities during the American-Indian War from Jamestown Colony to Wounded Knee* (New York: Random House, 2009).

nent, over the entire course of colonial and American history. These massacres also tended to come in clusters, normally during outbreaks of war.

Not only this, but often—as in the case of both the Mystic and Great Swamp Massacres—the perpetrators were colonists *and their Indian allies*. In many cases, it's next to impossible for anyone to say whether the majority of killings were carried out by colonists or by Indian warriors thirsty for revenge against their enemies. We have already seen how hundreds of eyewitness accounts attest to the brutality of Indian revenge killings, which often resulted in the assimilation or literal genocide of neighboring tribes. And certainly, when Indians and colonists were working together as allies during a time of war, to imply that slaughters perpetrated by the allies were "racially motivated" is farcical. As the historian James A. Warren reminds us, King Philip's War in the 1670s helped to destroy a "fascinating…bi-cultural experiment in Rhode Island that [the colonist Roger] Williams and the Narragansett leaders had worked so hard to maintain."[101]

The Indian wars of the 1670s destroyed decades of patient work, which saw both Indian and colonial leaders lay the foundations for a multiethnic society across New England. To pretend that destruction and division was one-sided and routine is to completely ignore the "lived experience" of thousands of New Englanders who wanted to create a multicultural society even in the seventeenth century.

As to causality, James Warren is at pains to point out that "the causes of the Great Swamp Fight were varied and complex." Warren explains that this was anything but simple colonist-on-Indian violence; it had much more to do with local power politics and the self-interest of various Indian chiefs than an overriding civilizational conflict. As to the question of whether the Great Swamp Fight was a battle or a massacre, Warren points out:

---

[101] "The Great Swamp Massacre, a Conversation with James A. Warren," Rhode Island Historical Society, December 19, 2020, https://www.rihs.org/the-great-swamp-massacre-a-conversation-with-james-a-warren/.

one could make a decent argument for either, and in a sense, it was both. The casualty figures among the Puritans confirm that the Narragansetts put up fierce resistance, which, to my mind, makes the engagement a battle. The Narragansetts had good reason to expect an attack, given the general turbulence that prevailed at that time in southeastern New England. The burning and the killing of non-combatants that followed after the Puritans [and their Indian allies] gained control of the fort, however, could certainly be called a massacre.

When war did break out, it often took the colonists by surprise. The largest scale colonial-Indian wars typically began with surprise attacks by Indians, which saw reeling colonists scramble to orchestrate a response.

In Virginia, the year 1622 saw the Powhatan Indians precipitate a war on the colonists, beginning with a surprise attack. The Virginians had settled in widely dispersed farmhouses, often very near Indian settlements, and the two peoples were used to trading and socializing with one another. This is why the English proved so vulnerable to ambush and massacre. In this case the Indians, whose intent was nakedly genocidal, managed to kill 347 people—one-quarter of the entire English population of Virginia. After signing a peace treaty, the Indians broke the peace again in 1644, managing to massacre some 400 colonists in the process. Another peace treaty was signed with them in 1646, and many of their descendants still live in Virginia today.

In the Pequot War of 1636–37, the Connecticut colony suffered months of raids on military forts and stockpiles without declaring an offensive war against the Indians. Only after the Pequots killed several women and children at Wethersfield did the colonists ally with local Indians to bring an offensive war to the Pequots. This campaign culminated in the above-mentioned Pequot or Mystic Massacre, when a force of some 77 Connecticut militia and over 250 Native allies attacked and massacred a Pequot stronghold.

King Philip's War in the 1670s also began with a surprise attack by Indians. It too resulted in the massacre of a large number of colonists. Like the Virginia colonists earlier, several generations of largely peaceful relations had taught the colonists that they had nothing to fear from their Indian neighbors; so the Massachusetts colonists had similarly settled in widely dispersed farmhouses that were vulnerable to Indian attack. In the series of massacres perpetrated in 1675–76, the death toll to the colonists was fully twenty-five hundred people—approximately one-third of the total population of New England.[102]

Both the Powhatan Wars of Virginia and King Philip's War in New England were calculated gambles on the part of powerful chiefs who hoped to deal a knockout blow to the English, thereby driving them from their territory forever. This was similar to how Indian chiefs dealt with neighboring tribes with whom they had a major grievance, when they believed they had a sufficient military advantage. The responsibility for the decision to go to war often lay with individual chiefs, and the logic they used made sense within the context of their social milieu.

After the 1670s, major conflict between the English and the Indians did not occur again until the French and Indian War of 1754–63—the better part of a century later. Hostilities once again began with Indian raids on widely scattered colonial farmsteads, resulting in the massacre and capture of colonists along long stretches of frontier. Many colonists were taken by surprise, because they were used to generations of peaceful relations and trade with the Indians who lived nearby.

While it is easy today to view this list of wars as an indication of continuous warfare, that is not how the frontier was experienced by the peo-

---

[102] See Robert Cray, "'Weltering in Their Own Blood': Puritan Casualties in King Philip's War," *Historical Journal of Massachusetts* 37, no. 2, 106–124. https://www.westfield. ma.edu/historical-journal/wp-content/uploads/2018/06/Weltering-in-their-Own-Blood-Puritan-Casualties.pdf

ple of that era. For them, brief and intense conflicts were flashpoints that interrupted long, mostly uneventful decades of peace, trust, and trade.

THE TRUTH ABOUT THE PILGRIMS

Historian David Silverman accuses the Pilgrim colonists of New England of ransacking Indian graves, stealing their food, and rummaging through their houses like common thieves. This allegation can be found in other well-known histories such as Roger L. Nichols's *Indians in the United States and Canada: A Comparative History* and in the writings of the Indian activist Frank James. What Silverman neglects to mention is that the lands in question were then covered with the bleached, unburied bones of people who had died in a massive plague only a year or two before the Pilgrims landed at Plymouth.

It's not as though Silverman was unaware of this fact. Elsewhere in his book, Silverman reports that the English captain Thomas Dermer passed along the New England coast after this plague, where he "found some ancient plantations [agricultural fields], not long since populous, now utterly void." He reports that a "great mortality" that the Indians "never heard of before" had left scarcely one in twenty people alive. The Plymouth Colony historian Nathaniel Morton wrote that "sad spectacles of that mortality" were evident throughout the country in the form of the "many bones and skulls of the dead lying above the ground." Evidently these people lay unburied in large numbers where they fell. Edward Winslow and Stephen Hopkins similarly reported how the entire route down the Taunton River was lined by formerly cleared fields being reclaimed by the woods, indicating that once "thousands of men have lived there," but that they had "died in a great plague not long since."

Silverman ignores the fact that the Pilgrims who "ransacked" Indian corn supplies and houses were going through areas that they believed to have been left waste by the recent plague, which had claimed perhaps 90 percent of the local population. He is honest enough to mention that the Europeans intentionally left some of the most important graves untouched; he also mentions that the English were careful to put most of the grave goods back in place, because they did "not wish to be odious" to the Indians.

It is also clear that by digging up a few of the graves, the English were mainly seeking to understand the Indians among whom they intended to live. Likewise, they were careful to leave the Indian homes undisturbed so as to cause minimal offense, while—believing them to be abandoned and unoccupied—they did take away some of the most useful implements they found.

Silverman alleges that the "theft" of a few bushels of corn would "leave the Indians starving," while it was obvious to all involved that a population reduced by 90 percent would not need every bushel; for all the settlers knew it had been totally abandoned. Time showed that the settlers did, in fact, pay the Indians back for this corn and other goods. As Nichols reports, the early Plymouth colonists were assiduous in policing their own people:

> The leaders of the Massachusetts Bay Company assumed that they would have peaceful dealings with the native people. As early as 1629 John Endicott received orders to "have a diligent & watchful eye over our own people, that they... demean themselves justly & courteous" toward the Indians. Colonial authorities took their directions seriously; during the first few years of settlement they strove sporadically to protect Indian rights and property from harm at the hands of the English. Individual settlers received such punishments as being whipped, branded, fined, banished, or even losing the title of Master for their misdeeds among the Indians. The colony even accepted corporate guilt in 1634 when Charleston had to pay damages

to nearby Indians because the settlers' swine had damaged the villagers' crops.

Nichols continues:

> Not only were the leaders admonished to limit the contacts their people had with the natives and to avoid trouble with them, but the company expected them to obtain land and settlement rights with care as well. This is clear from the instructions that directed the New England leaders to pay local chiefs for any claims they had for town sites and farmland.

When seen in this light, it seems more plausible that chiefs such as Massasoit had no misgivings about forging an alliance with the English during that first and subsequent Thanksgiving Days in early New England. Massasoit was not "crazy" or driven to "despair" as Silverman bizarrely suggests. Massasoit, like Powhatan in Virginia, was a very astute leader and a good reader of local power politics. His primary concern was how to maintain the stability of his own leadership and the integrity of his borders; in his mind the English were a relatively known and controllable entity, while his Indigenous enemies actually constituted a more pressing threat.

WERE INDIANS ENSLAVED BY THE ENGLISH?

In 1614, the soon-to-be-notorious English captain Thomas Hunt led a pillaging expedition down the coast of New England, in which he carried off twenty-four Indians as captives to be sold in Spain. Among these was Squanto, the very Indian who later introduced the Plymouth colonists to Indian agricultural techniques. According to Silverman, Hunt's name was still cursed among the locals years afterward; a woman from the village of Cummaquid, when she first saw the Pilgrims in 1621, "broke into a great passion, weeping, and crying excessively" because she had lost three sons in Hunt's raids, "by which means she was deprived of the comfort of her children in her old age."

Silverman portrays Hunt's actions as typical of English behavior. He suggests that New England in 1619 was a "place with a growing reputation for violence between Indians and European explorers," and alleges that "harrowing stories of the two peoples capturing and killing each other had been in circulation among sailors for years."

In reality, Hunt's actions were atypical; indeed, the fact that Hunt became infamous in local Indian lore for a generation suggests that his behavior was the exception rather than the rule. If Hunt's behavior was so typical, why was all of eastern Massachusetts still enraged at him years after the fact? And why did the subsequent shipwreck of a French ship lead to the murder and enslavement of the crew, in retaliation for his actions? In fact, Hunt's raid caused no end of headaches for subsequent traders and would-be colonists, since that single action caused unusual levels of ill will between Indians and Europeans for many years to come.

Thomas Hunt's "slave raid" belies a number of complexities that go unremarked in Silverman's account. For example, the reason Hunt wanted to sell Indians in Iberia is because no other port in Atlantic Europe had slave markets. Most European authorities did not allow slave markets in their territories; the ban on slave markets had become commonplace in most of Europe during the later Middle Ages. In England, a famous court case of 1559 determined that English air was "too pure for a slave to breathe in," and the custom became entrenched that anyone, of any race, became free from any taint of slavery the moment they set foot on English soil.[103] This "free soil" principle also became law in France and the Netherlands, for example.

---

[103] For the evolution of the "Free Soil" principle in Atlantic Europe, which held that any enslaved people entering a country were legally free from the moment they landed, see Sue Peabody and Keila Grinberg, "Free Soil: The Generation and Circulation of an Atlantic Legal Principle," *Slavery & Abolition* 32, no. 3 (2011): 331–339, https://www.tandfonline.com/doi/abs/10.1080/0144039X.2011.588468?journalCode=fsla20.

In deference to the modern CRT narrative, which avoids crediting Europeans with any virtue, biography.com mentions that Squanto was sold as a slave in Spain and then says that "he escaped." But even in Spain, the 1512 Laws of Burgos and the 1542 Laws for the Protection of the Indians outlawed the slavery of Indigenous Americans. Soon after they were sold, Squanto and most of his fellow Native Americans were in fact ransomed by Spanish friars, who had heard that an unscrupulous captain had illegally sold them in the local slave market. It was by these kind friars' efforts that Squanto was ransomed. He was clothed, fed, cared for, and given enough money to sail to England, where they told him that he would be able to find a ship bound for his homeland.

Squanto was able to convince an English captain to take him on board as an interpreter and guide, and in this way his passage back across the Atlantic was arranged and paid for. Considering the rough-and-tumble world of the early seventeenth century, all this charity should be seen as truly remarkable—an example of the strong strains of humanitarianism that were running through Western European culture at this time.

Rather than disappearing into the woods as soon as he returned, Squanto continued to deal with the New Englanders, and he proved invaluable to them in many subsequent negotiations. When he fell sick a few years later, he not only entreated the English to pray for him, but he also bequeathed to his English friends several of his items. Despite reports that Squanto had sometimes been duplicitous in his dealings with the English, it is reported that they mourned his loss and were deeply affected by it. It's difficult to avoid the conclusion that Squanto (Tisquantum as he was known in his own language) had developed a deep affection for aspects of European culture and found fulfillment acting as a bridge between the two peoples.

In sum, only a few hundred Indians are recorded as having been taken as slaves from New England during the seventeenth century; most were taken as prisoners during King Philip's War. What modern write-ups seldom mention is that a far greater number of New England Indians, almost certainly reaching five figures, were captured and enslaved by other Indians during this period. As Silverman himself mentions, "Indians in southern New England, as throughout North America, ranked captive taking among their primary war aims. Whereas they executed most adult male captives [and old people and babies], the women and children would have been spared and adopted after a period of debasement."

Families headed by such slaves suffered a lifelong, sometimes intergenerational stigma of being considered lower class and subject to the will of their captors. They were not allowed to attend communal hunts or be full members of the village council; in New England Indian society, the mark of slavery was real and ubiquitous. This reality is almost entirely ignored by modern journalists.

IS THANKSGIVING RACIST?

The original Thanksgiving was a sort of peace treaty, a celebration by two very different peoples of the hope that they would be able to get along together. Across several generations, this is for the most part what they did. Dozens of Indian schools—including the Harvard Indian College founded in 1655—attest to colonial New Englanders' concern for Indian children and their desire for Indian youth to have the same opportunities as their own.

Of course, the critics have a point. In the early twentieth century, Thanksgiving was used to paper over many of the sins of the European colonists and portray the Indians as though they willingly gave up their land and eventually their civilization to their European "fathers."

But it is equally misleading to read Thanksgiving in a universally negative and cynical light. Historical Europeans did plenty of horrible, murderous things, and we should not shy away from recounting these failings. But as this chapter has endeavored to show, the Europeans and Indians of New England really did forge many friendships and mutually beneficial ties. They were not "racist" in a consistent way that corresponds to modern notions of the term.

We have seen how thousands of Indians and colonists spent their lives forging peace between the peoples of colonial New England, going to great lengths to set up what has been described as a "biracial society." Surely it is unfair that these peoples' efforts go unremarked and unnoticed by the likes of *Good Housekeeping* and *Smithsonian Magazine*, while a handful of slaughters make front page news every November. It was these peacemakers' hope for goodness in spite of the world's evils that Thanksgiving was always meant to represent.

Given the complexities behind Indian-settler relations in colonial New England, is it appropriate to claim that Thanksgiving is a "racist" or "exploitative" holiday that ought to be replaced by a "National Day of Mourning"? To answer the latter question, we can point to the fact that the idea for a National Day of Mourning was popularized by the Red Power activist Frank James in the 1970s. The whole concept therefore reeks of a radical '70s indictment of capitalist society, which ought to be taken with a grain of salt. A better solution is to keep Thanksgiving for what it is—like most traditions, it can be adapted for modern sensibilities. This can be done by reminding children that while the holiday represents a symbol of hope and togetherness, that things did not always work out that way in practice. The holiday can therefore be a time of respect for Indigenous rights, while at the same time acknowledging that what the Europeans brought to the table was in balance somewhat more positive than Silverman's "trail of blood and mourning."

CHAPTER 12

WAS POCAHONTAS A
RACE TRAITOR?

*Long before Disney, white American popular culture
mobilized myths about Pocahontas to serve purposes
ranging from colonial conquest to Civil War, and
from racial segregation to white supremacy. Each usage
promoted an unequal society that benefited whites at the
expense of indigenous peoples and African Americans.*

—Honor Sachs, history professor at
University of Colorado, Boulder

*We understand the English and Americans think highly
of Pocahontas. For the Pamunkey tribe, [she] is not a big
deal. She doesn't mean a whole lot to us. Her contributions
to our way of life didn't really amount to much.*

—Chief Robert Gray

I t is easy to forget that the first permanent English colony in the New
World was not founded at Plymouth in 1621, but at Jamestown,
Virginia, in 1607. The English were latecomers to the game; the
Spanish already had a fort at Saint Augustine, Florida, by 1565. It was

partly to limit Spanish encroachment north of Florida that the English first looked to settle Virginia. Under Sir Walter Raleigh, they attempted to plant a colony at Roanoke (now North Carolina) in 1585 and again in 1587, but the second attempt was abandoned under mysterious circumstances. Returning to resupply the colony in 1590, the English found the fort abandoned and the mysterious word "Croatoan" carved on the side of the fort. It is assumed that these original colonists relocated to nearby Croatoan Island, where they were either massacred or assimilated into the local Indian population.

The early history of the Jamestown colony was mythologized in nineteenth- and early twentieth-century accounts of the United States, as America sought to create a national origin story. Some of the more colorful participants in this drama such as Captain John Smith and the regional Indian chief Powhatan were made larger than life. Overshadowing all of them, though, is the figure of Powhatan's daughter Pocahontas.

It will by this point come as little surprise that modern scholarship falls all over itself to read Jamestown, and the relationships between the colonists and the Indians there, in the most negative possible light. The 1619 Project is named after the fact that the first documented African slaves in the English colonies of the future US were brought to Jamestown in 1619. The project's lead author, Nikole Hannah-Jones, chose the name because she wanted to preempt the 1620 landing of the Pilgrims by a year. Her goal was to fix America's attention on the idea that even before the Pilgrims landed, slavery lay at the crux of American history. The Project's authors allege that Virginia colonists routinely enslaved Indians as well as African-Americans and that this was a core of the early colony's economy. Both of these claims are greatly exaggerated, since Indian slavery was and remained rare, and African slavery in Virginia remained nascent for the better part of one hundred years after the foundation of the colony.

As for Pocahontas herself, the University of Colorado, Boulder historian Honor Sachs recently published a piece in the *Washington Post* in which she argued that the entire purpose of the "myth of Pocahontas" is to "prop up white supremacy." She claims that throughout American history, the Pocahontas story was used to "promote an unequal society that benefited whites at the expense of indigenous peoples and African Americans" and thereby helped to "justify the subjection of nonwhite people." Later on, she claims, Pocahontas was used by older American families to distinguish themselves as "racially and ethnically superior" to immigrants from Southern and Eastern Europe.

In fact, for many years, Virginia elites claimed descent from Pocahontas as a badge of honor. Most of us would think of this as the opposite of racism...but of course commentators like Honor Sachs will employ tried-and-true New Left logic to make any good actions look bad. One has a sense that "white" Virginia elites could do no good in the eyes of Honor Sachs, even if they had made Pocahontas and her daughters the perpetual queens of Virginia.

Meanwhile, Amerindian activists have chosen to see Pocahontas as something of a "race traitor," similar to the role played in Mexico by Cortes's wife Marina. Their interpretations range from a deliberate downplaying of Pocahontas's role in history to accusations of treachery and "selling out." Pamunkey chief Robert Gray claims that Pocahontas, by deciding to marry an Englishman, "doesn't mean a whole lot" to the history of Amerindian peoples, and he dismisses her as "not contributing to our way of life." Does he mean to imply that every métis or mestizo person—including the millions of their descendants alive today—is somehow less of a person than a pure-blooded Amerindian? Millions of people across the centuries were to have experiences similar to Pocahontas. These people inhabited a world where cultural and "racial" boundaries were surprisingly fluid and permeable. This is because most people were not incorrigibly racist.

Chief Robert Gray might do well to remember that the majority of the descendants of Amerindians today are mixed-race, and that to marginalize this diverse group is to practice precisely the sort of racial prejudice and "erasure" the Left claims to be against.

POCAHONTAS AS A SOCIAL SUPERIOR

Due to a paucity of sources, we can know little of Pocahontas's life. The Englishman William Strachey is responsible for the oft-quoted claim that she would come naked into the fort as a preteen girl and unabashedly play with the English boys who were there. A few years later, during the First Anglo-Powhatan War, Powhatan and his allies captured a number of English prisoners. This led the English to place Pocahontas under house arrest, where according to the *True Discourse* of colonist Ralph Hamor, she was treated very well.

Pocahontas was used as a bargaining chip, and Powhatan soon recovered her in exchange for several colonists. During her captivity, the minister Alexander Whitaker introduced her to Christianity, and she later converted, taking the English name Rebecca. She is alleged to have told her father that she preferred to stay with the colonists, because of the good treatment they showed during her captivity. Given what we know of other early Indians such as Squanto and hundreds of others who would voluntarily join seventeenth-century colonial schools, the idea that Pocahontas preferred life among the English is not far-fetched.

Her father, consequently, agreed to have her marry the wealthy planter John Rolfe. Rolfe is an interesting character insofar as he professed to be in love with Pocahontas, while admitting his misgivings about marrying a girl who had grown up naked in the woods and whose manners and habits were far from what was expected of upper-middle-class Englishwomen of the time. Rolfe also knew that she had already had children with at least one other Native husband. Nonetheless he overcame all the supposedly patriarchal, Christian, and racial prejudices that liberals ascribe to colonists and took her into his home as his wife.

Despite his qualms, Rolfe felt the marriage to be advantageous because the English believed Pocahontas to be a Native American "noblewoman." This is a very important point that modern commentators anachronistically disregard. In seventeenth-century Europe, the distinction between nobility and commoners was fundamental. It was believed that nobles were innately superior. This is why the conquistadors were so ready to marry Indian "noblewomen" across Latin America—they believed that they were "marrying up" and therefore bequeathing their children a noble status. They further expected the Crown of Spain to award privileges to them based on the status of their Indian blood relations, just as was the case throughout Europe. Europeans who dealt with countries as far afield as Morocco, Turkey, and Russia also expected to find a noble or gentle class in those societies and expected to accord them special honors, just as they did at home.

We should expect nothing different in the New World. During the first two centuries of European exploration, Europeans from kings to scullery maids believed that Amerindian "nobles" were socially superior—that is to say, innately superior—to low-born Europeans. Across the Spanish, French, and early English encounters with Amerindians, we find a good deal of preoccupation with whether Indians came from "noble" families. For example, the French Baron of Saint Castin (d. 1707) married a daughter of a Penobscot Indian chief named Mechilde; his assumption was that she had noble blood and was therefore a good match for a French nobleman. He later brought his Indian wife back to France with him to live like a French baroness, and he intended to pass his noble titles on to his métis children.

In Virginia, many English were therefore ready to see Powhatan as a king and Pocahontas as a princess. According to the historian Robert S. Tilton, the marriage of Pocahontas and John Rolfe actually caused consternation in some English circles, because people believed it was improper for a commoner (Rolfe) to marry such a high-born noblewoman.[104] This is impossible to square with Honor Sachs's notion that Europeans felt themselves innately superior to Amerindians on account of race.

Furthermore, in this early pattern of marrying Indian "nobles" we may detect an assumption on the part of Europeans that Indian soci-

---

[104] Robert S. Tilton, *Pocahontas: The Evolution of an American Narrative* (Cambridge, UK: Cambridge University Press, 1994).

ety would be long-lasting and permanent—just like Islamic society had proven to be. There would be no point in marrying into the nobility of a society that one expected to disappear over the course of a few generations. This provides further evidence that European colonists did not arrive with any settler-colonial pretension of replacing or subordinating Indian society, but merely living alongside it.

INTERRACIAL LIFE ON THE FRONTIER

It is almost laughable how many writers have recently learned to assume that Indians and colonists loathed the very sight of one another, while feeling a sort of magical solidarity with everyone of their own "race." This cartoon view of history bespeaks a desperate desire to fit the square peg of historical evidence into the round hole of simplistic identitarian worldviews. It is a textbook example of the "presentism" that AHA President James Sweet was pilloried for warning against in 2022. And yet we know of dozens of tribal rivalries where Indians described their near neighbors as "devils," "dogs," "less than human," and "worthy of extermination." (Such sentiments often get attributed to colonists, such as the first governor of California for example, but are conveniently forgotten when they were uttered by one Indian against another.)

The Amerindian world of the seventeenth and eighteenth centuries was intensely local, and intensely tribal. The idea that they identified with one another in racial terms is completely anachronistic, based on a late nineteenth-century worldview that today's Amerindian and mixed-race people have adopted without recognizing its inapplicability to earlier periods. Today, many American Indians will tell you that they feel like a member of their tribe first and like an "Indian" second. This same inability to apply racial logic applies to most Europeans of the seventeenth and eighteenth centuries.

We have already seen how the Spanish formed interracial households with Indigenous people across Latin America. The English proved more standoffish than the Spanish and French, partly because the Indian populations of the English colonial areas were much lower relative to the numbers of English colonists. However, to pretend that English and Indian people did not regularly trade or communicate in a friendly manner is also wide of the mark.

Writing about early Massachusetts, David Silverman displays a schizophrenic attitude toward the question of whether the Indians and the English voluntarily formed friendships and trading partnerships. As we have seen, Silverman claims that the Indians must have been traumatized and even "psychotic" to enter into partnerships with the English. But if this was the case, then why does the historical record provide so many examples of Indians voluntarily wandering into English and Dutch camps, and even climbing on board ships where they knew they were easy targets for kidnapping? On the contrary, bands of Indians routinely met Europeans in their ships or along the shore, even prior to the arrival of the first colonists.

Such meetings always brought a certain tension, and both sides often arrived armed to the teeth. But the Indians were motivated to interact with the Europeans because they found their implements extremely valuable. And most Europeans proved trustworthy enough that the Indians readily accepted them as trading partners. Thus driven by economic incentive bolstered by sufficient levels of trust, many tribes jockeyed for position as middlemen between the Europeans and other Indian tribes; this was a major cause of the Pequot War of the 1630s, as with the intra-Indian Beaver and Fox Wars later on.

Fostered by trade, neighborliness, and a basic desire to avoid danger, early English colonial society featured a surprising degree of interracial comity wherever one cares to look, and from the earliest days there were friendships, adoptions, and intermarriages. Soon after they landed, the Pilgrims unearthed the skull of a European who had been shipwrecked and adopted by the Indians, and buried by them with honor. There were also many Indians such as Squanto who—despite being captured and sold into slavery in Spain—still chose to live among the English.

The phenomenon of the individual Indian living and working among the colonists therefore became commonplace during the seventeenth century. Indian children were adopted and taken into English households, where they eventually intermarried with the local population. Sometimes, Indian children were indentured to European families as surety for debts; this echoed a practice that was common among the Indians themselves. Modern commentators invariably cluck their tongues when they hear of such things, but they forget what we have already learned in an earlier chapter. Namely, that forced intertribal adoption—often as the result of kidnapping or raiding that resulted in the death of a child's father—was completely normative in Indian society.

Some Indians lived in communities that acknowledged the supremacy of English law; this included the Praying Indian villages, which will be discussed in a later chapter. Other groups maintained political alliances with the English that might last for generations. Justices of the peace in New England were appointed for the purpose of looking into Indian affairs, and these were empowered to appoint constables from among the Indians themselves. This system appears to have worked tolerably well, despite the tendency of Indian youths to raid or steal from farmsteads.

In early Virginia, we also see interracial associations everywhere we look. We already saw this in our glimpse of Pocahontas visiting the Jamestown fort as a child, which suggests that other Indian children were doing the same thing. Except during times of war, Indians and colonists traded, taught, relaxed, exchanged knowledge, and built friendships with one another. Men like John Smith sometimes spent months at a time living with the Indians, while bands of Indians might camp for several weeks in the vicinity of Jamestown. The same patterns are found in early Quebec and Massachusetts.

The historian David L. Preston has produced an illuminating book on frontier interactions of precisely this type along the Iroquois border, covering roughly the century between 1670 and 1770. Preston describes his project as follows:

My purpose in writing this book is to help readers understand the texture of human contact among ordinary European and Indian frontier settlers whose everyday lives were profoundly interwoven. The details of the tapestry can be gleaned from a host of meetings, scenes, places, and conversations described in eighteenth-century records: three French-Canadian sisters who lived among Catholic Iroquois for over two decades and operated a trading store in their village; Indians wandering the streets of colonial Montreal and drinking beer at Crespeau's tavern; German immigrants who approached Mohawks for permission to settle among them; Christian Mohawks who insisted that they would live out their lives as brothers with German Christians, who baptized and christened their children and were married in German churches; Indians who reveled with white settlers on Christmas Day; Scots-Irish squatters who lived peaceably with Indians and paid yearly rents to Indian landlords, in defiance of colonial landlords; Scots-Irish frontiersmen enjoying a friendly drink with Iroquois warriors at a backwoods Pennsylvania tavern; an Indian playing European tunes on his fiddle in a Mohawk Valley tavern; a Mohawk Indian with a European wife who lived among British frontier settlers in the Ohio Valley; a Palatine settler who refused to share a meal with an Iroquois in his home and pushed him away from the hearth; Palatine farmers in New York who made wampum belts, spoke Iroquoian languages, and negotiated with the French in Canada; a hatchet cleaving the skull of a Swiss settler, attacked at his frontier farm by English-speaking Delaware Indians with English names; a Scots settler murdered on an Ohio Valley farm while harvesting wheat with a man whose mother was a Delaware Indian, his father an Englishman.

What Preston's book drives home is the sheer variety of interactions between settlers and Indians. Far from the drab, one-sided victim narratives that get published today, the actual historical record presents a smorgasbord of human interactions of every conceivable type, ranging from true love and lifelong friendship to casual drinking and carousing, long- and short-term business partnerships, to animosity, violence, rape, and murder.

To impose a cynical and rigid calculus of racial absolutism, racial animosity, and oppression on these realities is to miss most of the richness and significance of early colonial life. Should historians once again choose to foreground the "lived experience" of interracial cooperation in colonial America, as Preston has, there is ample material waiting to be examined. For many centuries, across thousands of miles of territory, cooperation and coexistence between Indians and Europeans was a normal part of the fabric of life. The story of Pocahontas can and should be seen in this light.

CHAPTER 13

WAS AMERICA STOLEN?

It is high time for non-Native Americans to come to terms
with the fact that the U.S. is built on someone else's land.
Between 1776 and the present, the United States seized
some 1.5 billion acres from North America's native peoples,
an area 25 times the size of the United Kingdom. In the
Great Plains, the U.S. Army conducted a war of attrition,
with success measured in the quantity of tipis burned, food
supplies destroyed, and horse herds slaughtered. The result
was a series of massacres. "That a war of extermination
will continue to be waged between races, until the Indian
race becomes extinct, must be expected," [so said the first
governor of California to the state legislature] in 1851.

—Claudio Saunt, *Unworthy Republic* (2020)

O n the morning of September 19, 1737, three of the fastest
runners in Pennsylvania struck west from the Delaware River
along a prepared trail. Their goal was to reach as far west a
point as they could, because this would claim as much land as possible
for the colony of Pennsylvania from the Lenape Indians who previously
called the area home. The Lenape believed that the runners would likely
cover forty miles, but in the end, by sending some of the best sprinters

in the region, and by using preprepared trails, the runners were able to reach a point some seventy miles west of the Delaware, near the present-day Jim Thorpe, Pennsylvania.

This so-called Walking Purchase has long been recognized as one of the more egregious instances of fraud to be perpetrated on the North American Indians throughout the English colonial period. The question that stands before us in this chapter is: Was the Walking Purchase normative? Was this fraud typical of the way in which the English acquired Indian land?

As with many trends in history, this question does not lend itself to an easy answer. On the one hand, one can look at the map in 1500 and say "the Indians owned it," and look at the map in 1900 and say "the Europeans owned (most of) it," and conclude that the land was stolen. On the other hand, one can look more specifically, from generation to generation, and see exactly what was going on in this or that sphere of settler-Indian relations.

For example in Pennsylvania, the Walking Purchase was instigated by William Penn's sons Thomas and John. These two were eager to increase their landed holdings in the colony, and in order to do so, they reversed a decades-old policy maintained by their father, who had been decidedly pro-Indian. Before taking possession of Pennsylvania in 1682, William Penn sent a letter to the "Kings of the Indians of Pennsylvania," in which he promised to treat them fairly and to appoint officials who would act in a humane fashion. Penn's policy worked, and it inaugurated a fifty-year period of good settler-Indian relations known in Pennsylvania history as the "Long Peace." Penn writes:

> Now I would have you well to observe, that I am very Sensible of the unkindness and Injustice that hath been too much exersised [*sic*] towards you by the People of these Parts of the world…which I hear, hath been matter of Trouble to you, and caused great Grudgings and Animosities, Sometimes to the

Shedding of blood, which hath made the great God Angry. But I am not such a man, as is well known in my own Country: I have great love and regard towards you, and I desire to win and gain your Love & freindship [*sic*] by a kind, just and peaceable life; and the People I send are of the same mind, & Shall in all things behave themselves accordingly; and if in any thing any Shall offend you or your People, you shall have a full and speedy Satisfaction for the same by an equal number on both sides that by no means you may have just occasion of being offended against them.

True to his word, William Penn was assiduous in appointing land agents and other judges who would deal with the Indians fairly enough to avoid major offense, and in this, he must be accorded very successful indeed. It was only after the elder Penn's death, especially by the 1730s and '40s, that relations between the colonists and Indians began to turn sour. That being said, the first decades of the new towns of Bethlehem and Nazareth, founded circa 1740 in the middle of the Walking Purchase area, were marked by strong and cordial relations between the colonists and local Indians. Many of these converted to Christianity, learned trades, and settled down to live in the religious communes set up by the colonists. These Indians used tribal settlements to purchase farms and homes, while others were supported by the charity of the local religious foundations. Where, in this, do we find grounds for charges of fraud?

So, we can ask again: Was the Walking Purchase "typical"? Or was the Long Peace of 1682–1737 more typical? Was the defrauding of the Lenape "typical"? Or was the providence of food, shelter, education, and land to many individual Lenape more typical of colonial behavior? The simple answer is: it's complicated, but on balance, it is difficult to escape the conclusion that more colonists were kind to the Indians, more of the time, than they were cruel or treacherous to them.

But let us imagine for a moment that we agree with the fashionable and simplistic notion that America was "stolen." What precisely does this imply?

Is the United States fundamentally illegitimate as a result of the theft of Indian land, as Claudio Saunt argues in his 2020 book *Unworthy Republic*? Is it any less "worthy" than Russia, Iran, or China, which were built on the displacement and extermination of much larger minority groups than the Amerindians—some of which is still ongoing today? Is it less "legitimate" or "worthy" than an African country with a history of pre- and post-independence ethnic cleansing? What about Nigeria, whose slaving empire of Benin enabled the transatlantic slave trade by selling captured African rivals to Europeans and Muslims alike?

What about American institutions? Are they permanently tainted by this supposed theft of Indian land? Does American democracy mean nothing good? Can Americans take pride in the Constitution and the Bill of Rights, which have created one of the greatest, happiest, amalgamated people in history? Or are these ideas and institutions, as Saunt alleges, hollow promises designed to promote white supremacy over the American continent?

Then there is the question of racial guilt, which has become such a hot-button issue for the Left. Does every modern American owe a "blood debt" to Native American tribes? Does such a thing as an intergenerational debt exist? If such a debt is owed, was it settled when the Obama administration paid over $3.3 billion to settle longstanding treaty disputes with Native Americans between 2008 and 2016? If not, how could this debt be paid off? And who, precisely, is guilty? Are Latinos guilty? Black people? Recent immigrants? What about people whose ancestors tried to help the Indians or were massacred by Indians? What about the majority of Amerindians, who today are part European? Does Saunt include mixed-race Amerindians (who constitute the majority of Native Americans today) in his litany of people who must come to terms with the fact that they live on stolen ground? Who has a right to feel aggrieved? Only the Amerindians who live on reservations? What if that reservation is rich? What if the average Amerindian receives more money in handouts than the average American earns? Does this "blood debt" entitle Amerindians to be angry at the US government even as they receive historically high levels of aid in compensation for the sins of Americans past?

Lift the rhetorical veil, and the "stolen ground" myth raises so many logical absurdities that it becomes meaningless as a guide for modern-day policy. It is at base a new iteration of Chomskyism—the conviction that Western democracy is just as bad as any autocracy. For most on the Left, who don't bother to think through these questions, it seems that Native Americans are mere symbolic pawns who are useful to demonstrate that America and its capitalist system are bad.

As with many of the other anti-European myths we have addressed, the "stolen ground" myth began in earnest during the high point of academic Marxism in the 1970s. A key title is the Pennsylvania historian Francis Jennings's *The Invasion of America: Indians, Colonialism, and the Cant of Conquest*. This book was reissued in recent years and during the 2010s rose to new heights of popularity on Amazon. The 2010s saw a number of new titles push the "stolen ground" theme; one of these was *Violence over the Land: Indians and Empires in the Early American West* by Ned Blackhawk. Compared with later narratives, however, Blackhawk's book remains fairly cautious and scientific in its treatment of the southwest Indians in the years after 1750.

There followed a spate of much less temperate books pushing the stolen-ground genocide meme. In 2016 Benjamin Madley published a full-on indictment of US-Indian relations in California called *An American Genocide: The United States and the California Indian Catastrophe, 1846–1873*. A similar book by Jeffrey Ostler appeared in 2019 called *Surviving Genocide: Native Nations and the United States from the American Revolution to Bleeding Kansas*, while Claudio Saunt produced the aforementioned *Unworthy Republic: The Dispossession of Native Americans and the Road to Indian Territory* (2020). These books will be discussed in more detail over the next few chapters.

The "stolen ground" narrative has now become unassailable on university campuses. As American Historical Association President James Sweet found to his detriment in the summer of 2022, anyone who offers even a whiff of dissent to this and related narratives must expect to be ostracized from academic circles and faces a real threat of losing their job. Meanwhile, academic award committees fall over themselves to festoon books like Saunt's with accolades. *Unworthy Republic* was awarded the 2021 Bancroft Prize and the 2021 Ridenhour Book Prize, and was a finalist for the 2020 National Book Award; it was named one of the Top Ten Best Books of 2020 by the *Washington Post*, and a *New York Times* Critics' Top Book of 2020.

As the fawning treatment of Saunt's book shows, the (still majority white) American intellectual establishment is operating under the notion that the primary purpose of history writing is to atone for "racial guilt." This is done by producing and praising books which laud non-European peoples as much as possible, while simultaneously making Europeans look as bad as possible. It is sad, even pathetic, to think that so many intellectuals could fall into such a childish way of perceiving the world, where the only way to praise non-Europeans is to trash Europeans— as though history were a zero-sum game—but that's where we're at. It makes one wonder whether there is any value in getting a humanities PhD at all—if such a degree does not teach critical thinking, then what good is it? This "Indians are always good, Europeans are always evil" habit has become so ingrained, that the result is a sort of reality creep, where the academy gradually loses touch with historical facts, as they subsist year-in and year-out on a diet of books that continually stretch the truth in a single direction.[105] A side effect of this is that anyone who offers a balanced, truthful account of the past begins to look like an out-of-touch radical. In this environment of ideological uniformity, where is

---

[105] As of 2023, a major academic journal has finally dared to publish a critique of these grossly unscientific trends in post-colonial theory: Felsch, M. (2023). "The Scientific Shortcomings of Postcolonial Theory." *International Studies*. https://doi.org/10.1177/00208817221142485

there room to question? Where is there room for logical, fact-based, scientific critique? Has the entire historical profession abandoned objectivity on any matter where "race" is involved? If so, can they really continue to call themselves historians, or are they mere propagandists?

The narrative they push is so emotionally and politically charged that legitimate critics simply fall silent; they must self-censor. But the case against the "stolen ground" myth is obvious to any historian with a basic grasp of the facts, a sense of objectivity, and the willingness to tell the awards committees and the university administrations that the emperor has no clothes. This case will be presented in the following pages.

THE TIME FRAME OF COLONIZATION

The first inconvenient fact that confronts the "stolen ground" ideologues is that for most of the five hundred years since Columbus, over 90 percent of North America belonged to the Indians. In the early 1800s, fully three hundred years after Columbus discovered America, Europeans still inhabited only a fringe of the North American landmass. This has been amply attested by such beloved recent studies as Pekka Hämäläinen's *Indigenous Continent,* and it flies in the face of those who promote the erroneous idea that Europeans began stealing land with Columbus and Cortes, and continued in an uninterrupted orgy of theft until the Battle of Wounded Knee in 1890.

As attested by Hämäläinen, Kathleen DuVal, and other scholars, close to 90 percent of modern America changed hands from Indian to American ownership over a single fifty-year period between 1830 and 1880.[106] This may well be considered an act of rapacious dispossession, as we will discuss in more detail in later chapters. However, what this means in the *longue dureé* is that most generations of New World colonists were *not* responsible for dispossession of the Indians on a conti-

---

[106] DuVal, Kathleen. *The Native Ground: Indians and Colonists in the Heart of the Continent.* (University of Pennsylvania Press, 2011).

nent-wide scale by either action or intent—this was accomplished in the space of only two generations.

Anti-colonialist writers such as Noam Chomsky routinely claim that every generation of European Americans has stolen land from Native Americans in equal measure, as if this was a continuous and ongoing process of theft. Yet more than twenty generations have come and gone since the days of Christopher Columbus. Of those twenty generations, only two of them were responsible for the great majority of the "land grab" against Indians in the United States and Canada. The other eighteen generations occupied relatively little land that they had taken from Indigenous people or none at all. No generation since the 1890s has stolen land from the Native Americans in a significant way, and no single American generation before 1830 stole more than a tiny fraction of North America from the Native Americans. Even during the darkest chapters of the great land grab of the middle nineteenth century, there were many people who advocated for fair and just treatment of the Indians, including equitable land settlement.

It is therefore a basic fact of history that most European and American generations living in North America "stole" or occupied very little Indian land. This is backed up by the fact that a highly lauded strain of scholarship argues that most of North America remained Indigenous well into the nineteenth century. This highlights a question that every stolen land advocate must address: If Europeans were intent on displacing or exterminating the Natives over the entire course of European colonization, then how were the Indians still in possession of most of North America as late as 1830?

The answer depends on three factors. First is the historical goal of European colonization. Second is the technology factor, and third is a grudging respect for Indian land rights, which were simultaneously respected in some quarters even as they were violated in others.

The reason why most of the New World remained uncolonized for centuries after Columbus has to do with the model of colonization adopted by European powers in the New World. For the first two centuries at least, they were working from the same model they had employed in Asia and Africa. This model was based on trade rather than conquest, and its primary method was to create small trading forts in coastal areas, surrounded by a few external fields that could provide food for a handful of settlers. In Asia and Africa, Europeans realized that it would be futile to attempt any conquests inland—the people of those continents were too numerous and too formidable, even if less advanced technologically.

When French colonists first arrived in North America, they arrived with the plan to create a few trading stations along rivers at places such as Quebec and Montreal, whose primary role was to prevent rival European nations from claiming rights to the same territory. Their secondary purpose was to provide hubs for traders, who bartered with the Indians for furs in a small yet generally profitable trade.

The economy of fur trading required gathering furs from huge expanses of land. This meant that French traders ranged for thousands of miles inland, across the Great Lakes and down the Mississippi in search of fur supplies. The French founded a fort at New Orleans, near the mouth of the Mississippi, as a way of safeguarding their empire of fur. French traders first sought to assimilate themselves into existing Indian trade networks rather than replace them. As recounted by DuVal and others, the Indians long remained arbiters of European behavior in most of the North American interior. The Indians proved adept at transforming their economic life to supply furs to European agents. They accordingly forged new political alliances and claimed new territories based on the location of European trading stations. This change in economic orientation brought the Indians a wealth of European products that they quickly found they could not do without, including metal tools, textiles, firearms, and alcohol.

Following the French model, the first English colonists in New England also arrived with the idea that they would trade tools, guns, alcohol, and textiles for furs. It was only gradually, over the course of several generations, that the English shifted their focus toward farming and colonization. Most of this was simple opportunism, which occurred as

Indian populations dwindled through a combination of disease, warfare, assimilation, intertribal violence, and migration. While the New England model of small towns appears to have spread rapidly through some lowland regions, in fact it took several generations before the Indians had retreated from most of Massachusetts. While it may seem short in the grand sweep of history, sixty years is a lot of lived experience. The Indians' seminomadic lifestyle made it relatively easy for them sell their lands and retreat farther into New York State and the Green Mountains in the hope of avoiding contact with whites—as long as this could be negotiated with other Indian tribes along the way. Population densities in the region began low—highball estimates suggest that about ten thousand Indians were living in all of Vermont in 1500—so this meant that by 1680, there was space for Indians to migrate through the region after disease, migration, and assimilation had reduced their numbers.

We can now turn to our second factor that affected the pace of European colonization in North America: the technology factor. The Industrial Revolution marked a decisive turning point in the European ability to colonize the globe, but this did not happen until the mid-nineteenth century. Europeans clung to the coasts of Africa and Asia until very late. So it was in North America. In the Old World, the invention of modern weaponry such as howitzers and machine guns finally gave Europeans enough firepower to overwhelm traditional Muslim, African, and Asian armies. Before that time, European armies were kept in check by troops armed with primitive firearms and traditional weapons and sometimes suffered significant defeats.

Perhaps more importantly, the Industrial Revolution also brought a revolution in logistics. The invention of the steamship and the locomotive provided faster and more reliable transportation both at sea and on land. The invention of the telegraph provided instant communication across long distances. The dawn of modern medicine brought sanitation, vaccines, and medicines such as aspirin and quinine, which helped to make tropical areas more survivable. All these factors made American transcontinental expansion far more feasible than it had been only a few generations before.

Our third factor is the fact that Europeans did have grudging respect for Indian property rights, when these were properly spelled out. European court systems did not like to see property rights abnegated for no reason, and Indians quickly learned that deeds and treaties often gave them some form of redress against white land speculators. We have already seen how many European powers sought to limit the ability of Europeans to encroach on Indian land. The Spanish created separate "republics"—large tracts where Indians owned and managed land largely unmolested for the better part of three centuries. Farther north, both the French and the British for centuries treated Indian polities such as the Iroquois confederation as sovereign powers whose boundaries were to be respected. Dutch administrators made it a point of pride to respect Indian property claims in the Hudson Valley, and to gain land by voluntary sale rather than trickery. In this, they saw themselves as morally superior to their traditional enemies, the Spanish.[107] Respect for Indian political boundaries usually coincided with French and British policy goals, and so this tended to happen more often than not.

The famous Albany Congress of 1754 saw the British meet with delegates from the Iroquois nation. This eventually resulted in the British Proclamation Line of 1763, which forbade any European settlers from settling or even buying land west of the Appalachian Mountains. In creating and enforcing this line, the British government showed itself willing to defy the wishes of many American colonists in the interest of maintaining peace with the Indians. This was a decision that took a significant amount of political will, and it should be recognized as such. It renders ridiculous the theory of settler colonialism and the idea that Europeans were racially motivated to remove and exterminate all Indians.

The American government for the most part inherited this British sense of property rights and fair dealing. They therefore sought for sev-

---

[107] Meuwese, Mark. *Brothers in Arms, Partners in Trade: Dutch Indigenous Alliances in the Atlantic World. 1595-1674.* (Brill, 2011).

eral decades to create a barrier across which European settlers were not allowed to cross. Of course, there were many settlers who defied their governments and blazed into Indian territory despite these treaties, as we will discuss later on. This was basically inevitable in areas of political decentralization and sparse population. Nonetheless, the fact that both the British and American governments tried to enforce strict "no settlement" zones over a period of many decades deserves a prominent place in the mainstream narrative. Even Jeff Ostler, author of *Surviving Genocide*, admits that the US government did not begin to "prepare the ideological ground" for Indian removals until the decades of the 1810s.[108] And we will see that, in the 1830s, the US Supreme Court ruled against the removal of the southern Indians prior to the Trail of Tears on the grounds that the law granted the Indians permanent rights over their lands.

Taken together, these three factors of intent, technology, and respect for Indian land rights help to explain why Europeans and Americans did not "steal" most of North America from the Indians until as late as the 1830s. For the first three centuries of colonization at least—neither the will nor the logistical capability was there to make such a theft possible.

PURCHASED, NOT STOLEN

Another important fact that the stolen land theory overlooks is that the great majority of American land settled by Europeans before about 1810 was purchased from the Indians who willingly sold it via a bourgeoning land market. While some have argued that the Indians who sold land to Europeans were unaware of the long-term consequences of what they were doing, every historian who studies the facts of the matter concludes that such an interpretation is anachronistic and paints the Indians as far more naive than they in fact were.

The main way to acquire land in Europe since the later Middle Ages was to purchase it. Europeans developed the institution of the notary,

---

[108] Jeffrey Ostler, *Surviving Genocide* (New Haven, CT: Yale University Press, 2019), 183.

one of whose main jobs was to register land purchases at public offices in permanent form so that any disputed claims could be settled quickly. Europeans also developed different ways to finance the purchase of land, including mortgages. These institutions were centuries old when the English began settling North America, and to expect them to acquire land in any other way is to fundamentally misunderstand the British mentality during the first centuries of colonization.

At the very beginning of the settler-Indian encounter, a market had to be established. Since the Indians and English valued very different things, the prices originally paid can be exploited by modern-day commentators to look like fraud. But we need to remember the concept of relative value. A specific acre of land was relatively valueless to hunter-gatherer Indians, while agriculturalist colonists might value it highly.

This is the major principle behind the purchase of Manhattan and Staten Islands by the Dutch administrator Peter Minuit in the 1620s. People today call foul because the value of the trade goods given for the islands was relatively small, only a few thousand dollars in today's prices. However, the value of these trade goods to the Indians, who were encountering them for the first time, would have been close to inestimable. The Europeans offered them firearms; textiles; metal tools such as axe heads, hoes, and kettles; wampum, which the Indians already valued; and drills.

Modern critics get bent out of shape about this because they imagine that Manhattan Island is extremely valuable by nature. But like all things, Manhattan Island is only valuable if people find it desirable. The island only became valuable once people began to use it as the site of a prosperous city. To the Indians in question, the swampy, humid, bug-infested island would have formed merely a portion of their hunting grounds, and such land would have been worth merely a few dollars per acre. In the 1620s, there would have been no way to know whether the Europeans were there to stay or, like previous groups of Europeans who had been visiting North America for a century or more, they would prove nothing more than transient interlopers. So the deal very likely seemed a good one to them at the time. Meanwhile, within a few years, the Indians learned to drive a much harder bargain, as we have noted on multiple occasions. Subsequent transactions saw Europeans pay increasingly higher prices for an acre of Indian land.

In other words, the Indians quickly caught on to the idea of a land market. By the time of King Philip's War in the 1670s, we encounter Indians who were fully integrated into a money economy; they hoarded piles of silver coins, and they had long since learned that these could be used to purchase clothing, gunpowder, iron tools, and other useful items, even hundreds of miles from the nearest European settlement. Given this rapid monetization of the frontier, the Indians were also ready to part with scrub, waste, and disputed land in exchange for the money that would make their lives easier.

The majority of land that changed hands during the seventeenth and eighteenth centuries along the eastern seaboard was therefore not taken by some Walking Purchase–style fraud; instead, it was voluntarily sold by the Indians in just such a market. They did not for the most part feel as though they had been duped, or the market would not have worked as well as it did.

This process of marketization has been amply chronicled by any number of serious historians like Christopher Hannan, who has written about the land market in seventeenth-century Massachusetts:

> From the first decades of English settlement in the Plymouth and Massachusetts colonies to the end of the seventeenth century, norms of landholding were established and then maintained by both the English and the Indians.
>
> Starting at different conceptions of landholding and use in the 1630's, Indians and English had forged an important and lasting understanding about this most important asset by the 1670's. Over the course of the seventeenth century, Indians fought to put

forth their claims of natural and civil rights to retain their land, while the English gradually accepted a broader view of Indian land rights. Both got peace. King Philip's War, fought in 1675 and 1676, was an intense, short-lived conflict between Indians and English. It did little to alter the ways in which land was held and sold in Massachusetts or Plymouth. In fact, these colonies looked to restore the procedures by which Indians and English held and transferred land in the aftermath of war, rather than to change them. The war strengthened the Anglo-Indian community's faith in the system of stable landholding based on rule of law and due process.

While modern historians tend to emphasize the rare conflicts between Amerindians and settlers in the early years, far more Indians profited from selling land to Europeans than were victimized in such wars. Indigenous people such as John Wompas (died in 1679), whom we will meet below, made a career of speculating on the sale of Indian land to Europeans, and he was far from the only one to become wealthy and respected in European society as a result.

The historian of colonial American property formation Allan Greer has this to say about the process through which American land exchanged hands:

> We can hardly understand the colonial takeover of portions of the New World as a simple replacement: a European regime imposed in place of a native one. I prefer the term "property formation" as a means of more fully historicizing matters. Of course, this was a massively unequal encounter, one in which force and violence were rarely absent; almost invariably people of settler stock flourished at the expense of indigenous populations; yet the triumph

of settler tenures was not instantaneous, nor was it completely conclusive, nor was it the outcome of unilateral settler action.

Greer reminds us that while this exchange was often unequal, it was not unilateral. Though it was often done under duress, it was more often done on a voluntary basis.

We also need to remember the time scale of land exchange, which seems compressed in hindsight but might have seemed very long in the course of "lived experience." The process of land exchange before the 1800s took a very long time, and in any given generation, the boundaries between settler and Indigenous land might move little or not at all. Indians continued to have agency throughout this period, and the process was generally much less violent—and certainly less genocidal—than the sensationalists like to claim. The idea that the land market that created the thirteen original colonies in itself constitutes out-and-out theft is therefore purely ridiculous.

A final note on land markets is to remind us how they work. In every country with land markets, owners seldom remain in possession for more than a single generation. Longstanding family seats in places such as England represent a tiny proportion of the land. With the creation of land markets in New England, Virginia, Quebec, and the other colonies, the Indians became actors in an inherently fluid market. Once Indians became outnumbered by colonists, a process that occurred in much of lowland New England after a generation or two, then as soon as it became legal for Indians to sell land it was inevitable that they would eventually do so. The only way to prevent this in perpetuity is to create some type of overriding clause that says the land can never be alienated—something that today's activists increasingly want to do, though this brings with it a host of philosophical, legal, and social problems, as we will discuss.

Many Indians did settle down to farm, either by marrying farmers or by making a decision to shift lifestyles. For many individuals, this meant becoming regular paid laborers on farms, which went on until they or their children eventually assimilated into farming society.[109] We know from early examples such as John Wompas, and later examples such as Major Ridge (whom we will meet below), that Indians throughout the colonial and early American periods were purchasing and working land as Europeans would. Just like Pocahontas, many Indians did not necessarily cling to their traditional lifestyles but saw the advantages of farming over hunter-gathering and quickly adapted to European methods. Modern scholars lament this as "de-indigenization," but if this lifestyle was voluntarily chosen, then how is any such judgment not a form of gross hypocrisy?

The Mohican tribe is a well-documented example of this gradual assimilation. As Algonquin Indians, the Mohicans were not part of the Iroquois confederation.[110] Meanwhile, the Iroquois-confederated Mohawks outnumbered the Mohicans and saw them as rivals in the bourgeoning fur trade with eastern colonial settlements. During the seventeenth century, the Mohawks waged a number of genocidal wars against the Mohicans, eventually driving their remnants into the arms of the European colonists. Many of the remaining Mohicans—who by this point only numbered a few hundred—settled down in the area of Stockbridge, Massachusetts, where they became known as the Stockbridge Indians. Their chiefs held regular discourse with colonial authorities, and one of them even participated in a state visit to Queen Anne of England in 1710. Later in the century the Stockbridge Indians accepted missionaries and gradually converted to Christianity. During the American Revolutionary War, the Stockbridge Indians formed a militia party who sided with the Patriots against their traditional ene-

---

[109] For a pessimistic spin on the surprising prevalence of Indians working as paid laborers east of the Appalachians, see Ostler, 131. See also Stephen W. Silliman and Thomas A. Witt, "The Complexities of Consumption: Eastern Pequot Cultural Economics in Eighteenth-Century New England," *Historical Archaeology* 44, no. 4 (2010), 46–68, https://www.jstor.org/stable/25762268.

[110] In his novels, James Fenimore Cooper amalgamated the Mohicans and the Mohegans, who were separate Algonquin-speaking tribes located in two separate areas.

mies the Iroquois, who had sided with the British. By this point, the Mohican warriors were dressing and arming themselves in a manner scarcely distinguishable from American frontiersmen. During one battle in 1778, the Stockbridge brigade lost some forty warriors, which was about half of their number. Other small groups of Mohicans befriended the Moravians of Bethlehem, Pennsylvania, and went to live with them on various settlements. Over the next several decades, continued contact with European society saw the remainder of the Mohicans either assimilate without a trace into mainstream society, while a few moved westward and settled on reservations. James Fenimore Cooper's famous *Last of the Mohicans* was therefore more of a legend, while the reality was defeat in war at the hands of a rival tribe, followed by centuries of gradual assimilation.

This tale of assimilation of American Indians into the new farming culture was normative and generally advantageous to the Indians who adopted the new lifestyle, even if modern purists such as Patrick Wolfe wish that they had stayed in the Stone Age. Gradual acculturation was a continuous process, which moved as the frontier moved. We see similar changes much later, when, beginning in the nineteenth century, many Plains Indians decided to embrace cattle ranching as an economic strategy.[111]

The descendants of Indians who purchased property in earlier centuries continue to own American land down to the present day. The majority of Indians in America today are mixed-race, and almost every part-Indian in America now owns or rents land just like every other American.

Therefore the idea that the Indians have been "defrauded" is a historical anachronism based on the modern idealization of primitive lifestyles, a cherry-picked sample of the minority of Indians who chose to move onto reservations, and a fundamental inability to understand how markets work.

---

[111] Peter Iverson, *When Indians Became Cowboys: Native Peoples and Cattle Ranching in the American West* (Norman: University of Oklahoma Press, 1994). This mostly focuses on the twentieth century.

THE PROBLEM OF POPULATION

We have already seen how many Indian tribes gradually lost their cultural distinctness via a combination of warfare and assimilation into the numerically superior society. This touches upon our final elephant in the room, which is the precipitous dwindling of the North American Indian population during the period between 1600 and 1800. This left the land between the Appalachians and the Mississippi practically vacant by the time Jefferson made the Louisiana Purchase in 1803. By 1810, the entire Iroquois nation probably amounted to some ten thousand individuals. These inhabited an area encompassing more than eight modern US states along the southern Great Lakes, with large swaths of modern-day Ontario in Canada thrown in.

Besides the Iroquois, the only other significant Indian populations on the borders of the United States in 1783 were the so-called Five Civilized Nations of the Cherokee, Choctaw, Chickasaw, Creek, and Seminole Indians. They were called "civilized" because as heirs to the Mississippian customs, they tended to be more sedentary, to rely more heavily on farming, and therefore to build more permanent villages. It was believed by Americans of the day that these tribes would more readily take to farming and other types of "civilization." Indeed, they were making steps toward this when the Jackson administration decided to uproot them and drive them all to Oklahoma, precipitating the infamous Trail of Tears (discussed in a later chapter).

Still, these tribes only amounted to some seventy thousand individuals, spread over what are today several US states including Georgia, Mississippi, Alabama, and Florida. Apart from the Iroquois, these made up the bulk of Amerindians living east of the Mississippi in the early nineteenth century, bringing the grand total to less than one hundred thousand individuals even before their forced expulsion. This number is widely attested and is not in serious dispute.

Meanwhile, by 1800 the population of the United States was over five million and growing at a rapid pace. This happened not primarily through immigration but by natural increase. (After a few colonial waves that were small by later standards, large-scale immigration to the United States began again in the 1820s and hit a peak with a wave of Irish migration in the 1840s. It picked up again on a larger scale in the 1870s and 1880s, reaching another peak in 1900–1910.)

During the first decades of the nineteenth century, the main reason that US population increased was due to an abundance of food. The agriculture practiced by the colonists was very efficient and produced many calories per acre. By 1810 the US census registered over seven million people, and by 1820, the population was nearly ten million. While the Indian population east of the Mississippi actually began to grow somewhat during this time—in part because of the robust Indian-protection policies of the US government—the Indians nonetheless remained hopelessly outnumbered by a factor of one hundred to one.

This ratio, incidentally, is similar to the Indian population ratio of the United States today. Today it is estimated that perhaps one million Indians live on reservations in the US (including Alaska); meanwhile, perhaps four to five claim to be "American Indian" on their US census forms. For those who wish to claim a nineteenth-century "genocide," the fact that the US Indian population has remained steady proportional to the overall US population since 1810, despite massive immigration from Europe in the later nineteenth and early twentieth centuries, is a simple and clear refutation.

Sensationalists claim that the Indian population of the United States was small due to European aggression in the early settlement period. However, it is true that no European army had ever been through most of the regions inhabited by Amerindians in the pre-1820 period. Many areas had been visited by trappers and traders, to be sure, but for the most part these men visited the tribes as guests who were welcomed because the Indians benefited from hosting them.

The frequency of intermarriage can only be guessed at, but the fact that most people who claim American Indian status today are mixed-race, suggests that this has been going on for a long time, just as it has in Mexico. The propensity to intermarriage is why so many "Indians" such as Major Ridge and John Ross were actually mixed-race by the time we encounter them in early nineteenth-century accounts. Many historians hold that mixed-race marriages were normative beyond the frontier, where European men were often alone on their farmsteads and single or widowed women felt unsafe. Hundreds of drawings and portraits of mixed-race couples can be found in American archives of the early west. Intermarriage was encouraged by the nearly universal Indian practice of adopting people from other tribes to make up for their own lack of numbers. This incidentally suggests that for them the important issue was the survival of a tribal way of life, rather than any concept of racial purity.

Specialists know that massacres and other deliberate acts of violence accounted for less than 1 percent of Indian population decline. With a mere ten thousand to twenty thousand Indians falling in European-instigated massacres over four centuries of English and American colonization, out of an overall population of millions, it is difficult to blame massacre and murder for the fact that Indian populations did not recover.

The real reason the Amerindian population east of the Mississippi was already so small by 1800 is not due to the theft of Indian land, or genocidal policies, but to a combination of more mundane factors. First was the inefficiency of hunting and gathering. Second was Amerindian susceptibility to disease. Third was Amerindian aggression by the likes of the Iroquois, which reshaped Amerindian society from within, and made population replacement difficult. Fourth was gradual assimilation into farming society.

WAS INDIAN LAND STOLEN?

When all this evidence is added up, we get a portrait of colonial-Indian land exchange that is much more nuanced than the "genocide and theft" narrative would have us believe. The ideas that Europeans were ready to steal Indian land from the start, that they were unrelenting in their assault on Indian land rights, that they were racist, that they always wished to displace the Indians, that most of their transactions were driven by fraud, that land was usually taken by force, that European and American governments turned a blind eye to the plight of Indian landholders, that Indian populations fell because of massacre and violence, and that Indian populations were at all comparable with European populations by the early nineteenth century—all these simplistic notions have been debunked in this chapter.

The "stolen land" chorus cherrypicks two generations out of twenty-odd which saw the flipping of most of North America from Indigenous to settler control. They write as though these two generations are representative of the other twenty. These historians crow about how most of North America remained under Indigenous control until the nineteenth century, and in the same breath lambast every generation of European settlers as thieves, even if they lived at a time when the borders were relatively static. They ignore the fact that by this time the population ratio of Europeans to Indigenous had fallen—through no one's fault—to a ratio of roughly 100:1. They forget that market forces would have redistributed land until Natives held far less than they originally had, and they forget that most Natives at the time wanted it this way (or else they would not have traded with Europeans, which they did). They cheer the agency of Indigenous people throughout the encounter period, but ignore Indian agency whenever Indians voluntarily traded land for other goods they wanted. They seem to think that all Indigenous areas should have been defended against market forces, in perpetuity, and they therefore fall into the thorny trap of whether Natives should have been allowed to sell their land (historically, inability to commodify land is a recipe for abiding poverty). They ignore the fact that in most eras, most land changed hands via land markets, rather than through fraud. They ignore the reality that hunter-gatherer tribes claimed the majority of the modern American land area, but that such landholding patterns have become unsustainable everywhere in the world once agriculture has been introduced. They also ignore all government and citizen action—

much of it effective—which attempted to defend the Indians against rapaciousness.

This is not to say that Europeans were guiltless—far from it. I agree completely with Allan Greer that the odds were generally tilted against the Indigenous people of the Americas and that Europeans by dint of their superior numbers, technology, and organization tended to hold more of the cards. Many people cheated when they thought they could get away with it—as is unfortunately the case with people throughout the world today.

All the same, this chapter has revealed a much more complex picture than fashionable historians would like us to take away. The overriding conclusion is that despite all appearances, land in the colonial and early American periods was "not stolen" in the sense that most Left-wing historians and pro-Indigenous activists would have us believe.

CHAPTER 14

WERE THE FOUNDING FATHERS ANTI-INDIAN?

*"George Washington Owned Slaves and
Ordered Indians to Be Killed."*

—*Washington Post*, August 25, 2019

*Washington knew that he must build his nation on
Indian land, and by war and diplomacy, he helped set
the United States on a path of westward expansion that
transformed tribal homelands into American territories and
then into states. The primary goal of Washington's Indian
policy was to acquire Indian lands. In that, he succeeded.
His second goal—and it was a distant second—was to
establish just policies for dealings with Indian peoples.*

—Colin Calloway, "George Washington's
'Tortuous' Relationship with Native Americans"

One of the main things that glues a democracy together are the stories its citizens share. These animate the institutions and social norms that keep a democracy democratic.

For over two hundred years, Americans realized the value of their democracy, and this helped to ensure that the Founding Fathers were portrayed fairly. Yet in a few short years, the media establishment of the United States turned overwhelmingly against the Founding Fathers. We've seen how as late as 2016, Bernie Sanders could gush about the "grandeur" of Mount Rushmore. By 2020, major news outlets such as CNN were slandering Jefferson, Washington, Lincoln, and Roosevelt as slave owners, murderers, thieves, and criminals. What used to be a fringe opinion of the Far Left has suddenly become mainstream.

The same holds true of the American historical establishment. Historians who used to be marginalized as radicals are enjoying a degree of attention they have not known since the 1970s. A typical opinion was expressed by the historian Jeff Ostler in his book *Surviving Genocide*, when he said it is a "particular genius" of the American people "to inflict catastrophic destruction all the while claiming to be benevolent." This is Chomskian moral relativism and ideological projection at their worst.

One thing has long been clear to historians who study the Founding Fathers with a modicum of objectivity: they were exceptional men to whom every person alive owes a deep debt of gratitude. Of course they had their faults, sometimes glaring ones. Historians have written many books analyzing these faults and shortcomings. Few serious historians in recent decades have sought to whitewash or conceal these imperfections. Yet, as a rule, historians before circa 2016 concluded that the American founders were for the most part principled, moral, upright, well-intentioned, wise, humane, and effective at advancing the cause of democracy. So much so that the American pantheon compares favorably with any comparable political elite in history.

How then did our culture become so blind to their obvious virtues? According to the *Washington Post*, which has run numerous articles and opinion pieces on "Native American genocide" in recent years, the only thing we need to know about George Washington's relationship with Native Americans is that at some point, he ordered a number of them to be executed. Likewise, according to CNN, the only thing worth knowing about Lincoln is that he ordered the execution of thirty-eight men of the Dakota tribe—which they sensationalize as the "the largest mass execution in American history."

Far Left academics have lately had a field day as the zeitgeist propelled their pet theories to audiences they never hoped to influence. In *The Indian World of George Washington*, historian Colin Calloway admits that Washington tried to enact some humane policies to promote Indian welfare, but he insists that Washington's overriding goal was to steal as much land as possible from the Native Americans.

Yet Calloway's sweeping statement glosses over a fundamental truth, namely that Washington's attitude changed over time. It's true that Washington began his career in the Shenandoah Valley as a surveyor and land speculator and fought Indians as a British officer in the Seven Years War. He had an eye for continued westward expansion and as such might well be thought to have an interest in the displacement of Indigenous peoples. But as his experience with leadership grew, he became increasingly protective of Indian welfare, and as president he put a great deal of energy into protecting Indian land from white encroachment. His major preoccupation in that regard was to create a permanent boundary between Indian Territory and the United States, which white settlers were not allowed to cross.

Because founder-bashing is in vogue, many nonhistorians have gotten in on the act. A veritable avalanche of dubious academic studies is being rushed to press by people with next to no qualifications. In late 2021, the political scientist Michael A. Genovese published a helpful guide to *US Presidents and the Destruction of the Native American Nations*; his coeditor is an assistant professor of English literature at Diné College in Arizona, which is located on Navajo land. The book's introduction mocks the idea that the United States is a reasonable and good country, using the "stolen ground" myth as the basis of their attacks.

Activists have also been emboldened to post increasingly one-sided and thinly researched opinion pieces online that paint the Founding Fathers as nothing more than racists and murderers. One such writer is Mark Anthony Rolo, who wrote an anti-founder diatribe for the *Montana Great Falls Tribune* based on a single phrase in the Declaration of Independence. As it lists the many sins of King George III, the Declaration mentions that the British king has incited the "merciless Savages" to slaughter men, women, and children along the frontier. Out of this two-word phrase Rolo spins an indictment of the entire American enterprise. He paints the Declaration as a "call to war against the Indigenous people of America," which it certainly was not. Jefferson's language was aimed at creating maximum sympathy for the colonists' cause in both England and America. The British were actively encouraging Indian violence against the colonists, resulting in the massacre of women and children and the torture of captives.

Nor does Rolo seem to recognize that in the eighteenth century the word "savage" had a different connotation than it does today. In French, *sauvage* does not mean brutal and ignorant but simply "people who live out of doors, and close to nature." This is the sense in which the popular epithet "Noble Savages" was used. The idea derived from the influential writings of Rousseau, who argued that civilization had corrupted man's natural innocence, which could still be observed in the unspoiled peoples of the New World.

Let us try to counter some of this modern hysteria by examining the founders' actual words and actions regarding the Indians.

THE WISDOM OF BEN FRANKLIN

Ben Franklin has gone down in history as a prolific scientist, inventor, author, publisher, entrepreneur, and statesman. One of the foremost intellectuals of his generation, he traveled widely in Europe, where he was celebrated by royalty and other leading lights. He was one of the most cosmopolitan and broadminded members of the founding elite.

Franklin also left us with some telling remarks on the American Indians, which display his characteristic humanity and common sense. We have already been introduced to Franklin's letter to James Parker, written in 1751, in which he expresses his admiration for the Iroquois confederation. In the same letter, he also endorses a proposal to send a number of blacksmiths to live among the Indians. He hoped that this would set an example, which would encourage Indian men to take up blacksmithing themselves. Practical man and deist that he was, Franklin felt that providing the Indians with tools for economic independence was much more important than sending missionaries.

Franklin's philosophy was thus a variant on the modern-day aid worker's mantra: give a person food, feed them for a day; teach a person to farm, feed them for a lifetime. Franklin points out that the Indians were by this point completely dependent on the whites for the upkeep of their guns and that as soon as their gun broke, they might have to travel hundreds of miles in order to find a smith who could repair it. Franklin believed that if the English could encourage Indians to learn smithing—perhaps by having their children grow up around blacksmiths—this would lead them to become self-sufficient as a society and less vulnerable to white encroachment. In this, one sees nothing except respect for the Indian way of life, a desire to strengthen and protect it, and an expectation that it would continue in a similar fashion for decades if not centuries to come. (One also gains yet another hint that Indian traditions of warfare led Indian men to eschew work such as smithing and farming—which ultimately contributed to the impoverishment and downfall of their civilization.)

But it is in another passage, written toward the end of his life in the 1780s, that Franklin's thoughts on the Native Americans come out in more detail. In this passage, written while Franklin was serving as US Ambassador to France, just after the successful conclusion of the Revolution, he compares Indians favorably with Europeans. Though he is guilty of promoting the "Noble Savage" stereotype, which was idealized and unhistorical, this was partly done to make North America—and the fledgling United States—look good to our French allies. Isn't that better than calling them godless heathens?

For the modern Left, of course, nothing a European does is good—it will always be read in the most negative possible light. So it is best to look at Franklin's words themselves:

> The Indian Men, when young, are Hunters and Warriors; when old, Counsellors; for all their Government is by the Counsel or Advice of the Sages; there is no Force, there are no Prisons, no Officers to compel Obedience, or inflict Punishment. Hence they generally study Oratory; the best Speaker having the most Influence. The Indian Women till the Ground, dress the Food, nurse and bring up the Children, & preserve & hand down to Posterity the Memory of Public Transactions. These Employments of Men and Women are accounted natural and honorable. Having few Artificial Wants, they have abundance of Leisure for Improvement by Conversation. Our laborious manner of Life compared with theirs, they esteem slavish and base; and the Learning on which we value ourselves; they regard as frivolous and useless.

Franklin praises the Indians and their society on a number of points, including their simplicity and lack of bureaucracy. He admires their apparent lack of need for a system of criminal justice, arguing that Indians know what to do without being compelled, and that both men and women believe their distinct roles to be honorable. He also praises them for their eloquent speech—high praise indeed during the eighteenth century, when European society valued rhetoric above all else. Franklin appreciates that Indians do not show greed or acquisitiveness and that they enjoy leisure to converse and "improve their minds"—something eighteenth-century gentlemen also held in high esteem. Furthermore, he pointed out that from the Indian's point of view, the European lifestyle seemed tedious and wearying. In other words, Franklin was clearly capable of a high degree of cultural empathy.

Franklin goes on to praise Indian culture for its politeness, its order, its respect for the old, and the fact that Indians were more than capable of recognizing when Europeans were cheating them. Franklin also disparages Europeans who deal fraudulently with the Indians or treat them with rudeness and incivility.

Esteemed as one of the greatest American minds of the late colonial period, Franklin's remarks did much to set the tone for how Native Americans would be viewed both in Europe and America. Anyone looking for evidence of prejudice, racism, meanness, cultural chauvinism, greed for Indian land, or a desire to replace their culture and religion with those of Europe will be sorely disappointed.

Since he was too old to hold political office in the new United States, Franklin did not get a chance to put his thoughts about the Indians into action. We therefore turn to some other founders who did.

WASHINGTON AND THE BEGINNINGS OF US INDIAN POLICY

A recent book by Richard Harless called *George Washington and Native Americans* lays out how Washington's views on the Indian question evolved over the course of the later eighteenth century. At first he was more desirous to acquire Indian lands, but later he became increasingly protective of Indian welfare. His greatest fault, according to Harless, is that like John Eliot and many others before him he believed the only practical solution for the increasingly outnumbered Indians was that they eventually learn how to farm.[112] This he advised both for their own

---

[112] Considering that the Indians had already adopted innumerable "white" ways of living by this point, including the use of firearms, metal tools, textiles, money, and various modes of thought and education, to take a stand on the issue of farming, as many modern critics do, seems a bit naive.

protection and material improvement and so that they would stop being a security threat to American citizens.

Registering Indian land with an actual notary was considered one way to establish irrefutable legal tenure. Even though this was sometimes violated (as it would be by the Jackson administration), the logic behind land ownership and the protection of Indian land rights was generally sound. And while modern activists might find fault with this policy—in reality, was there any other solution on the table? What would these activists propose instead?

The first problem facing President Washington was securing his own vulnerable borders. This was a major problem for the new nation, whose strategic situation was dire. Washington knew better than any man alive that the US Army and treasury were exhausted in the later 1780s. The US had barely squeaked a victory over Great Britain, and only with massive subsidies from France.

Meanwhile, Great Britain owned Canada, where thousands of Indians still lived. The Spanish after 1762 owned all the land west of the Mississippi River, including New Orleans, and many French agents still acted in the Mississippi basin. France would reacquire all of Louisiana again in 1800. As Washington well knew, many Indians preferred the French, partly because they were better providers of guns and other European goods than the British proved to be. The Indians had already proven themselves devastating as allies of the French during the French and Indian War of 1754–63.

In this, as in many other things, Washington's instincts proved correct. Twenty-five years after he assumed the presidency, the British would invade the US and burn Washington, DC, during the War of 1812. As Washington feared, the British stirred the Indians living on the Canadian border to begin the attack. The threat to US security from Great Britain and its potential Indian allies was very real.

This is why Washington—and Jefferson after him—was keen to secure key tracts of land as buffers to protect American settlers from Indian massacres. Washington's concerns were not for the frontier settlers alone, however; the mere threat of stirring up Indian anger on the frontier was an effective foreign policy tool for any European power who wished to threaten the United States. To this end, Washington's chief Indian policy was to create a new version of the Proclamation Line of 1763. Washington at the time had no way of knowing that the US would soon purchase Louisiana. Even Jefferson's agents in Paris were shocked when Napoleon offered the whole territory to them early in 1803.

In 1790, the US border with the Indians extended over fifteen hundred miles of complete wilderness. We have seen that that the US population was already four million, while the Indian population east of the Mississippi was now less than one hundred thousand.[113] In these circumstances, was there any power on Earth that could restrain the hordes of settlers and speculators who were streaming into Indian lands? Farming is a land-intensive business, and a self-sustaining farmer might manage between fifty and two hundred acres. More than that was physically impossible. Those four, eight, and twelve million Americans were spreading farms across the North American continent almost as fast as a prairie fire.

Washington was a realist. He was a surveyor and an Indian fighter, and as a young man he had practically grown up on the frontier. And as president, he was a humanitarian—a humane person who wanted to see as little bloodshed, indignity, and starvation as possible. He cared deeply about the soldiers and the women and children who would lose their lives if the Indians were treated badly.

In 1783, Washington was still hopeful that a strong line could be established to protect both settlers and Indians. As soon as the Revolutionary War was over, Washington wrote to James Duane, arguing for the establishment of a firm line of settlement between the US and the Indians. He also noted that the US was going to be magnanimous in peace—even though by right of war, they could have expelled all Indians

---

[113] In 1600, this population had probably been about four hundred thousand. Most of this reduction was due to disease.

across the border to Canada, since many tribes had allied with the British during the war. Washington wrote:

> As (the Indians) [despite] all the advice and admonition which could be given them…during the prosecution of the (Revolutionary) War could not be restrained from acts of hostility, but were determined to join their arms to those of Great Britain and to share their fortune; so, consequently, with a less generous people than Americans they would be made to share the same fate; and be compelled to retire along with them beyond the Great Lakes.

> But as we prefer peace to a state of warfare, as we consider them as a [misled] People; as we perswade [*sic*] ourselves that they are convinced, from experience, of their error in taking up the hatchet against us, and that their true interest and safety must now depend upon our friendship. As the country is large enough to contain us all; and as we are disposed to be kind to them and to partake of their trade, we will from these considerations and from motives of compassion, draw a veil over what is past and establish a boundary line between them and us beyond which we will endeavor to restrain our people from hunting or settling, and within which they shall not come, but for the purposes of trading, treating, or other business unexceptionable in its nature.

> And if they should make a point of it, or appear dissatisfied at the line we may find it necessary to

establish, compensation should be made them for their claims within it.

As to how to administer Indian Affairs, Washington advised that American officials must be held to the strictest standards of discipline and morality:

> How far agents for Indian Affairs are indispensably necessary I shall not take upon me to decide; but if any should be appointed, their powers in my opinion should be circumscribed, accurately defined, and themselves rigidly punished for every infraction of them. Nor should the agents be permitted directly or indirectly to trade; but to have a fixed, and ample salary allowed them as a full compensation for their trouble.[114]

Washington therefore strove throughout his presidency to encourage the Indians to live in ways that would help them better resist the settler onslaught. He realized that the major problem was—just as it had been in Massachusetts some 150 years earlier—that the Indians' unsettled lifestyles encouraged young warriors to conduct raiding expeditions on settler farms, which in turn provoked settler retaliation. Due to the superior technology, organization and numbers of the settlers, this kind of provocation almost always turned out badly for the Indians.

Like Franklin and his blacksmiths, Washington therefore encouraged the purchase of farm equipment and spinning wheels for the Indians, and fostered policies that would teach them to live settled, agricultural lives. As the historian Mary Thompson put it: "Washington felt that as the cultures got closer together and got more alike, it would make them easier to live together." Who today could reasonably fault him for this combination of wisdom, humanity, and realism?

---

[114] George Washington, letter to James Douane, September 7, 1783, https://founders.archives.gov/documents/Washington/99-01-02-11798.

JEFFERSON THE PRAGMATIST

While many acknowledge that Washington was well-disposed toward the Indians, especially as president, others see in Jefferson a shrewd, calculating man who said nice things in public but was anti-Indian in private. In a now-famous confidential letter to the first governor of the Indiana Territory, the future president William Henry Harrison, Jefferson reveals his Indian policy:

> This letter being unofficial, and private, I may with safety give you a more extensive view of our policy respecting the Indians.
>
> Our system is to live in perpetual peace with the Indians, to cultivate an affectionate attachment from them, by every thing just and liberal which we can do for them within the bounds of reason, and by giving them effectual protection against wrongs from our own people.
>
> The decrease of game rendering their subsistence by hunting insufficient, we wish to draw them to agriculture, to spinning & weaving. The latter branches they take up with great readiness, because they fall to the women, who gain by quitting the labours of the field for those which are exercised within doors. When they withdraw themselves to the culture of a small piece of land, they will perceive how useless to them are their extensive forests, and will be willing to pare them off from time to time in exchange for necessaries for their farms and families. To promote this disposition to exchange lands—which they have to spare and we want—for necessities, which we have to spare and

they want—we shall push our trading houses, and be glad to see the good and influential individuals among them run in debt, because we observe that when these debts get beyond what the individuals can pay, they become willing to lop th[em off] by a cession of lands.

In this way our settlements will gradually circumscribe and approach the Indians, and they will in time either incorporate with us as citizens of the U.S., or remove beyond the Mississippi. The former is certainly the termination of their history most happy for themselves. But in the whole course of this, it is essential to cultivate their love.

This letter lays out Jefferson's Indian policy warts and all. Jefferson clearly wanted the US to take over Indian land. But he wanted this to be done legally, by purchase, with goodwill, and over time. He foresaw that ultimately, only a few "wild" Indians were going to remain inside the borders of the United States. Like Washington, he preferred not to have them there for obvious security reasons.

Like Franklin and Washington, Jefferson knew that the Indians were long since dependent on the Americans for many of their "necessities." He was also correct in judging that they were going to have to settle down sooner or later, not only because of their own desire to use European-manufactured items but simply because game was disappearing—largely through their own use of firearms. Jefferson was also at pains to ensure that US government agents, rather than private speculators, supplied the Indians and bought their excess land, because as Jefferson said, this could be done by the US government without profiteering. This would provide the maximum price to the Indians for their land, while charging them the minimum price for the necessities they needed.

Jefferson repeatedly attempted to ensure that Indians would be left with more than enough land to make them prosperous as farmers.

He only intended to purchase for the United States the land that the Indians, in their unavoidable transition to a farming people, could have no hope of making use of. On numerous occasions Jefferson revealed his intention to set up every friendly and cooperative Indian household with enough land to make them financially independent—indeed, much wealthier than the majority of European Americans of his time. His goal, in other words, was to leave Indian families at least as wealthy as the average American family, if not more so. As president, Jefferson wrote to the Cherokee Deputies in 1809, urging them to "make a law for giving to every head of a family a separate parcel of land, which, when he has built upon and improved, it shall belong to him and his descendants forever, and which the nation itself shall have no right to sell from under his feet."

Nor should we have any doubt that Jefferson was sincere in his affection for the American Indians. He wanted their gradual "civilization" and introduction to the global culture to proceed as humanely as possible.[115] Jefferson elaborates on this in a letter written to John Adams during Tecumseh's Rebellion, in which he argues that the US should conquer Canada in order to remove the British agents who it was widely believed were responsible for "inciting" the Indians to make war on the United States:

> So much in answer to your enquiries concerning Indians, a people with whom, in the very early part of my life, I was very familiar, and acquired impressions of attachment and commiseration for them which have never been obliterated.
>
> Before the revolution they were in the habit of coming often, and in great numbers to the seat of our government, where I was very much with

---

[115] In the eyes of Dave Graeber, Jefferson was wrong to believe that most humans prefer the opportunities and comforts of modernity to the illiteracy and continuous danger of subsistence living.

them. I knew much the great Outassete, the warrior and orator of the Cherokees. He was always the guest of my father, on his journeys to and from Williamsburg. I was in his camp when he made his great farewell oration to his people, the evening before his departure for England.

That nation, consisting now of about 2000 warriors, and the Creeks of about 3000, are far advanced in civilisation [*sic*]. They have good Cabins, enclosed fields, large herds of cattle and hogs, spin and weave their own clothes of cotton, have smiths and other of the most necessary tradesmen, write and read, are on the increase in numbers, and a branch of the Cherokees is now instituting a regular representative government.

This passage sheds more light on the conditions between the US and the Indians in the early decades of the nineteenth century. The first thing to notice is that like Franklin, Jefferson is sincere in his appreciation for Indian oratory, culture, and the general gravity and pride of the Indian peoples.

Even more importantly, Jefferson and many other Americans believed that the Indians were making "great strides towards civilization." To their minds, their civilizing policy of, for example, introducing Indian women to spinning wheels was working. Jefferson observed how the Indians were learning to read and write, and they were practicing democracy among themselves. These points were calculated to produce maximum sympathy for the Americans in Adams and any other readers of his letter.

In this letter, Jefferson endorses the idea that the southern Indians, who lived in the region of Georgia, Alabama, and Mississippi should be allowed to keep their lands within the United States and should not be removed. Many in the American elite agreed with Jefferson's assessment that the southern Indians should be left in their places. Alas, Jefferson's line of thought would not be sustained, and the election of Andrew Jackson in 1829 turned American policy in favor of Indian removal.

THE HUMANITY AND BRAVERY OF LINCOLN

In recent years, activists and journalists have seized upon a specific incident from the presidency of Abraham Lincoln to tar him with the brush of anti-Indian bigotry. This is the case of the so-called "Dakota 38." Long an obscure footnote in Lincoln's presidency, it has become famous enough among Twitter activists that "Dakota 38" was spray-painted on the base of a toppled Lincoln statue during the George Floyd riots of 2020.

The background to the story is the Dakota War of 1862. At that time, the Civil War was going badly for the North and the government fell behind in making its prearranged welfare payments to the Dakota and other Indians in the west. At the same time, US government agents took advantage of the chaos to make massive profits for themselves at the expense of various Indian tribes. A US commission of early 1862 found that the previous governor had enriched himself to the tune of roughly $100,000 in only four years, on a salary of $2,000. Clearly, much injustice had been done; at the same time, the desperate political situation was a primary reason why things had gotten so far out of hand so quickly.

Faced with starvation, a faction of the Dakota opted for war and began massacring settlers. Some thirty thousand settlers fled the violence, which claimed the lives of over one hundred soldiers and militiamen and over three hundred and fifty noncombatants. Hundreds of women and children were also taken into slavery; many women were raped or forced into nonconsensual sexual relations with their captors. (Modern activists seem to think that mass rape is okay, as long as the victims were "settlers" who deserved it. One thinks of Ward Churchill's "little Eichmanns" sentiment and wonders in what direction the moral compass of such people actually points.)

In the aftermath, nearly four hundred Dakota warriors were sentenced by hastily conducted military tribunals. After a review, President Lincoln pardoned 90 percent of them, leaving only thirty-eight to actually be hanged. As Lincoln himself stated, he wished to pardon all men except those unequivocally guilty of rape or who took part in massacres of unarmed civilians. He determined to spare all those whose only proven offense was taking part in pitched battles; he argued that these men were simply soldiers doing their duty. Lincoln would take a very similar tack with Confederate soldiers during the Civil War, hoping that humane treatment would induce them to create a lasting peace after the horrors of war were over.

Lincoln's policy toward the Dakota was thus lenient and humane by most standards. It was also brave, because it put him directly at odds with public hysteria over the recent massacres. It shows no sign of "racism," but treats Indian warriors with as much humanity as was later shown to Confederate POWs. Lincoln was well aware that his clemency would dispose many people against his government at a crucial period during the war, but he did it anyway. Such moral bravery in a politician should be celebrated, not condemned.

***

Looking at the writings and actions of the greatest American Founding Fathers, headlines such as "George Washington Owned Slaves and Ordered Indians to Be Killed" are revealed for the pathetic propaganda that they are. Such headlines have almost nothing to do with historical reality or historical complexity, or indeed with the science of uncovering historical truth. We have seen from the greatest founders' own words that they were—to a man—exceptionally humane, exceptionally wise, and concerned with finding practical solutions to the vexing problems of Indian welfare and keeping the peace during troubled times. The fact that they usually had very limited resources and had to grapple with lines of communication which stretched across thousands of miles of trackless territory reveals just how daunting the task that fell to them actually was.

Could any of our activist historian friends have done better or been significantly more humane when placed in the shoes of a Washington or Lincoln? The answer is: of course not. By any historical standards, the likes of Jefferson, Franklin, Washington, and Lincoln continue to merit their exceptional reputations, and anyone who would question this on the grounds of an anti-Indian prejudice is blinded by ideological animus and impervious to evidence.

CHAPTER 15

WAS THE TRAIL OF TEARS GENOCIDAL?

Long before the "Trail of Tears" occurred, Native Americans were forcibly removed from their land in the name of conquest and American Manifest Destiny, or the belief that white settlers had the right to expand and occupy all territory in the Western hemisphere. This belief of conquest was ingrained in American culture, rearing its ugly head time and time again in American history. But the Trail of Tears was one of the most jarring incidents of Native American genocide, and not only left thousands of Native Americans dead, but destroyed vibrant culture.

—Maeve McGuire, "Contemporary Review of Genocide and Political Violence"

The Trail of Tears is a label for the policy of Indian removal inaugurated by President Andrew Jackson in 1830 and continued by Jackson's second vice president and successor, Martin Van Buren. The main groups affected were the Five Civilized Tribes of southern Indians, who had been granted lands in the modern US states of Georgia, Alabama, Mississippi, Florida, and neighboring areas.

In all, about sixty thousand Indians were removed from these areas to the new "Indian Territory" in Oklahoma. These removals were for the most part direct violations of earlier treaties made with the Indians. Even the US Supreme Court declared them illegal. They were instigated after gold was discovered in North Carolina and Georgia, which put massive political pressure on state authorities to allow encroachment on Indian land.

This was particularly unfortunate, because the various southern Indian tribes had for several decades settled in to do precisely what the likes of Washington and Jefferson had hoped for: to farm, to own property, to become businesspeople, and generally to assimilate into the American lifestyle of the time, while maintaining distinctive ways of their own. All of these tribes had lived in their territories for a generation or more as independent nations within the United States; the communities that were ripped apart by the relocation were vibrant and beginning to thrive.

Now, it is true that the Jackson government made several proposals to the southern tribes offering them land and money in compensation for their lands east of the Mississippi. No matter how you slice it, however, the removal was grossly unfair, and the way it was enforced was cruel and capricious.

An eyewitness, the Reverend Evan Jones, described the following scene as the troops arrived in 1838:

> The Cherokees are nearly all prisoners. They have been dragged from their houses and camped at the forts and military posts all over the Nation. In Georgia, especially, the most unfeeling and insulting treatment has been experienced by them, in a general way. Multitudes were not allowed time to take anything with them but the clothes they had on.
>
> It is a painful sight. The property of many has been taken and sold before their eyes for almost nothing;

the sellers and buyers being in many cases combined to cheat the poor Indian. The poor captive in a state of distressing agitation, his weeping wife almost frantic with terror, surrounded by one group of crying, terrified children, without a friend to speak one consoling word, is in a very unfavorable condition to make advantageous disposition of his property even were suitable and honest purchasers on the spot…the truth is the Cherokees are deprived of their liberty and stripped of their entire property in one blow.[116]

Once the Indians got to Oklahoma, the chaotic nature of the relocations meant that border disputes flared up among various tribes and factions. This resulted in a series of high-profile murders and internecine conflicts. The entire affair remains one of the darkest stains in the entire history of US-Indian relations. That said, the events in question have been significantly distorted and misrepresented for political effect.

Most reporters today assume that the majority of these Indians died on the way to Oklahoma from the hardships of the journey. Fortunately, the death toll was relatively low for such a forced march, given the conditions of the times. The total number who died en route was in the neighborhood of three thousand people, which amounted to some 5 percent of the total population. Most of these unfortunate souls died of cold, exposure, and disease, which were exacerbated by the fact that some marches were cruelly conducted by soldiers during the winter months. Eyewitnesses describe pitiable scenes during the forced migration, in which children and old people lay down to die or were shot by their own relatives because they could not go any farther. Many others struggled on with inadequate clothing, bare feet black with frostbite.

---

[116] Quoted in *Slate*: Rev. Evan Jones, "'Work of Barbarity': Here's What the Trail of Tears Was Like, According to Someone Who Was There," *Slate*, February 10, 2019, https://slate.com/culture/2019/02/trail-of-tears-eyewitness-evan-jones.html.

Sensationalist historians paint the Trail of Tears as though it was typical of US Indian policy. They brand it unabashedly "genocidal" and write as though no European Americans stood up for Indian rights during the whole debacle. They also act as though the Indians in question were broadsided and given no choice except to be frog-marched halfway across North America at a moment's notice.

The questions that lie before us in this chapter are therefore: Was the Trail of Tears "genocidal?" Was it typical of US Indian policy? Were the Indians given any viable alternatives? Were they surprised by the removal order? And were there any American citizens or institutions that put up an effective fight against the injustice? To paint "America" as uniformly bad due to the Trail of Tears, given that substantial numbers of Americans did indeed fight against the Trail of Tears policy, is to engage in propaganda rather than history.

DIVISION AMONG THE INDIANS

Most accounts—including that of Reverend Jones quoted by *Slate*—portray the Trail of Tears as a forced removal by the United States government against Indians who were innocent victims caught completely unaware in the middle of the night. What these simplistic (and propagandistic) accounts fail to mention is that the issue of removal fiercely divided the Indian leadership of the day. The leadership had known that this was coming for years, if not decades, before it actually happened, and many offers and counteroffers were made before any soldiers actually showed up at someone's door.

Many Indian leaders had been educated outside the tribal areas, and many believed (as had Franklin, Washington, and Jefferson) that the eventual removal of the Indians was inevitable, considering the tremendous economic and demographic pressure that was being put on a few thousand Indians by hundreds of thousands of covetous white settlers.

The divisions over Indian removal were only one facet of a major debate that had been going on in Indian society for the better part of one hundred years. Just like their American counterparts, most tribal leaders by the end of the eighteenth century were aware that their way of life was disappearing, that they had voluntarily become economically dependent on the whites, and that the advance of writing and education was changing their culture irreversibly. The sheer numbers of whites versus Indians meant that by the early nineteenth century many were already part white—what in Mexico would be called mestizo and in Canada métis.

Among the prominent Cherokee in the 1820s and '30s were Major Ridge, John Ridge, Elias Boudinot, Sequoia, and John Ross. Most of these men were part European; they had received European educations, and many married European women. Major Ridge for example was part Scots. He was nonetheless raised as a warrior by the tribe, earning distinction in battle and gaining the nickname "He Who Slays the Enemy in His Path." He later married a part-white woman named Suzannah Catherine Wickett, and they had several children together.

During the War of 1812, Major Ridge served alongside United States troops under Andrew Jackson—the same man who as president would later order the Indian removals—and was awarded the honorary title "major." Ridge first served with Jackson against a faction of the Creek Indians who rejected the ongoing Americanization of their culture. Later, he helped Jackson fight against Seminole holdouts in 1818, leading a faction of Cherokee warriors against them. This use of Indian troops against Indians was not unusual but rather a standard pattern. At every stage of American history, the annals of warfare bristle with Indians who proved eager to test their mettle in battle against other Indians. This, after all, is what their ancestors had been doing since time immemorial.

As early as the 1810s, Jackson and others began to offer financial settlements to the southern Indians in return for their consent to move beyond the Mississippi. While Ridge initially opposed this plan, he was later persuaded that the best path forward for the Cherokee as a people was to maintain good relations with the US government. This is why both Ridge and his son John later supported the conciliatory faction during the negotiations of the 1830s. The aim of this faction was to accept the inevitable from a position of strength, thereby hoping to gain as much land and financial support from the US government as possible.

During the 1810s and '20s, Major Ridge achieved considerable economic success. Near the Cherokee town of Coosa in Georgia, he developed a plantation of nearly three hundred acres, purchasing some thirty African American slaves to serve as a labor force. There he grew corn, tobacco, and cotton. A keen entrepreneur, Ridge also operated a successful ferry company and a trading post that served as the regional general store.

During the 1830s, the Ridge faction supported the Treaty of New Echota, which was signed by the US government with the Cherokees in 1835. It offered generous terms to all Cherokees, including the right to become full US citizens and to settle in the states where they then resided. Each household was to receive a farm of 160 acres and part of a $5 million settlement amounting to over $300 per individual. In 1830, the average wage of a farm laborer was about ten dollars per month, meaning that every Indian received not only enough land to build a large farm but nearly three years' wages each, in cash. In contemporary terms, the median US household income is $68,000; triple this is over $200,000. Today, the median US household's total savings is only $5,300. This deal was nothing to sneeze at.

In addition, those who chose not to stay, receive a farm, and become US citizens would be granted territory in Oklahoma equal to that which they had vacated in Georgia, in addition to their share of the indemnity. An additional $500,000 was set aside for an education fund that was to provide educations as the tribal elders saw fit.

For all its generosity, this treaty did come at the expense of the Cherokees' ancestral lands in Georgia. It was by any civilized standard illegal and unfair for Jackson to force the Cherokees to move. The Treaty of New Echota aroused the ire of Jackson's opponents including, as we will see, Ralph Waldo Emerson. It was also opposed by a traditionalist faction of Cherokee led by Chief John Ross.

Also part-European and married to a European American, Ross served as the rallying point for all those who opposed New Echota. The divisions opened up by the treaty within the Cherokee and other nations had been ongoing for decades and had already caused a great deal of intertribal bloodshed. When they arrived in Oklahoma, the unsettled state of the Indian tribes in the new territory was something that few had foreseen and that no one had planned for. Partly for this reason, the newly settled Indians began to wage war against each other; tribe fought tribe and faction fought faction. In addition, Plains-dwelling tribes such as the Comanche also conducted raids into the newcomers' territories.

It was this unforeseen chaos that helped foment a new civil war among the Cherokee. The John Ross faction held the Ridge faction responsible for selling out to the US government, and Major Ridge, John Ridge, and Elias Boudinot were all murdered in the later 1830s.

MASS RESISTANCE TO JACKSON'S POLICIES

Sensationalists who wish to view the Trail of Tears as a sign of long-standing genocidal intent on the part of colonists neglect to point out one significant fact: the decision by President Jackson to remove the southern Native Americans beyond the Mississippi was hugely controversial.

Because of the prevalence of Zinnism in American historiography, it is next to impossible to find a recent academic book about the anti-Jacksonian opposition to the Trail of Tears. However, there is one gap in the anti-American armor here, namely that many women's groups were part of the anti-Jacksonian party during the Indian removal debates. This has led feminist scholars to write about opposition to the Trail of Tears in a way they never could if "minorities" were not involved. As the feminist scholar Mary Hershberger put it in 1995:

> Andrew Jackson's request to Congress in December
> 1829 for federal monies to remove Southeast
> Indians beyond the Mississippi River generated

the most intense public opposition that the United States had witnessed. In six short months, removal opponents launched massive petition drives that called on Congress to defeat removal and to uphold Indian rights to property. To block removal, Catharine Beecher and Lydia Sigourney organized the first national women's petition campaign and flooded Congress with antiremoval petitions, making a bold claim for women's place in national political discourse. The strength of antiremoval forces stunned Martin Van Buren who, writing of the events over twenty years later, portrayed the government's side as besieged from all quarters and stated flatly that "a more persevering opposition to a public measure had scarcely ever been made."

Pretty much everything you need to know about the extent of contemporary opposition to the Trail of Tears is present in this summary. Hershberger implies that women were opposed to the Indian removals while men were generally complicit. But her own write-up betrays this misleading conclusion. According to Jackson's second vice president, Martin Van Buren, the policy had stirred up such a hornet's nest of opposition that the US government felt besieged on all sides. Public sentiment in the North was largely, and in many places vehemently, anti-removal.

Even Van Buren's conscience was pricked by his role in this debacle.[117] He was aware, in later years, that historians' judgment on the Trail of Tears was likely to involve moral censure of his and Jackson's actions for as long as the United States would endure. In his autobiography Van Buren admitted that he and Jackson had made the US government "unjustifiable aggressors" in the matter. He was fully aware, in other words, that he and Jackson had been on the wrong side of history.

---

[117] Jackson's first vice president, John C. Calhoun, was an architect of the Trail of Tears removals and did not, to my knowledge, appear to have repented in later life.

RESISTANCE IN CONGRESS: DAVY CROCKETT

In the course of the debates that raged across the US in the lead-up to the Trail of Tears, some people made arguments that would today be recognized as explicitly racist; for example, that Indians were not entitled to their land because they were a naturally inferior people. This should be seen in the context of the leadup to the US Civil War, which pitted slaveholders and defenders of slavery against abolitionists who argued that the "universal rights of man" as set forth in the nation's founding documents applied equally to all races. Because debates in the 1830s included a number of such racist arguments, activists like to portray them as typical of American attitudes at the time. One master's thesis on the subject reflects what most students and academics currently want to believe about white American racial attitudes in the 1830s:

> The U.S. treaty commitments to the Indians were argued to be invalid; because the Indians were an inferior race the agreements with them could be annulled by a superior race. The arguments for Georgia's superior rights and U.S. expansion, based on principles of white supremacy and colonial rights of discovery and conquest, won the day.[118]

While nakedly racist opinions were widespread at the time, they were far from universal. In the US Congress, opposition to the Indian removal was pervasive, and the debates dragged on for years.

One of the most prominent opponents to Jackson's policy was the US Representative from Tennessee and former Indian fighter Davy Crockett. In an 1834 letter, Crockett shows his disgust with Jackson's Indian removal policies; what he finds even more depressing was the fact

---

[118] This is from a master's thesis for the University of Massachusetts Boston by George William Goss, called "The Debate over Indian Removal in the 1830s," submitted 2011. https://scholarworks.umb.edu/cgi/viewcontent.cgi?article=1045&context=masters_theses

that Van Buren was likely to continue them as Jackson's successor (which he did). Crockett writes:

> The time is come that man is expected to be as transferrable and as negotiable as a promissory note... I have no doubt that Martin Van Buren thinks that Andrew Jackson has full power to transfer the people of these United States [i.e., the Native Americans] at his will, and I am truly afraid that a majority of the free citizens of these United States will submit to it, and say "Amen, Jackson done it."

> ...I have almost given up the ship as lost. I have gone so far as to declare that if Martin Van Buren is elected that I will leave these United States, for I never will live under his kingdom. Before I will submit to his government I will go to the wilds of Texas. I will consider that government a paradise to what this will be. In fact, at this time, our republican government has dwindled almost into insignificancy. Our boasted land of liberty has almost bowed to the yoke of bondage. Our happy days of republican principles are near at an end.

> This is Van Buren's principle: that a few have the power to transfer the many.

> I must close in the hope of seeing better times.[119]

Note Crockett's deliberate use of the term "man"—which in the conventional fashion of the time he meant to apply universally to people of all races. In Crockett's view, Indians were entitled to the same rights as

---

[119] "The Gilder Lehrman Institute of American History." *To Charles Schultz | Gilder Lehrman Institute of American History*, https://www.gilderlehrman.org/collection/glc01162.

European settlers, and race had nothing to do with it. For Crockett, this was true whatever their legal status might have been.

Soon after writing this letter, Crockett lost his seat in the House of Representatives, which prompted his plan to move farther west to Texas. He was instrumental in helping it to declare independence from Mexico, and would later die at the Alamo fighting for the new republic.

Crockett appears here as a radical democrat, a man who fervently believed in a sort of perpetual revolution and a need for people to throw off the yoke of bureaucracy and corruption. He believed that just like European Americans, Amerindians were entitled to their lands by nature, law, and custom; he found the Jacksonian removal so morally repugnant that he was willing to leave the territory of the United States in order to make his point.

RESISTANCE BY THE US JUDICIARY

Jackson came to power as a populist and a states-rights advocate; not to mention he personally wanted to see the Indians removed as far west as possible. All of this made him popular in the south, which formed the basis of his support in the 1828 election. In concert with southern state legislators who stood to gain the most from Indian removal, Jackson pushed ahead with the removal of the Cherokees.

Even before Jackson announced his intention to begin Indian removal in 1830, anti-removalists had been planning to resist his actions in the courts. After all, the Indians had been granted their land in perpetuity by previous treaties. This showdown culminated in one of the most famous Supreme Court cases from the era, the 1832 decision in Worcester v. Georgia.

The case was brought by Samuel Worcester, a missionary to the Indians who declined a pardon from a lower court and underwent a sentence for hard labor, all so that the Cherokees could bring their case to the Supreme Court. The laws in question are somewhat obscure and complicated, but Chief Justice John Marshall made sure to use the occasion to make a resounding defense of the right of the federal government to determine Indian policy, partly in the hope that this would override the often harsher policies of state governments. Marshall argued that the United States government had succeeded to the rights of the British Crown in America, and therefore had the right to deal with the sovereign nations of the American Indians. He thereby also set the foundation for the idea that Amerindians remain, to some extent, sovereign nations—a precedent still cited by Indian activists to this day.

The main question before the court was whether or not the state of Georgia had the right to contravene federal treaties guaranteeing the Cherokee the right to live in perpetuity on large sections of northern Georgia. We have seen that gold had recently been discovered in the North Carolina and Georgia mountains, prompting a massive push by locals to encroach on Cherokee land. It did not help that the Cherokee were vastly outnumbered by the European Americans. Not only did prospectors range across Cherokee territory, but speculators were covetous of other lands that were becoming increasingly valuable as the population of Georgia increased and the market gained depth. Swayed by local interests, the State of Georgia accordingly passed several laws that limited Cherokee rights to their own land.

Marshall's verdict made Jackson's removal of the Cherokees illegal. In a move that today would be considered highly irregular, Jackson chose to ignore the Supreme Court and press ahead with removal anyway. But this does not erase the fact that the removal was declared illegal by the highest US court and was performed in defiance of the legal authority of the American court system.

RESISTANCE BY INTELLECTUALS

It was not only members of Congress and the US Supreme Court who opposed Indian removal; we have seen how a large swath of the American public also opposed it. Spearheading the resistance were a number of intellectuals, including the Concord group of New England writers and thinkers that included Ralph Waldo Emerson, Louisa May Alcott, Henry David Thoreau, and Nathaniel Hawthorne. Other progressives of the time, such as Herman Melville and Walt Whitman, were involved in a wave of social utopianism that was then gripping the United States and Europe. Their utopianism was in turn part of the Transcendentalist Movement, which put the individual's soul and personal experience at the center of all things.

Davy Crockett was one of the thousands who tried to put their utopian dreams of a better society into practice at this time. The English poet Samuel Taylor Coleridge formed a plan to create a utopian community on the banks of the Susquehanna in Pennsylvania as far back as 1794. Brook Farm, founded in 1841 by the Unitarian minister George Ripley, was one of dozens of idealistic communities across the country that aimed to pool labor and provide time for every person to better themselves through reading and scientific experiments.

For many other Americans, the Second Great Awakening of the 1830s and 1840s brought religious focus to this desire to build a better world. Mormonism and Adventism were manifestations of this fervor. Many Christians now interpreted the message of Jesus as advocating universal equality and the alleviation of all human suffering. Abolitionism became a key part of many reformists' platforms. *Uncle Tom's Cabin*, written by the evangelical progressive Harriet Beecher Stowe, humanized black people by personalizing the agonies they faced under slavery and did more than any other thing to tip the US public toward abolitionism.

This fervor for human rights that gripped the United States also extended to the Indians. It motivated thousands of young European Americans to dedicate their careers to the improvement of Amerindian lives. It also motivated Ralph Waldo Emerson to write a letter to President Van Buren in 1838, which included the following:

Sir:

My communication respects the sinister rumors that fill this part of the country concerning the Cherokee people. The interest always felt in the aboriginal population has been heightened in regard to this tribe. We have learned with joy their improvement in the social arts. We have read their newspapers. We have seen some of them in our schools and colleges.

It is not to be doubted that it is the good pleasure of all humane persons in the republic that [the Cherokee] shall be duly cared for; that they shall taste justice and love from all to whom we have delegated the office of dealing with them.

It now appears that the government of the United States choose to hold the Cherokees to [a] sham treaty. In the name of God, sir, we ask you if this be so. Do the newspapers rightly inform us? Men and women with pale and perplexed faces meet one another in the streets and churches here, and ask if this be so. Such a dereliction of all faith and virtue, such a denial of justice, and such deafness to screams for mercy were never heard of in times of peace and in the dealing of a nation with its own allies and wards, since the Earth was made. Sir, does this government think that the people of the United States are become savage and mad?

The soul of man, the justice, the mercy that is the heart in all men, from Maine to Georgia, does abhor this business.

Ralph Waldo Emerson[120]

---

[120] "Letter to President Van Buren." *Ralph Waldo Emerson*, 14 Feb. 2023, https://emersoncentral.com/texts/miscellanies/letter-to-president-van-buren/.

The context of this letter was Van Buren's inauguration in March 1837, after which he pressed forward with the removal of the Cherokee Nation to Oklahoma. Northern intellectuals like Emerson might have hoped, until this time, that the matter would be resolved in favor of the Cherokees. No doubt Emerson exaggerated the universal opposition to the Indian removal. But it is undoubtedly true that millions of Americans, especially in the North, were deeply dismayed at the news that Van Buren was going to go ahead with the removal of the Cherokees.

Modern activists who casually dismiss all those who came before them as brutish and ignorant racists should perhaps take the time to learn details such as these before preening themselves on their moral superiority to previous generations.

RESISTANCE BY CHRISTIAN MISSIONARIES

Among the many private individuals who dedicated their careers to the improvement of relations between Amerindians and the European majority were Christian missionaries like Samuel Austin Worcester, who brought the landmark suit in *Worcester v. Georgia*. The son of a minister from Vermont, Worcester had also learned printing in his youth, and after graduation he was sent as a missionary to the Cherokees in Georgia, where he moved with his wife and children. Later, when the Cherokees were forced to move to Oklahoma, Worcester and his family went with them; his new base was Park Hill. One of Worcester's children became famous in her own right as a missionary to the Indians, and his granddaughter Alice Mary Robertson became a Native American rights activist and the second woman elected to Congress, soon after women received the vote in 1921.

After moving to Georgia, Worcester collaborated with the Cherokee leader Elias Boudinot to help create the newspaper known as the *Cherokee Phoenix*. Boudinot had been educated at a missionary school in Connecticut, along with many other prominent Cherokees including John Ridge, David Carter (Tah-wah), and David Brown. The reputation of this paper reached across the United States. Emerson mentions it in his letter to Van Buren.

The *Phoenix* was bilingual in English and Cherokee and utilized the Cherokee alphabet created by the Indian polymath Sequoia in 1821. It was then taught in Cherokee schools and learned by missionaries like Worcester, with the result that literacy in Cherokee was increasing in the years before 1830.

We have already met another Christian missionary who decided to share the fate of the Cherokee, namely the Reverend Evan Jones. Jones was born in Wales in 1788 and immigrated to Philadelphia in 1821 with his wife, Elizabeth Lanigan. Jones was sent by the Baptist Foreign Mission Board to work with the Cherokees of North Carolina, where he taught school.

When the US government decided to remove the Cherokees to Oklahoma, Jones and his family agreed to lead a group of some one thousand Cherokees to Oklahoma, in part to protect the Cherokees from the caprice of the soldiers as much as possible. Some seventy-seven of his band were lost during the migration. Once they arrived in Oklahoma, Jones set up a new school and mission, converting many Indians to Christianity by his hard work and evident goodness. He and his family remained advocates of the Indians to the US press and government for many decades afterwards.

Worcester and Evans were just some of the many European Americans who risked their lives in the defense of the southern tribes during the Trail of Tears era. Their story—and the widespread opinions that they represent—surely deserves to be heard, despite the efforts of Ostler, Saunt, and the rest to treat them as mere historical footnotes.

THE TRAIL OF TEARS: A BALANCED READING

Was the Trail of Tears genocidal? Jackson and his supporters may have been driven by covetousness, political expediency, and a large dose of genuine racism, but the real history surrounding the Trail of Tears reveals that terms like "genocide" are unhelpful for understanding what actually happened to the southern Indians in the 1830s.

Then as now, almost everyone agrees that the Trail of Tears was one of the more tragic and dishonorable events ever engaged in by the United States government. That being said, it remains true that the Indian-removal policy was opposed by a great many members of the US Congress, by members of the American intelligentsia, by millions of private citizens, and even by the US Supreme Court. The treaties and offers that preceded the removal contained a number of stipulations that are much more generous than they might have been.

Meanwhile, the great majority of Indians who went along the Trail of Tears either went voluntarily or without incident. Many of those who died were victims of infirmity, disease, and exposure to the elements, which was fairly normal for any mass movement of people during the early nineteenth century, voluntary or otherwise. A 95 percent survival rate hardly counts as genocide, especially when most of these deaths were indeed situational rather than premeditated. People who are given a choice to become farmers and US citizens but who then choose to be relocated to Oklahoma on principle can likewise hardly be called victims of genocide. Some US officials and soldiers were truly cruel during the forced sales and migrations, but a surprising majority were not. These outliers are seized upon by modern-day propagandists such as the writers at *Slate* quoted above and made to look typical when they were not.

The more one learns about the Indian leaders of this time, the more one realizes that most had long interpersonal histories with the American elite. This was hardly the one-sided, us-vs-them affair that most modern journalistic accounts make it out to be. Major Ridge fought alongside Andrew Jackson as his ally in more than one military campaign. Ridge's own son was educated in Connecticut. Most of the Cherokee leadership was part European. And everyone involved knew what was at stake for years before it happened—there was a long, drawn-out political process, which helped to ensure that traditionalists like Ross would be pitted against assimilationists like Ridge.

Many of those who opposed the removal—whether they were European, Indian, or mixed-race—did so for reasons of personal and political gain. The same went for many of those who supported it. In short, the real story of the Trail of Tears is complex and not nearly as cut-and-dried as sensationalists would have us believe.

This is not to say that Jackson, Van Buren, and their supporters do not bear a heavy responsibility and that it was not a serious tragedy. Martin Van Buren recognized his error, at least in later years, and he was big enough to admit that he had been egregiously wrong. But to continue to evoke the Trail of Tears as a massacre, a genocide, an inevitable product of deep-seated American racism against non-Europeans, as typical of American treatment of the Indians, and as unopposed by US institutions or public opinion, perpetrated by capitalist Europeans against unsuspecting and innocent Natives who were unanimous in their opposition—all these common themes are an almost total misrepresentation of the facts.

Moreover, to call anyone who cites these qualifications an "apologist for genocide" is no more than a facile attempt to shut down scientific debate and an admission that their case does not stand up to critical scrutiny.

CHAPTER 16

DID EUROPEANS STARVE, MASSACRE, OR SPREAD DISEASE AMONG THE NATIVES?

Buffalo were hunted almost to extinction as a means of genocide in the Plains Indian Wars.

—Adrian Jawort, Indian Country Today, 2018

During the solar eclipse of January 1, 1889, the Paiute shaman Wovoka had a vision. God appeared to him in the guise of a Native American man and promised Wovoka that both the living and the dead sprits of Native Americans would unite to drive the white man out of North America forever. According to this prophecy, which came to be known as the Ghost Dance, a new age of peace and prosperity would descend upon the land, and the tribes would live together in a world without evil. The Ghost Dance quickly went viral among the remaining Indians of the western United States, and political leaders such as Sitting Bull encouraged their tribespeople to embrace this ideology as a means of resisting white encroachment.

The United States government, for its part, recognized the danger represented by the Ghost Dance movement and issued proclamations banning the ideology and the ritual dances that went along with it. Upon learning that Chief Sitting Bull had adopted the Ghost Dance among his Sioux tribe, he was shot by US policemen for fear that he was about to lead an insurrection.

Two weeks later, the US 7th Cavalry under Colonel James W. Forsyth surrounded the Lakota Sioux encampment near Wounded Knee Creek. On the morning of December 29, a number of US soldiers went into the Lakota camp in order to enforce a disarming order on the Sioux. During the tense minutes that followed, a deaf warrior known as Black Coyote refused to give up his rifle, on the grounds that he had paid a lot for it. Black Coyote's rifle went off, and the troops, some of whom had a superior tactical position, began to fire on the Lakota.

By the time the firing stopped, some two hundred and fifty Lakota men, women, and children lay dead. Some twenty-five US soldiers also died during the fighting, and another thirty-nine were wounded, despite the fact that the Lakota had been partially disarmed at the beginning.

Modern-day commentators portray the Wounded Knee Massacre as just another slaughter of helpless Indians by racist United States troops. But the numbers of US dead remind us that the situation on the ground was often more fluid than we like to think. This is true even during the later decades of the nineteenth century, when the Indians were usually outnumbered and outgunned. The high number of US casualties at Wounded Knee suggest that many soldiers had waded into the group of Lakota warriors expecting there to be no resistance—just like hundreds of similar actions that had taken place across the west in previous decades.

The Wounded Knee Massacre also shows the role of political ideology and political ambition among the tribespeople of the American West. Even as late as 1890, there were still many Indians who were willing to fight and die rather than submit to the reservation system that was being offered as an alternative by United States officials. (More on this below.)

If a politically free people choose to resist with armed force rather than surrender—even if they are hopelessly outnumbered and out-gunned—do lopsided battles count as massacres—especially on occasions when most of the dead are enemy warriors? For many decades, both the Indians and the Americans took it on faith that what happened between circa 1830 and 1880 was a series of Indian wars rather than Indian massacres. And while these battles generally did not go well for the Indians, it remains true that the overall casualty count during five hundred years of North American expansion ended up with surprisingly equal numbers of Indians and Europeans dead at one another's hands.

The internet is filled with web pages on the "Indigenous genocide" of the later nineteenth century—as though most of the victims were murdered, unprovoked and in cold blood, by Europeans. These articles often claim that Americans intentionally spread disease among the Indians via smallpox blankets or intentionally starved them by slaughtering buffalo and burning crops. As we have seen in countless other scenarios, most of this is an exaggeration. Most of the "missing" Indians in the population tallies will simply not have been born during the upheavals of the period, while others will have been victims of naturally occurring disease and malnutrition. War casualties therefore made up a small minority—usually less than 5 percent—of the "deaths" that are routinely cited.

There is also the fact that Indian casualties in the mid-nineteenth century included a great number of men, women, and children who were massacred at the hands of rival tribes. One of the things that the 1990 Kevin Costner film *Dances with Wolves* gets right is that most tribes were being continually pressed by traditional Indian enemies, who might often slaughter and kidnap with more ruthlessness than white troopers or vigilantes.

In the southwest, the border with Mexico led to a complex web of alliances that encouraged intertribal raiding with the promise of legal impunity. Many tribes lost more people to such rivalries than they did to the whites—the only difference being that no one today bothers to write web pages on intra-Indian warfare and slaughter, despite the abundant evidence for conflicts of this nature.

The squeeze that many tribes felt with the arrival of large numbers of whites after 1850 often served to intensify traditional rivalries, as hunting grounds and food supplies were threatened. This led to an increased casualty count, at a time when Amerindian tribes could least afford to suffer population decline. The result was a downward population spiral that reached a nadir of perhaps two hundred and seventy thousand Indians by the turn of the twentieth century.

THE ROLE OF TECHNOLOGY

The fifty years from 1830 to 1880 constituted a decisive and turbulent era in the history of US-Indian relations. This brief period saw the great majority of US land flip from Indian to settler proprietorship. The population of the United States was about thirty million and growing every year, while the Indian population was perhaps three hundred thousand. In other words, whites outnumbered Indians by one hundred to one. About half of these Indians were already settled on reservations, making the proportion of settlers to "wild" Indians even more disproportionate. Apart from Oklahoma, California contained the greatest numbers of Indians in 1850. The numbers of Indians roaming the Plains fluctuated in the few tens of thousands, a tiny population that was spread among a dozen or more large US states. That said, they occupied territories that were increasingly coveted by farmers and ranchers, as the value of property continued to increase.

The frontier remained dangerous throughout this time period, and Indians were frequently the aggressors. This led to dozens of massacres of European Americans by Indians that often get overlooked. We can count the Indian Creek massacre of 1832, in which fifteen settlers were massacred by Potawatomi Indians; the Fort Parker Massacre of 1836, in which seven European Americans were killed by Comanche; the Killough Massacre of 1838, in which eighteen settlers were killed by a party of Cherokee; the Webster Massacre of 1839, in which ten settlers were killed by a party of Comanche; the death of twenty-three settlers at the hands of the Comanche during the Linnville Raid of 1840; and so forth. This steady litany of outrages at the hands of Indian bands goes far to explain why the American public had little sympathy for independent Indian bands during these decades.[121]

As the nineteenth century wore on, the tide turned rapidly against the Indians. By the 1850s we find increasing numbers of massacres in which dozens or even a few hundred Indians were killed by whites at one time. California, as we will see in the next chapter, saw the worst of this action.

But were these massacres typical of US-Indian relations during the mid-nineteenth century? Were they part and parcel of a larger policy of "genocide"? Should they be taken as emblematic of US policy as a whole? Did Americans make no attempt to broker peaceful and humanitarian solutions? Was ongoing government support for the Indians insignificant to the point of irrelevance? Were the active and manifold "Friends of the Indians" charitable societies set up across the US good for nothing?

The main factor that "doomed" the western Indians of these decades—just as it doomed the buffalo—was the rapid advance of Western technology on the heels of the Industrial Revolution. Few people take the time to recall that whites and Indians had been mixing across huge swaths of the American interior for the better part of two hundred years before the Trail of Tears was instigated in 1830. Few also realize that for the most part, this generations-long intermingling of white and Indian had done little to destroy Indian political independence.

---

[121] In nineteenth-century newspapers, anyone who wants to can find op-eds, written in the aftermath of yet another massacre of settlers by Indians, which declare that "the only good Indian is a dead Indian." Yet these sentiments were far from universal, and context does matter. As we have seen, many Indians can be found throughout colonial history who stated that this or that rival tribe were subhuman and worthy only of extermination. Such pronouncements by Indians about rival tribes, though commonly held, rarely make it into write-ups in the likes of History.com or Smithsonian.com. Why is this?

After 1830, the rapid advance of canals and railroads brought a huge influx of European Americans to the Mississippi and beyond. The creation of a massive metropolis and railroad hub at Chicago opened the US interior to settlement and a massive influx of eastern capital, which had repercussions throughout the west. Property prices soared as accessibility increased. Even before the Omaha-Sacramento railroad was completed in 1869, settlers had been ranging across the American west in their tens of thousands during the Oregon Trail era of the 1840s and '50s. The first transcontinental telegraph was completed by Western Union already in 1861, meaning that news could now be relayed rapidly from virtually any point in the United States.

The telegraph and the railroad gave an enormous logistical advantage to United States troops, who could report Indian movements and move supplies with a much greater rapidity than ever before. Such circumstances rapidly closed the circle on the remaining politically independent Indians, making their sphere of operations dramatically smaller in only a few short decades—a much faster time scale than envisioned by Jefferson only a few decades before.

POISONED BLANKETS: THE SMALLPOX MYTH

Even most activists recognize that much of the Indian population decline of the nineteenth century was due to the spread of novel diseases rather than massacres. They therefore encourage—or do not discourage—the myth that Americans and their governments intentionally spread disease among the Natives, whenever they get the chance. Nearly every mention of disease in this context contains at least an implication that Europeans spread pathogens intentionally. For example, an article on science.org called "How Europeans Brought Sickness to the New World" leads with this sentence: "In the Americas, the arrival of Europeans brought disease, war, and slavery to many indigenous peoples."

Note the rhetorical sleight of hand that lumps a passive event (the spread of disease) with active wrongs such as waging war and taking slaves. Note also how this sentence implies that Europeans were always the aggressors in war, that the Europeans only warred on Indigenous peoples, that Indigenous people never allied with Europeans for their own advantage, and that disease was unknown in the New World and Indians never warred on one another before Europeans arrived.

These rhetorical tricks notwithstanding, specialists know that the spread of disease during these centuries was mostly beyond the control of any party, whether European or Indian. Waves of disease often spread for hundreds of miles away from European-Indian contact points. It was therefore common for infections to rage among Indian populations that had no contact with Europeans at all. However, it is certainly the case that Europeans carried unknown diseases to which the Indians were vulnerable. Typhoid, measles, flu, and other diseases were all unknown to the New World before European contact—although it also worked the other way, as in the case of syphilis, a virulent infection that was almost certainly brought back to Europe by Columbus's crew, spreading across the continent with devastating effects.[122]

The worst of the Old World diseases was smallpox, which ravaged settlers and Indians alike. As we will see, smallpox among the Indigenous population of the Americas was a major cause for government concern throughout the eighteenth and nineteenth centuries. As the Enlightenment and the Scientific Revolution advanced across the West, officials in some countries gained a greater awareness of the spread of smallpox, the numbers of cases involved, and also the potential to treat diseases through various types of inoculation. What we find is a longstanding concern for Native victims of smallpox that gives the lie to narratives of "genocide."

---

[122] Charles Q. Choi, "Case Closed? Columbus Introduced Syphilis to Europe," *Scientific American*, December 27, 2011, https://www.scientificamerican.com/article/case-closed-columbus/.

The archival research of hundreds of historians has only turned up a handful of instances where Europeans may have spread smallpox as a form of biological warfare—and all of these are inconclusive.

The most notorious is the alleged gift of smallpox-infected blankets to Natives in the area of Fort Pitt during the French and Indian War. In letters between General Sir Jeffrey Amherst and Colonel Henry Bouquet, Amherst suggested that Bouquet take advantage of an outbreak of small-pox in the area to attempt to infect the local Indians. Bouquet for his part agreed that he would look into the possibility, though he admitted to Amherst that he was afraid lest he get smallpox himself. Biological warfare, then as now, carried with it the distinct possibility of killing friend and foe indiscriminately.

While we have no records of Bouquet pursuing the matter further, apparently a trader and militia captain at Fort Pitt known as William Trent did attempt to deliver two blankets to the Indians. It is not known whether Trent's attempt was carried out, let alone whether it helped to spread smallpox in the way that Trent and Amherst might have wished.

Historian Paul Kelton is author of several books and articles on the dissemination of disease among the American Indians, including the 2007 book *Epidemics and Enslavement: Biological Catastrophe in the Native Southeast 1492–1715*. Meanwhile Philip Ranlet of Hunter College wrote an article in the year 2000 on the Fort Pitt incident. According to both historians, this is the single documented case of Europeans or Americans attempting to sow disease among the Native Americans—in all of American history.[123]

While evidence for Europeans spreading disease among the Indians is almost nonexistent, there is, on the flip side, ample evidence that Europeans went out of their way to inoculate Indians against smallpox as soon as a vaccine became available.

---

[123] This is written up in Patrick J. Kiger, "Did Colonists Give Infected Blankets to Native Americans as Biological Warfare?" history.com, November 15, 2018, updated November 25, 2019, https://www.history.com/news/colonists-native-americans-smallpox-blankets.

The smallpox vaccine was perfected by the British doctor Edward Jenner in 1796. This was an improvement on an earlier technique called variolation, which had been practiced since 1721. Jenner's lab sent some samples to US president and amateur scientist Thomas Jefferson, who became an enthusiastic early adopter of the vaccination technique. Meanwhile variolation was used—sometimes to good effect—throughout the Americas both before and after vaccines were invented.

For the first several decades, Jenner's vaccine was both hard to come by and highly perishable. Variolation was a technique of inserting smallpox scabs into small cuts in the skin; it was found that this often provided immunity—though it sometimes resulted in death. It was therefore only used when a smallpox epidemic was raging so severely that the odds seemed worth the risk. In Mexico and Latin America, a terrible smallpox epidemic of 1797 threatened millions of Native people, and it is reported that some sixty to seventy thousand Indians were induced to undergo variolation, supposedly with good success. However, many Indians continued to resist these efforts, resulting in the deaths of tens of thousands.

Thomas Jefferson, for his part, used the smallpox vaccine on his own children and the rest of his household, including his several hundred slaves. Soon afterwards, he became the first person to introduce smallpox vaccine to the Amerindians. He convinced a great delegation of warriors, who were staying in Washington DC in the winter of 1801–02, to get vaccinated, and the program was a success. He thereupon encouraged the chiefs to spread the news of the vaccine to their people, hoping to induce them to inoculate themselves.

In 1803, Jefferson sent some smallpox vaccine along with the explorers Lewis and Clark. He gave them instructions to vaccinate as many people as possible and to encourage the Indians to accept vaccination as soon it became available. Lewis later wrote to Jefferson requesting additional vaccines, since the stuff he had brought with him appeared to have spoiled.

It can therefore truthfully be said that the United States government pursued a policy of inoculating the Indians against smallpox almost as soon as the vaccine was invented. This policy was continued at government expense throughout the nineteenth century, not only in the United States but in Mexico and Latin America as well. As early as 1803, the king of Spain authorized a massive expedition whose purpose was to travel throughout New Spain, inoculating as many Indians as possible. This provides substantial confirmation of the longstanding Spanish policy of attempting to maximize the Indian population—and once again flies in the face of claims of intentional genocide.

By 1806, the expedition's leader, Dr. D. Francisco Xavier de Balmis, could report in the *Madrid Gazette* that the vaccine was now established in every part of the New World empire as far north as Sonora. De Balmis claims to have vaccinated fifty thousand Indians in Peru alone. The reason this could be done so rapidly compared with the US was that the Spanish practiced "arm to arm" vaccination, where a few vaccinated people were used as human incubators. Their blood was taken and injected into other people's arms, which provided immunity. The Americans meanwhile used a vaccine stored in a cotton thread, which could spoil after a few months or faster through exposure to the elements. By the 1820s, agents such as James Patie were active in California vaccinating Indians across the territory; in his journal he claims to have vaccinated no fewer than twenty-two thousand people across the mission district.

After a false start under President Monroe in the 1810s, the US government under President Jackson began to fund an Indian vaccination program in 1832. Yes, the same president who is vilified for the Trail of Tears was the one who authorized the first federally funded mass vaccination program for the purpose of saving the Indians from their greatest scourge.

According to an act dated May 5, 1832, "It shall be the duty of several Indian Agents and sub-agents under the direction of the Secretary of War to take such measures as he shall deem most efficient to convene the Indian tribes at their respective towns, or in such other places and numbers and at such seasons as shall be most convenient to the Indian population, for the purpose of arresting the progress of smallpox among the several tribes by vaccination." The secretary of war was empowered to employ as many physicians and surgeons as necessary; the Indian agents were to be supplied with "genuine and effective" vaccine matter. According to Stearn and Stearn, who wrote on this program back in the 1940s, the Indians in some areas had been vaccinated by the federal program earlier than many white people in the region, with the result that the white settlers might experience mass death from smallpox, while the Indians proved resistant.[124]

It is probable that the federal Indian vaccination program of the nineteenth century saved tens of thousands of lives—a significant proportion of all Indians who remained in the United States by 1900. Recent historians have been noticeably silent on this critically important policy, because it does not support their aim of portraying Europeans and Americans in the worst possible light.

One of the few recent articles on the topic drives home the schizophrenic logic behind this "damned if you do" mentality. According to a 2004 article by J. Diane Pearson, an ethnic studies lecturer at Berkeley:

> The Lewis and Clark expedition was part of a global effort that used imperial medicine to advance colonization and the politicization of Western medicine among indigenous populations. The medical program was designed to serve as a diplomatic tool to convince indigenous populations of the United States' power and superiority. Powerful physicians, politicians, and religious leaders associated with the expedition also used imperial medicine to expedite

---

[124] E. Wagner Stearn and Allen E. Stearn, "Smallpox Immunization of the Amerindian," *Bulletin of the History of Medicine* 13, no. 5 (1943), 601–613. https://www.jstor.org/stable/44440816

federal policies that endangered the lives of American
Indian diplomats.

The mind boggles at how someone could write this sort of nonsense
with a straight face. Of course, one could always argue that a purpose of
Lewis and Clark's medicinal intervention was to impress Native peoples
with the prowess of Western science. But such an argument can only be
made by someone whose life has been so comfortable, so free from real
hardship or want, that they can treat the miracles of modern medicine
as mere ideological tools. It is yet another case where modern Western
academics spend so much time in a rhetorical bubble, that they forget
that reality exists.

The cold, hard fact is that the US government's long-term, widespread vaccine policy saved a substantial portion of all American Indians
in the nineteenth-century United States. People lament the fact that the
Indian population dipped below a few hundred thousand by 1900, but
it might easily have dipped far lower, had the federal government not
intervened to provide medicine, food, and other material support to the
remaining Indians. It is indisputable that the US government's vaccination policy saved far more Indians than were massacred during the
entire nineteenth century, including in California. In the end, Pearson's
argument is so contrived that it leads her to the conclusion that the US
government would have been morally superior had it withheld lifesaving
vaccines from the Indians, resulting in tens of thousands of prevent-
able deaths.

THE OREGON TRAIL

The experience of the Western Trails gives the lie to another modern
stereotype, which is the destructive migration of European Americans
into the west. Travel along the Oregon, Mormon, and California Trails
began in earnest during the 1840s and then became a flood during the
1850s. It is estimated that up to four hundred thousand people migrated

along the Oregon Trail to the Pacific Northwest, with some sixty thousand taking the Mormon Trail to Salt Lake City, and some two hundred thousand are supposed to have taken the California Trail. The outbreak of the Civil War in 1860 saw US troop protection decrease and a diminution of immigration to the west. By the end of the Civil War, immigration picked up again, until the coming of the railroads a few years later spelled the end of large-scale overland travel by wagon.

One might imagine that with hundreds of thousands of settlers moving across the American west, this would engender a good deal of friction with the Plains Indians. However, John Unruh, author of the classic 1979 study *The Plains Across*, argued that relations between Indians and settlers were largely peaceful during the pre–Civil War era. We know that Indians regularly visited Fort Laramie in Wyoming, for example, from the fort's founding in the mid-1830s until tensions increased after the outbreak of war in 1860. The war caused many Indian tribes to side with either the US North or the South; meanwhile many troops were withdrawn from outlying areas to more strategic strongpoints, while at other times, raiding parties caused many people to go into hiding.

Prior to the war, however, Indians often sheltered around forts such as Laramie for long periods, while engaging in peaceful trade with the European Americans. The reason the Indians were disposed to trade, is because they had already been trading with the French for centuries. The French economy accepted furs and animal products from the Indians, in return for guns, gunpowder, rum, metal tools, and other useful implements.

According to Unruh, during the entire period between 1840 and 1860, over all three major trails across thousands of miles of rugged territory, only about 325 settlers were killed by Indians, while about 426 Indians were killed by settlers.

These figures are hardly indicative of all-out war, let alone a genocidal mentality. Instead, they betoken ongoing restraint and a desire for trade and peaceful relations on both sides. The fact is, the Great Plains were so vast, and the resident Indian population so small, that both groups could choose to avoid each other if they wished, and for the most part—outside of traditional trading areas—that is what they chose to do.

THE CIVIL WAR AND THE LONG WALK

The outbreak of the Civil War in the United States led to a heightening of tensions across the American west. In "Indian Territory" (Oklahoma), the majority of tribes actually sided with the Confederacy, because a minority of wealthy and influential Indians owned African slaves and did not wish to give them up. This however stoked tensions with the few tribes who sided with the Union and, of course, with the Union Army itself.

Many Native Americans enlisted with both the Confederate and Union armies during the Civil War. This was due to the fact that many Native Americans were already skilled warriors and also because the armies would issue regular paychecks. As a result, it is estimated that no fewer than ten thousand Amerindians—a significant portion of the total Native population—enlisted as officers or soldiers during the war. About two-thirds of these fought for the Confederacy.

The Confederate States considered Arizona and New Mexico to be part of their territory; they therefore planned and executed an ambitious campaign of conquest in New Mexico, which took place in the spring of 1861. This soon petered out, however, though the last Confederate militias and other rebel groups were not defeated until 1862. For several years after, the area remained rife with danger for the few US troops in the area, and the maintenance of order was fraught at best.

In this precarious situation, prospects for political opportunism were widespread. Various Mexican forces, Indians residing in both Mexico and the United States, and groups of US and Confederate militia all vied for power in a wide, sparsely populated territory.

One of the most notorious incidents to come out of this tangled history is the so-called Long Walk of the Navajo, which took place as the US Army was attempting to reassert control over the region in 1864.

As with the Dakota 38 incident two years earlier, most write-ups of this event downplay the fact that it was unusually harsh because it occurred during the chaos of wartime. Wikipedia predictably portrays this event as an act of "ethnic cleansing" against the Navajo that was genocidal in its scope.[125] The Native Voices website, funded by the US government, calls the event a "forced removal," in which the US Army drove the Navajo three hundred miles at gunpoint. It quotes from Ruth Roessel's 1973 *Navajo Stories of the Long Walk Period*, in which one Navajo stated that "our ancestors were taken captive and driven for no reason at all. They were harmless people, and even to date, we are the same, holding no harm for anybody."

What these and other write-ups downplay is the fact that New Mexico at the time of the Long Walk was rife with Confederate sympathizers, many of whom were actively attempting to enlist the Navajo to their side. The Navajo of this time were not harmless, as it happens, but rather a band of armed warriors keen to maintain their political independence. They had to be dangerous, because they were continually under threat from Mexican raiders and enemy tribes such as the Apache.

The US government repeatedly gave warnings to the Navajo to surrender and remain near US forts where they could be monitored; if not, they would be treated as enemy combatants. The problem from the Navajo point of view is that US forces failed to provide more than a modicum of protection and necessary supplies in order to keep them from starving. Often times, Navajo livestock were carried off, and US officials were only sometimes able to recover them. This led to increasing frustration with American officials and a desire to maintain independence despite US demands.

Those Navajo who surrendered early and cooperated with the US troops were cared for to an extent in camps, though the conditions in such places will have been appalling by modern standards. Those who did not surrender immediately were made victims of the infamous Long

---

[125] "Long Walk of the Navajo," Wikipedia, https://en.wikipedia.org/wiki/Long_Walk_of_the_Navajo.

Walk—another low point in US-Indian relations. Over the course of dozens of different forced marches, up to nine thousand Navajo were relocated from their homelands to a fort up to three hundred miles distant. Making matters worse, the Navajo arrived to find several hundred of their Apache enemies already stationed at the fort. The lack of food and other necessities soon inflamed tensions between the two groups, leading to numerous outbreaks of Indian-on-Indian violence.

Modern accounts vilify the US Army leaders who supervised the Indian removals of these years. Probably the most infamous of these leaders is the frontiersman Christopher "Kit" Carson. According to history.com, Carson "was responsible for waging a destructive war against the Navajo that resulted in their removal from the Four Corners area to southeastern New Mexico."[126] In this telling, Carson and other US officials were cruel, heartless Army officers whose goal was to exterminate as many Indians as possible.

Few realize that Kit Carson had previously been an Indian agent for the US government in northern New Mexico and southwest Colorado. By all accounts, he discharged this office with a good deal of compassion for the Indians, many of whom he got to know personally and some of whom he befriended.

As an Indian agent, Carson was supposed to help settle disputes among the Natives and generally keep the peace, not least to prevent reprisals against them from white vigilantes. Usually, incidents of vigilantism outside California were contained to lesser offenses than murder, and a great deal of this was due to the efforts of US officials. This is why the number of massacres outside California in these decades remains surprisingly low, especially considering the longstanding tensions between so many different parties.

Carson was given responsibility for protecting the Ute, Apache, and Pueblo Indians in his territory. One of the major problems he faced was

---

[126] "This Day in History—July 07, 1863: Kit Carson Begins His Campaign against Native Americans," history.com, https://www.history.com/this-day-in-history/kit-carsons-campaign-against-the-indians.

the ongoing war between the Utes and the Apaches, and the fact that the Apaches had been responsible for a series of attacks on their Indigenous neighbors as well as nearby white settlers. In 1854 the superintendent of Indian Affairs wrote of the Apaches that "no other single band of Indians has committed an equal amount of depredations upon, and caused so much trouble and annoyance to the people [both Indigenous and white] of this Territory." He concluded, "whenever there is any mischief brewing, invariably the Apaches have a hand in it."

Carson's correspondence has been reported on by Tom Dunlay in his 2000 book *Kit Carson and the Indians*. Dunlay's account of Carson and his world is balanced; it admits that the whites of this time were highly ethnocentric and mostly assumed their own civilization was superior (something that was not always true in earlier periods). Carson believed that the only realistic policy by the 1850s was for Indians to be removed to areas remote from white settlement—i.e., onto reservations. He also repeats the old truth that Indians would have to be enticed to settle down and farm if they were not to starve, since game was becoming increasingly scarce.

However, much of Carson's time was spent settling day-to-day disputes between Indians. He was often preferred by them as a judge. Carson observed that most of the disturbances in the region, including cattle theft, were the work of a few bad apples and that most Indians only wanted peace and quiet. He also argued at various points that the whites in the region were in the habit of cheating the Indians, and "unwilling to do them justice." He saw it as the role of the US government to prevent such fraud and give the Indians a fair price for their merchandise. The role of trusted white traders, including those who intermarried with various tribes, was also valuable to many Indian groups.

Another part of Carson's job was to dole out US-mandated supplies to the Indians under his protection. This was part of an ongoing policy to prevent them from starving, although the logic behind it was not entirely altruistic. Experience showed that hungry Indians were more likely to conduct raids. Having no administrative headquarters, and forced to range around his enormous territory, Carson would often come upon bands of Indians who were "in a very deplorable state." He would provide as many supplies as he could, though the US government's Indian relief efforts were notoriously underfunded—especially during the Civil War. As Carson put it, "if the government will not do something for them to save them from starving, they will be obliged to Steal."

In all, the Carson papers show the situation in much of the west in the later nineteenth century to be a very difficult one. Many Indians had been displaced by the new technologies; many whites were streaming into the region as a result of the same. However, the US government's policy was certainly not to starve them genocidally. It repeatedly encouraged Indians to take up farming or ranching in order to improve their food security, but many groups refused or found the transition too difficult. Having been raised as warriors, many Indian men continued to find the idea of farming abhorrent. While understandable, the persistence of such an attitude was bound to cause additional suffering for Indian bands given the state of the world in the 1860s and '70s. Matters were not helped by the fact that one of the Indian warriors' main pastimes was to raid other tribes' food supplies, leading to a near-continual friction between Indian groups. In the interim, despite many Indians' refusal to settle down and farm, the US government went to considerable lengths to distribute food and other supplies in order to relieve their condition.

THE COMING OF THE RESERVATIONS

Even prior to the formation of the United States, the British and colonial governments attempted to settle various Indian groups east of the Mississippi. Despite the tales of woe that nearly always accompany the history of these settlements, many treaties were honored in the long run, as can be attested by the numerous Indian reservations that exist in eastern states to this day. Many of these date from the seventeenth or eighteenth century.

Many treaties were indeed later reneged upon. Often, however, due to population decline and assimilation, lands that had been set aside as "reservations" were simply divided up into individual lots and given to Indian householders. After this, the land would eventually be sold to non-Indians on the property market.

Participation in the property market, which still forms the basis of many American Indian households today, can hardly be considered a great evil. During the 1820s and '30s, a popular mentality in the United States favored the removal of large groups of Indians farther west, opening land to European American settlement. We have also seen how this mentality was not universal and how it was bitterly opposed by many Americans.

By the 1850s, the idea of "pushing the Indians farther west" was becoming a logical absurdity. Many Americans had by this point reached the West Coast via the western trails, and it was increasingly obvious that there could be no more punting the Indian problem westward in hopes that it would go away. As the west rapidly opened in the years around 1850, the US government scrambled to figure out how to minimize friction between armed settlers and warlike Indians. As a result, the Indian Appropriations Act of 1851 was passed with the aim of providing places for various western tribes to settle.

The goals of the act were to protect Indians from white encroachment, to reserve some Indian land, which would remain legally out of the reach of American land claims, and also to protect European Americans from Indian aggression. It was also hoped that the reservation system would encourage Indian groups to settle down and farm. By 1871, an additional appropriations act had been signed, which ceased to recognize Amerindian tribes as independent political units.

It is entirely understandable, given the Trail of Tears and other treaty abrogations by the US government in recent decades, that many Indian groups were suspicious of various US initiatives toward them. And while in the end definite reservations were settled on, it took several decades of wrangling—often at the expense of Indian rights and claims—before these took a final form.

Many US government officials were openly anti-Indian, but many were not. Prominent figures such as President Grant sympathized with the Indians and did everything they could to ensure an equitable peace. After assuming the presidency from 1869, Grant implemented a new policy toward the Indians, which he dubbed the "Peace" policy. The goal was to minimize the armed conflicts and incidents that had gotten out of control during the Civil War years. A secondary goal was to gain as much intelligence on the state of Indian affairs as possible, in the interest of avoiding future conflict. Grant's policy included the appointment of General Ely S. Parker, a full-blooded Seneca Indian, as the first Native American commissioner of Indian Affairs. Grant also appointed a Board of Indian Commissioners to help ensure that federal commitments to the Indians would be equitably carried out.

Events eventually spiraled out of Grant's control to some degree, though not for want of trying. By some measures, Grant's peace initiative enjoyed success. According to the *Encyclopedia of Indian Wars*, settler-Indian incidents dropped from over one hundred per year in 1869 to a mere fifteen per year by the mid-1870s. The last large-scale conflict was the Great Sioux War of 1876–77, which included Custer's Last Stand. Wounded Knee, mentioned above, was the last coda to this drawn-out conflict with the Sioux.

By 1887, the Dawes Act, or General Allotment Act, was signed into law. This time, the goal was to break up tribal Indian reservations altogether. The policy once again aimed to assign 160 acres of farmland and/or 250 acres of grazing land to each Indian household. This provided Indian households with the same amount of land that was made available to white settlers under the various homestead acts of the same era. The idea that this was prejudicial to the Indians or treated them as second-class citizens can therefore be put into dispute. One supposes that modern critics would have preferred if the average Indian household was given ten times more land than the average non-Indian household?

Perhaps twenty or fifty times more land? There are limits to what a political system can hope to achieve, and it would seem that equity between Indians and settlers—coupled with the fact that Indians continued to benefit from many targeted federal programs—is fairly generous by nineteenth-century standards.

The goals of the Dawes Act were severalfold. First, it would free up a lot of "unused" Indian land for the property market, and in fact some two-thirds of the Indian land base of 1887 was sold to non-Indians as a result of the act. The other aims were to break up tribes, reduce administration costs, and attempt to induce individual Indians to take responsibility for their own betterment. This latter point is obviously a thorny issue, given the subsequent history of Indian reservations in North America. We will see in a later chapter that Indians have, since well before the 1880s, been the recipients of a great deal of US federal funding, which amounts to a welfare system. Reformers of the 1880s already believed that the reservation and tribal systems tended to encourage dependency and decrease the scope for individual initiative.

Left-leaning critics of the reservation system are philosophically at odds with the notion that welfare payments discourage human capital formation. Right-leaning critics meanwhile argue that handouts create a moral hazard that rewards an unproductive lifestyle. They argue that this is why problems such as alcoholism, drug use, and violence have remained endemic in many tribal areas today, while Left-leaning critics invariably blame "racism" or some other systemic wrong—anyone but the alcoholics themselves. The Dawes Act reformers were certainly heavy-handed; but to assume that their arguments had no validity, is to assume that one side of a live political debate is correct while the other side's arguments have zero merit. It's not a very sophisticated point of view.

In the end, the Dawes Act was not fully enforced, and the tribal units were not entirely broken up. Many Indians volunteered to pursue an education at an "American-style" school because they believed this would provide a higher standard of living. In hundreds of thousands of cases, it did. By 1900, the majority of "Indians" were mixed-race, and their culture was extremely hybrid. To discuss "pure-blooded" Indians as though these were some pristine cultural and genetic group that was being ruined by European-American contact is by this point in history rather out of touch with realities on the ground. Cultural assimilation was attempted in many quarters but never "completed," if for no other reason than the United States is not a totalitarian state and democracy found a middle ground to accommodate people who wished to maintain some of their traditions.

By 1934 President Franklin D. Roosevelt had gotten an Indian New Deal passed, whose centerpiece was the "Indian Reorganization Act." The purpose of the Indian New Deal was to reconstitute viable land bases for remaining Indian tribes, with the express purpose of encouraging them to preserve something of their traditional cultures. Things had now come full circle: an American public that used to fear Indians for their violence or despise them for apparent poverty was now—in hindsight—ready to appreciate Indian cultures for the richness these provided to the American experience. Even at the nadir of Indian fortunes at the end of the nineteenth century, some 2 to 3 percent of all US territory remained in Indian hands as reservations, a figure that remains similar today. It is easy to lose sight of the fact that even at the very worst of times circa 1900, American Indians still controlled between two and three times more land per capita than European Americans did. Now, some ninety years on from the Indian New Deal, the Indian population is growing by leaps and bounds, and the American tribal scene is more vibrant than it has been at any time since the nineteenth century. Clearly, the American propensity to evil must have some limits.

THE SLAUGHTER OF THE BUFFALO

One of the most poignant scenes in the 1990 Kevin Costner film *Dances with Wolves* occurs when a band of Sioux hunters on horseback rides over the crest of a hill, only to find a panorama of slaughtered and skinned buffalo left to rot in the sun, stretching as far as the eye can see.

According to Andrew C. Isenberg, author of *The Destruction of the Bison* (2000), it is possible that there were forty million buffalo roaming across the Great Plains of the United States in the year 1800. By 1900, less than one thousand were left. Most of these were slaughtered during the early 1870s, in the space of only a few years. In terms of sheer biomass, it is probably the most substantial and rapid massacre of megafauna ever to occur in global history.

Across the American plains, many groups of Indians made a living from hunting buffalo. They relied on them not only for meat: their skins were used for clothing, mats, and shelter; their bones were used for tools; their horns were used for cups and fire-carriers; their fat was used for candles; and their stomachs were used for waterskins. The effects of the buffalo slaughter on these peoples were immediate and catastrophic to their way of life. Within the space of a few short years, the buffalo-hunting lifestyle became impossible, and the Plains Indians were forced to relocate to farmsteads and reservations reserved to them by the white men.

The modern Left has seized upon this historical event and spun it with maximum ferocity against European Americans. Some public officials and newspaper editors of the 1860s and '70s full-throatedly advocated the extermination of the buffalo, because they saw it as a solution to the "Indian question." Seizing upon this hysteria and hyperbole, activists now charge that the American government, supported by the American public, wanted to starve all American Indians into extinction during the later nineteenth century. This was supposedly done as an extension of their ongoing racist war of extermination and genocide. The overall goal was not merely to starve the Indians but also to seize their empty land for use as capital.

In recent years, prominent magazines such as the *Atlantic* have published exposés on the slaughter of the buffalo; usually these have been sympathetic with the most anti-American interpretations of the event.[127]

---

[127] J. Weston Phippen, "'Kill Every Buffalo You Can! Every Buffalo Dead Is an Indian Gone,'" *Atlantic*, May 13, 2016, https://www.theatlantic.com/national/archive/2016/05/the-buffalo-killers/482349/.

Such accounts invariably focus on the gung-ho pronouncements of men such as "Buffalo Bill" Cody, who made a living out of leading buffalo-hunting expeditions in the 1870s. According to the *Atlantic*, "One colonel...had told a wealthy hunter who felt a shiver of guilt after he shot 30 bulls in one trip: [to which the response was] 'Kill every buffalo you can! Every buffalo dead is an Indian gone.'" This was a popular phrasing of a supposed US Army stratagem. According to the *Atlantic*, the Civil War had reemphasized to US generals the importance of logistics; so, after the war generals such as Sherman and Sheridan began to squeeze the buffalo supply as a means to bring the Plains Indians to heel.

Before we assess how much truth there might have been to this—and the short answer is that there was some—it also behooves us to remember the historical origin and functioning of the Plains Indian buffalo economy.

Only about 10 percent of all American Indians in 1870 actually lived off the buffalo, so the idea that killing the buffalo would starve the majority of Indians is wide of the mark from the outset. Prior to the rapid decline of the buffalo herds in 1870s, certain Plains tribes including the Sioux, Cheyenne, Comanche, Crow, Shoshone, and Blackfoot Indians took a significant portion of their calories and resources from the buffalo herds. They followed these herds on horseback, setting up camp at certain points in the year and intercepting the herds whenever they would need to harvest buffalo for resources. They were therefore, for all practical purposes, nomadic peoples, who were living a sort of augmented hunter-gatherer lifestyle. Prior to the mid-nineteenth century, most of these Plains Indians hunted buffalo with a bow and arrow from horseback, though trade with the French, the Spanish, the Mexicans, and the Americans brought increasing numbers of working firearms into the picture.

The popular imagination (including Hollywood portrayals like *Dances with Wolves*) assumes that these tribes had been hunting buffalo in this romantic fashion since time immemorial. What most people do not realize, however, is that the buffalo-hunting Indians were only able to take up a nomadic herd-following lifestyle *after* the introduction of horses to the Great Plains by Spanish adventurers during the sixteenth and seventeenth centuries. Prior to this, the tribes in question had practiced regimes of mixed farming and hunting, which tended to be more settled and agricultural in fertile parts of the southwest and more nomadic in the less fertile north and center.

The highly romanticized Plains buffalo lifestyle, in other words, was artificial, based on European interventions, and relatively new. It was created by the introduction of European horses, and it was only a few centuries old when it disappeared in the 1870s. Buffalo hunting is therefore not an ancient indigenous practice as many assume, but a perfect example of the hybridization of European and North American culture. To pretend that its passing was yet another blot on the record of Europeans in the New World is to forget that it never would have existed without Europeans in the first place.

The driving force behind the disappearance of the buffalo is the same that drove the near-extinction of African megafauna during the decades around 1900. Namely, the advance of firearms technology during the Second Industrial Revolution. A major turning point came in the 1860s with the introduction of breech-loaded repeating rifles. These could fire much more accurately and frequently than the older-style muzzle-loading weapons that were still in use during the US Civil War. From 1873 the Winchester rifle was mass-produced to the extent that it became the staple firearm of the west. Improvements in cartridges also enabled the classic six-shooter revolver to be introduced.

With new tools came new opportunities for personal enrichment. The mass killing of buffalo increased dramatically during the early 1870s. This was mostly conducted by free-ranging white hunters, who took advantage of the new advancements in firearms technology to supply a massive uptick in European demand for buffalo leather. These hunters were going to kill buffalo for the simple reason that it was lucrative. It is doubtful whether any force on Earth would have been able to stop them in such remote areas, even if the US government was unanimous in its opposition. As with many environmentalist causes since, the problem is that public opinion was divided, so inertia led to an undesirable outcome. Local opinion was likewise divided due to the fact that buffalo hunting was lucrative for an interested minority.

Between 1872 and 1874, more than one million buffalo were killed by white hunters per year. The Indians were also quick to take advantage of the new firearms technology; so, despite their much smaller numbers, they are believed to have killed fully one-quarter as many buffalo as the white hunters. Indian culling of buffalo during these years was therefore not negligible, and it's difficult to reconcile this with ideas of Indian environmentalism. Even if buffalo hunting by whites had been made illegal, it is questionable whether the great buffalo herds could have survived the more efficient killing of them by Indians themselves using the new repeating rifles. And around the globe, including Africa and Asia, the new firearms initiated a precipitous decline in megafauna populations.

For all the press the "killing of the buffalo" receives, the slaying of the bison was not an official policy of the US government, nor did government agencies turn a blind eye.[128] To the contrary, many states and territories in the High Plains had already begun to restrict hunting during the 1850s and '60s, even before the buffalo trade went into high gear. However, the buffalo slaughter rose so meteorically after 1871 that by the time most government agencies could act, much of the damage had been done.

At the national level, there were various conflicts of interest on the buffalo question in the US Congress. Certainly there were some who believed that the last unsettled Indians could be better subdued if the buffalo were dramatically reduced in numbers. Others, however, sought to reduce the wanton destruction of game both for its own sake and because they knew it would cause conflicts with various Indian tribes.

---

[128] John Hanner, "Government Response to the Buffalo Hide Trade, 1871–1883," *The Journal of Law & Economics* 24, no. 2 (October 1981), 239–71, https://www.jstor.org/stable/725325.

As reports of the slaughter grew more alarming in 1872 and 1873, several bills were introduced in Congress that would have restricted their slaughter. By 1874, a law was introduced that would protect the buffalo for the purpose of providing white settlers with meat and of protecting a public resource. As one representative put it:

> The fact is that the value of these animals roaming
> the plains is not to the Indian, but to the settler who
> is compelled to subsist on the meat of the buffalo,
> and who desires this law passed to protect the herds,
> just as you would desire a law passed to protect the
> herds of the East if they were assailed by vandals.

The law stated that it was henceforth illegal for white settlers to kill female buffalo on federal land, and the purpose was to prevent "over-kill" by focusing hunting on male buffalo only. In the end, President Grant was convinced by one of his secretaries to veto the bill, and it was never enacted. However, it should be noted that both houses of Congress passed a bill in 1874 that was aimed at protecting buffalo herds. Their goals might not have been very noble, but the law shows that any desire to "exterminate the Indian" through elimination of the buffalo herds was of secondary importance in the minds of most US congressmen, even during the 1870s.

In sum, Americans have been taught to believe that the mass slaughter of buffalo in the 1870s was the result of a deliberate US policy aimed at starving the remaining American Indians to death. In fact, the US government proved that if anything it was determined to *stop* the buffalo slaughter, or at least render it more sustainable. Congress even passed a law prohibiting the slaughter, in a timely enough fashion that it might have made some difference. Political wrangling saw the law get vetoed and rendered ineffective, but this was not for lack of political will by the majority of US legislators. In addition, only a tiny proportion of surviving Indians lived off buffalo hunting in the 1870s—perhaps 10 percent of all surviving Indians. So the idea that slaughtering buffalo would have harmed the majority of Indians is yet another misconception.

Moreover, US government food subsidies for Indians had been ongoing for decades and continue to the present day. It seems rather daft to accuse the government of attempting to starve Indians out of some sort of racist hatred when the US government had been supplying food to many disparate tribes throughout the later nineteenth century. If the US had any buffalo strategy at all, it was to force Indians to give up buffalo hunting so that they would have to settle down and take up farming. As in earlier periods, it was widely believed that this would solve everyone's problems. Farms would make it easy for the government to enforce Indian property rights; it would entice young Indian males not to range, steal, and raid; and it would make the Indians economically prosperous.

Earlier we debunked a number of other myths about the US treatment of Indians during the bleak decades of the mid-nineteenth century. Far from attempting to exterminate the Indians through the deliberate spread of smallpox, the US government supported a decades-long vaccination project against that same disease—a project that sometimes saw Indian vaccination take precedence over European American vaccination. Rather than massacre Indians on sight, hundreds of thousands of settlers on the Oregon and other western trails actually suffered about the same casualty figures as the Indians. The reservation system, often maligned as "antithetical to the Indian way of life" or worse, was in many ways an inevitable consequence of the end of hunting and gathering in the American west, which itself was determined by the inexorable march of modern technology. A core tenet of the Dawes reformers was to give Indian families the same amount of land that was granted to European American homesteaders.

To argue that any of this is "genocide" is once again to seriously misunderstand the messiness of historical reality, especially in a decentralized democracy such as the United States.

CHAPTER 17

DID THE GOLD RUSH TRIGGER AN INDIAN GENOCIDE?

Peter Burnett, the first governor of California, proposed a war of extermination against Native Americans, triggering rising calls for the extermination of Indians in the state. In California in the 1850s and 60s, an Indian skull or scalp was worth 5 dollars, while the average daily wage was 25 cents. From 1846 to 1873, the Indian population in California dropped to 30,000 from 150,000. Countless Indians died as a result of the atrocities.

—"The American Genocide of the Indians— Historical Facts and Real Evidence," from the website of the Ministry of Foreign Affairs of the People's Republic of China

Benjamin Madley's *An American Genocide: The United States and the California Indian Catastrophe, 1846-1873* has been one of the most influential books on the topic of settler-Indian relations in recent years. It has led to a rebranding of what used to be called the "California Indian Wars" toward a near-universal acknowledgment that what happened in California between 1848 and the 1870s was indeed a "genocide."

California was ceded to the United States by Mexico at the conclusion of the Mexican-American War in 1848. Even before the war was officially over, gold was discovered at Sutter's Mill. This sparked a massive exodus of prospectors, adventurers, and ne'er-do-wells who sought to get rich quick in California.

It has long been recognized that this massive influx of rabble spelled trouble for many among the Indigenous population. As early as 1885, a book called the *Indian Wars of the Northwest: A California Sketch* by A. J. Bledsoe lamented how "the pioneers of civilization, rudely unmindful of the prior rights of those who first possessed the soil, see in the savage inhabitant of a new country only a legitimate object of oppression and injury." Under the influence of Benjamin Madley's prose, the first decades of American presence in California now register as the greatest catastrophe to befall North American Indians at the hands of settlers during the entire history of colonization and displacement. Indeed the "California genocide," as it is now being called, looks fair to topple the Trail of Tears as the most shameful episode in US-Indian history.

Rising awareness of the tragedy of early California history has led to a great deal of soul-searching in present-day California, not all of it unwarranted. For example, the University of California Hastings Law School recently changed its name to "College of the Law, San Francisco." This was done to avoid referencing the name of Serranus Hastings, the first chief justice of California who also—according to Madley—helped to organize and finance some particularly egregious raids and massacres against the Yuki Indians in 1859. These raids resulted in the deaths of up to six hundred Indians in the region, many at the hands of settlers whose express purpose was to kill every Indian they could find.

It is easy to see why Madley's book has made such a splash. The pacing is relentless as its 350 pages describe murder after killing after massacre. The chapter structure likewise provides a ruthless, unrelenting chronology of genocidal intent, with chapter titles such as "Prelude to

Genocide," "Rise of the Killing Machine," and "Perfecting the Killing Machine." A typical incident is described by Madley as follows:

> In the predawn hours of December 31, 1854, as many as 116 militiamen, accompanied by an unknown number of Smith River Valley whites, quietly surrounded Etchulet and took up concealed positions in the brush. At daybreak, as men, women, and children emerged from their houses to begin the day, the militiamen and vigilantes opened fire. They shot them down as fast as they could reload. Unable to see their attackers and possessing only three guns, the Indians could not defend themselves. Amid the carnage, a few evaded the crossfire and plunged into Lake Earl. There too they became targets, and those who swam across the lake encountered a second group of well-armed killers laying [*sic*] in wait. This was a slaughter of men, women, children, and elders—every one in sight. When the shooting stopped, perhaps "hundreds" were dead; not more than five seem to have survived. The attackers apparently suffered only a single casualty.

Clearly, there is no way to excuse behavior like the Etchulet (Achulet) Massacre, and it must be concluded that a great deal of what went on in early California was morally reprehensible. This is true even if many of the participants would argue that they were "at war" with Indians who had precipitated fights by raiding livestock or occasionally killing settlers. The fact of the matter is, while the US Army did sometimes try to protect Indians in California, oftentimes they were understaffed and underequipped, and top Army commanders were not always willing to protect Indians to the extent they should have.

But was it "genocide"?

The major problem with Madley's book lies in its myopic focus on the nitty-gritty of individual killings and slaughters. Madley calls himself a "genocide studies" specialist, and his narrative framework assumes a priori that what happened in California was "genocide." It continually downplays state and federal efforts to corral, disarm, congregate, feed, and protect the Indians; it downplays various ways in which Indians assimilated into California society or fled altogether; it downplays the danger that the Indians themselves posed to settlers at various times, it downplays the distinction between war and massacre; in short it provides hardly any countervailing evidence, despite the fact that Madley's interpretation comes down hard on the side of what used to be considered an extreme interpretation of events.

Madley's purpose in focusing on killings with no mention of Indian wrongdoing or benevolent American officials is obvious: his book aims not at balanced history but at a propagandistic, shock-value impression of what went on during this twenty-year period in California.

The extent of Madley's can be gleaned from an op-ed in the *San Francisco Chronicle* by a professor named John Briscoe, who was prompted by the Hastings dispute to write the following summary:

> Between the first European "contact" in 1542 and 1834, the native Californian population dropped from 350,000 to 150,000. The causes of the population collapse were European diseases, abuse at the hands of the Spanish and suicides. After 1834, however, when the native population plummeted from 150,000 to 18,000 the cause was different: Indian hunting was sport for the mostly white gold-seekers and settlers. Indian-hunting raids nearly annihilated the population and had the added benefit of ridding the state of those who

might assert their land rights, rights guaranteed under international law.[129]

Herein lies the crux: Madley's book gives the impression that in 1849, there were some one hundred and fifty thousand Indians living peaceably in California—but that twenty-odd years later, most of these had been hunted to near extinction for sport by gleefully genocidal white hunting parties, including those organized by Serranus Hastings. This is certainly the impression that the law professor Paul Caron got from Madley's book, and the figure of "100,000 killed" can be found splashed liberally across less-cautious corners of the internet.

The problem is, the number of Indians who were killed outside of active warfare during the entire course of the "genocide" was in reality less than five thousand—meaning that some 97 percent of California Indians were *not* massacred during this time period. A 3 percent slaughter rate is horrendous enough—but it's a far cry from the 88 percent slaughter rate that Paul Caron claims in his blog post.

Not only that, but the 1996 *Cambridge History of the Native Peoples of the Americas*, which discusses the California Indian Wars and other southwestern engagements at length, does not at any point call these conflicts a "genocide."[130] Even the term "massacre" is used sparingly. The authors describe the onset of the "massacres" as a series of military raids which were often provoked by Indian pillaging expeditions. They introduce the situation as follows:

> Shortly after the onset of the gold rush, a number of California Native groups found themselves

---

[129] Paul Caron, "The Moral Case for Renaming UC-Hastings Law School Due to 'Indian Hunting' by Serranus Hastings in the 1850s," *TaxProf Blog*, July 11, 2017, https://taxprof.typepad.com/taxprof_blog/2017/07/the-moral-case-for-renaming-uc-hastings-law-school-due-to-indian-hunting-by-serranus-hastings-in-185.html.

[130] Howard R. Lamar and Sam Truett, "The Greater Southwest and California from the Beginning of European Settlement to the 1880s," in Bruce G. Trigger and Wilcomb E. Washburn, eds., *The Cambridge History of the Native Peoples of the Americas, Volume 1* (Cambridge, UK: Cambridge University Press, 1996), 57–116.

embroiled in a series of skirmishes conducted by local militia or gangs of miners. In 1850, California Governor Peter Burnett authorized the sheriff of El Dorado County to call up 200 men as a volunteer militia to punish Miwoks who had harassed emigrants on the Salt Lake to California trail, and had stolen and butchered their cattle. Over 300 men enlisted and engaged Indians in a series of skirmishes that cost the new state an exorbitant amount of money. A year later in the southern district, a local group organized to fight the Mariposa War, a military expedition that eventually gained the approval of the California legislature. Subsequent militia campaigns launched against California Indians were numerous, some twenty occurring during the Civil War period alone. Instead of solving the problem of Indian livestock theft, however, these expeditions often pushed Native peoples far from their traditional subsistence bases, increasing their dependence on raiding for survival. Anglo-American Californians responded with new invasions, leading to a deadly cycle of violence between Indians and their new neighbors.[131]

Notice there is no talk of genocide here, no discussion of this as though it were a particularly egregious episode. Tragic and sometimes horrific to be sure, but most of what went on was at least somewhat understandable as a response to Indian raiding, given the anarchic and violent situation on the ground.

Since the *Cambridge History* represented the mainstream of historical opinion on the California Indian Wars prior to the appearance of Madley's book in 2016, this should be more than enough to give us

---

[131] Lamar and Truett, 98–99.

pause before we rush with the likes of Briscoe and Caron to call the event a "genocide." Madley himself resorts to claiming that the "genocide" of his text has been "hiding in plain sight"—despite decades of serious scholarship that concluded against using this term. Cautious and scientific historians know better than to take a single author's interpretation as grounds for completely upending a century or more of historical interpretation. While such a reinterpretation sometimes proves to be warranted—the fact is, other authors will have to sift through this mountain of references before their true scope can become apparent. Preferably this will be done by authors who have not decided a priori that the California Indian Wars were a "genocide."

Instead of sober reflection, however, what we have encountered in the California genocide debate is a species of internet-driven presentism, which falls over itself in order to embrace the most radical possible interpretation of events. Good history, it ain't.

SPANISH AND MEXICAN OPPRESSION

As with other Indian population figures we have encountered, a basic problem is that we have no idea how many Indians were actually living in California when Mexico ceded it to the United States in 1848. We also have no idea how many fled the state and how many intermarried or otherwise assimilated with the Mexican American and European American populations. All of these are significant variables that call for caution. The main population figures that we have are based on the estimates of a few early nineteenth-century adventurers, who went around to the various Spanish missions and counted some of the Indians who were living there.

According to our best guess, before the arrival of the Spanish in the 1760s, there were perhaps three hundred thousand Indians living in California. The great majority of these lived in the fertile central valley and certain coastal regions, since this provided the Natives with an abundance of food. Early observers noticed that while California itself provided some of the most bountiful sustenance anywhere in North America, the California Indians were among the most "primitive" of all North American people. The going theory is that the abundance of food, in this case, made life so easy that the Indigenous people of California did not bother to innovate. Instead, they took advantage of the Eden-like conditions to live relatively simple lives.

All this changed with the arrival of the Spanish during the second half of the eighteenth century. The principal goal of the Spanish missions in California was to establish a presence that might help ward off the English and Russians, who had been sniffing around in the northern reaches of the territory. Because they were organized under ancien régime Spain, the various religious orders—especially the Franciscan friars—were given authority over the California Indians.

The principal goal of Father Junipero Serra and other missionizing friars was to encourage the local Indians to live near Spanish missions, where they could be taught the Holy Catechism, the use of writing, and basic techniques of farming. The missions distributed food and clothing, and reduced intertribal violence by keeping order and dispensing justice. In Mexico, such a system had been in place for several centuries, and the Indigenous population, so far as anyone understood in the 1760s, had adapted to this institutional framework with a minimum of difficulty.

Junipero Serra used to be held up to California school children as a benign bringer of civilization to California. He was even sainted by Pope Francis as recently as 2015. In recent years, Serra's overly rosy reputation has plummeted—sometimes quite literally. During the 2020 iconoclasm, for example, a major statue of Serra was pulled from its pedestal in San Francisco's Golden Gate Park. The mission system over which Serra presided has recently been likened to a series of "concentration camps," outposts of white supremacy, and loci of slavery. Native activists have taken to decrying them as "places of death" to local newspaper reporters.[132]

---

[132] Carly Severn, "'How Do We Heal?' Toppling the Myth of Junípero Serra," KQED San Francisco, July 7, 2020, https://www.kqed.org/news/11826151/how-do-we-heal-toppling-the-myth-of-junipero-serra.

Serra himself wrote a set of instructions to mission overseers, dictating that the Indians should be physically punished for infractions against the system. This was hardly unusual, since both recalcitrant monks and petty criminals were similarly punished during the eighteenth century. Of course, Serra's quote has been taken out of context, and this has been used to paint him as an anti-Indian sadist.

But there is no need to see Serra as a particularly evil man. In his canonization speech, Pope Francis defended Serra as a defender of Indigenous people against some of the harsher abuses to which they were subjected by Spanish and Mexican overseers—and in this the pope is absolutely correct. In general, the historical record bears out Serra's reputation as a mild-mannered but determined administrator. He certainly ordered whippings and shacklings of recalcitrant Natives, and it is arguable that the entire process of luring Indians to the missions—and later keeping some of them there by force—was misguided. All the same, from a humanitarian point of view, there have certainly been worse men in history than Junipero Serra.

Probably the major problem with the mission system is that it concentrated California Indians into particular locales. This rendered them that much more susceptible to European diseases—though, as we have seen, it also made it easier to administer vaccines as these became available. At the same time, the system did provide shelter, clothing, protection, and a regular quantity of calories to the Indians, all of which meant that their numbers did not collapse precipitously for several decades, despite their increased susceptibility to disease.

Another frequently cited problem with the Spanish mission system was the fact that it treated Indians as second-class citizens. They were definitely under the authority of the Franciscans and other Spanish officials, and they were subject to forced-labor requirements similar to a medieval peasant. Newspaper articles paint this labor regime as "brutal" but in reality, it was probably no more harsh than that endured by many wage laborers in the eighteenth and nineteenth centuries. Experience in Spain shows that labor on church estates might be lax or harsh, depending on the individual personalities and local traditions involved. But it is true that the mission system gave ample scope for abuse and was hardly conducive to encouraging self-reliance.

According to the sources we have, it seems that a major downturn in the California Indian population occurred during and after the Wars of Mexican Independence, which broke out in 1810 and carried on until 1821. Soon after independence, the Mexican governors then proclaimed the "secularization" of the mission system in California, although this proved a decidedly mixed bag for the California Indians. Under the Mexican system, California Indians remained subject to forced labor by secular landowners who rapidly purchased the old mission lands.

It was the Mexican government, then, that created the custom whereby Indians could be indentured and "sold" for their labor. Under this system, Indian children were often sold outright as slaves. The Mexican custom was carried over into the American period, and it became the grounds for much abuse. What few writers wish to emphasize is that this indentured servitude was outlawed by the California legislature as a follow up to the Emancipation Proclamation in 1863—less than fifteen years after the Americans took over in California. It took another decade, partly due to the lack of resources brought about by the Civil War, for this emancipation to be effectively enforced however. In the chaos created by the harsh and anarchic situation left by the retreating Mexican government, a great number of California Indians seem to have disappeared—to the extent that a population, formerly three hundred thousand strong, melted away, mostly during the brief Mexican period between circa 1810 and 1848. By the time the Americans got hold of the territory, the Indian population in California is believed to have been between one hundred thousand and one hundred and fifty thousand people. Of course, modern critics opt for the higher number because this makes the Americans look worse.

What happened to the approximately one hundred and fifty thousand California Indians who disappeared during the last few decades of Spanish and Mexican rule in California? No one knows for certain.

As the mission system broke up, many Indians were subject to forced relocation, and birth rates probably fell precipitously. At the same time, the dissolution of the old mission system likely encouraged many Indian families to flee. Most likely, since they were familiar with the Spanish language and institutions, these Indian families fled farther south toward the more "civilized" parts of Mexico. Throughout this process many groups fought with one another, and in the interest of protecting their own meager food supplies, many Indian groups will have set upon stragglers who wandered through their lands.

Madley does spend a few pages discussing the fate of the California Indians under the Spanish and Mexican regimes, and he notes that there is a debate in certain circles as to whether the mission system and its breakup constituted a genocide. It seems that the number of Indians who disappeared from California prior to 1848 was equal to or greater in number than the Indians who disappeared after 1848. In this regard, then, the Spanish and Mexicans seem just as culpable of destroying the California Indian population and culture as the Americans who came after them. The fact that we have fewer records of outright slaughter from the Spanish and Mexican periods does not mean that these things did not happen.

However, the main reason Madley and others are less keen to throw the Mexican government under the bus for its treatment of the California Indians—even though they "killed" at least as many Indians as the Americans did—is that many of the Spanish and Mexican officials who mistreated the California Natives were themselves Indigenous or part Indigenous. By the 1820s, most Mexicans were mixed-race; yet here they were, mistreating California Indians alongside the most egregious European taskmaster. This is a rather glaring case of cherry-picking to fit the narrative.

In order for Madley's "California genocide" story to be complete, it has to be understood in its entirety—not simply by focusing on the twenty-five years that make white European Americans look worst. It has to be fully acknowledged that the Indian population dropped precipitously during the Spanish, Mexican, and American periods. This will require historians to acknowledge that race and racism are not really arguable as causes of slaughter and decline to nearly the extent that modern popularizers wish to portray.

What about the population figures themselves? How certain can we be that California contained three hundred thousand Indians in 1760, one hundred and fifty thousand in 1848, and twenty thousand in 1880? How sure can we be of Madley's death toll, which he claims was over ten thousand Indians? Once again, we cannot really be sure of these figures at all. Sherburne F. Cook, for example, estimated that the California Indian population had fallen from one hundred and fifty thousand in 1845, to one hundred thousand by 1850, and fifty thousand by 1855, which surely indicates a mass exodus rather than genocide.[133] As Madley himself relates, Cook estimated some forty-seven hundred deaths of California Indians during the course of the Indian Wars. Madley goes on to more than double that in the appendices to his book, which are available online.

To his credit, he is cautious with many of his figures, and discounts many of the wilder reports. But the appendices are presented in an extremely awkward format that trickles out his data on "killings" across nearly two hundred pages and leaves little room for fact-checking. There is a strong possibility that many reports of Indian deaths were exaggerated by the "hunters" out of sheer bravado or in pursuit of a financial reward, and there is undoubtedly double-counting involved, to a significant degree. The most incriminating appendix is Appendix 3, which purports to show something in the neighborhood of ten thousand Indians murdered at the hands of nonfederal US forces.

How many of these were double-counted and how many exaggerated is difficult to tell, but it does seem credible that at least half this figure were actually killed over the period from 1846–73. How many of these were killed during "wars" of various kinds in which Indians were

---

[133] Sherburne F. Cook, *The Population of the California Indians, 1769–1970* (Berkeley: University of California Press, 1976), 44.

resisting with armed force is difficult to make out from the way Madley arranges the material, and one suspects that this was done on purpose to blur the line between military and nonmilitary engagements. Cook for his part estimated that "military deaths" outstripped civilian massacres (which he called "social homicide") by a ratio of some six or seven to one—a figure which Madley seems to reverse.[134] Naturally, Madley's highball estimate of sixteen thousand dead is the one which now makes all the headlines, including a major write-up on history.com, and mentions in several newspapers and university publications.[135]

The fact is, many Indian groups knowingly and willingly went to war rather than submit to some type of sedentary existence. Among the various raids and battles that this situation created, we have the Gila Expedition of 1850, a "costly failure by California militia to punish the Yuma for the Glanton Massacre, that nearly bankrupted the state." (John Glanton was a European-American murderer and scalp hunter who richly deserved his fate at the hands of the Yuma.) We can also mention such conflicts as the Owens Valley Indian War, which after innumerable campaigns resulted in the deaths of some two hundred Natives, and about sixty American soldiers. It is difficult to call such actions "massacres" in any traditional sense of the term.

In sum, the breakup of the mission system meant that the political situation in California was highly unstable to the point of anarchy when the first Americans began to arrive en masse. The Mexican system was already rife with abusive legislation, including the notion that Indians could be indentured and essentially sold as slaves. This idea of Indian slavery was not an American invention as is often portrayed; in fact by 1870, the Americans made this custom illegal. But during the first two decades of American presence in California, the anarchic political situation provided plenty of opportunity for adventurism, vigilantism, and

---

[134] Sherburne F. Cook, *The Conflict between the California Indian and White Civilization* (Berkeley: University of California Press, 1976 [orig. pub. 1943]), 262–67.

[135] Erin Blakemore, "California Slaughtered 16,000 Native Americans. The State Finally Apologized for the Genocide," history.com, June 19, 2019, https://www.history.com/news/native-american-genocide-california-apology.

other forms of outlawry associated with the Wild West. The sheer chaos of the situation helps to explain why historians prior to 2016 were reluctant to pronounce the whole affair a "genocide," but rather to see it in terms of a society in flux.

A RETURN TO NUANCE

All told, the worst period of violence in California lasted less than twenty years. Much of the stage for this abuse was set by the Mexican government's secularization of the mission system and the indentured labor system that it created. Many of those who bought, sold, and abused Indians in this period were part-Indigenous Mexicans. Undoubtedly, it was a time of sorrow for many California Indians, and it was one of the most shameful episodes in the entirety of American history. But other forces besides racism and white supremacy were at work. By the time the United States government got more control of the situation in the 1870s and '80s, most of the violence was over, and an era of consolidation and coexistence could begin.

After the 1870s, the major "problem" faced by Indians in the coming decades was the enforced education of their children in an effort to incorporate them into American society—an issue we will take up in the next chapter.

When confronted with scholarship such as Madley's, a final and very serious question arises. We can see from the website of the Chinese Ministry of Foreign Affairs quoted at the beginning of this chapter that such scholarship undoubtedly justifies real, ongoing modern-day genocides in the minds of Russian and Chinese officials, by making US and Western claims of moral superiority seem hollow. This makes it far easier for non-Western officials to justify present-day massacres and deflect Western protests based on humanitarian grounds as baseless posturing. "You were just as bad as us," they can rightly say after reading Madley et al. Thus, it is arguable that while modern "genocide scholarship" has done next to nothing to help the plight of modern-day American Indians (who as we will see are already the most highly compensated group in the US today), it has real "blood on its hands" when it comes to ongoing genocides and massacres from Ukraine to Tibet, and from Syria to Sudan. This is where academic historians sometimes need to step back and think through the full implications of what they are doing before grinding their ideological axes with such single-minded fury.

***

In Part III we have debunked a number of myths about the nature of colonial English and American expansion between roughly 1600 and 1900.

The idea that the first Thanksgiving is a cause for shame and mourning is likewise demonstrably false. Narratives that claim otherwise are guilty of deliberate misreading of the meager sources for early New England history. Most of the history of early New England was surprisingly peaceful; most of the time, both Indian and New England authorities managed to keep violence from boiling over. Indian desire to trade with Europeans was extensive and drove much of this interaction.

Most of the time, the colonists did not steal or cheat the Indians out of their land. The standard way to acquire land from the Indians was therefore to purchase it from them; this was done in almost every instance east of the Appalachians that was not occasioned by the outbreak of war. Indians for their part were not naive or gullible dupes; they were well able to understand the nature of these transactions and usually able to drive a good bargain.

In Pennsylvania, William Penn inaugurated over half a century of fair dealing with the Indians known as the Long Peace, a period of good relations, which is almost universally ignored.

In New England, colonists set up several layers of jurisdiction to protect Indians; they almost immediately set up Praying Villages to teach them to farm and to provide them with enough property to set up as farmers equal to any colonist. Others set up schools for the Indians, to which many Indian parents voluntarily sent their children. As a result of this exchange, European ideas permeated Indian culture, just as European tools and weapons had done.

Many Indian children grew up alongside European pupils and often thrived and intermarried with their neighbors. A great percentage of the "missing Indians" of this time period were simply assimilated into the local European population, which is why so many East Coasters have trace amounts of Indian blood even today.

Colonists were not consistently "racist" in any meaningful sense of the term toward the Indians. French and other traders were welcomed by tribes across North America and often married into those tribes with the blessing of Native elders. This resulted in a significant métis population, from whom were drawn many prominent chiefs of the nineteenth century.

The American Founding Fathers have been frequently abused of late. But in dealing with Native Americans, they showed a great deal of humanity and wisdom, as their writings and actions demonstrate.

The Trail of Tears occasioned one of the most heated debates ever witnessed in US history, anticipating the heated rhetoric over slavery that was soon to characterize US public life. Some members of Congress were so incensed by the removal policies of Presidents Jackson and Van Buren that they left the United States altogether.

Despite the horrors and inhumanity of the removals, perhaps 5 percent of the Indians who moved actually died; this compares favorably with the death rate of settlers on the Oregon Trail, which was higher. Even before the removals, the US government offered relatively generous terms to various tribes who left voluntarily, including offers of land, cash payments, annuities, and ongoing government support.

During the entire period of the Oregon Trail, contrary to Hollywood portrayals, only a few hundred settlers and an equivalent number of Indians were killed during violent disturbances, despite the fact that hundreds of thousands of settlers were on the move into Indian territory. Most of the period was characterized by a surprising level of restraint on both sides.

In California, the Gold Rush of 1849 led to a mass migration of settlers into previously highly populated Indian country. The result was several decades of war and massacre that left several thousand Indians dead and resulted in one of the darkest chapters in the history of US-Indian relations. All the same, many of the casualties claimed for this period in fact occurred under Spanish or Mexican rule. And even Madley's figures show that maximally only about 10 percent of California Indians were massacred or killed during the conflict period, against frequent internet claims suggesting 80 percent or more.

In Part IV, we turn to contemporary issues, including the question of whether or not educating Native Americans in "modern," European-dominated culture is morally justifiable. This issue has recently rocked Canada, causing major cultural upheaval and leading to the vandalization of numerous historical monuments. We then turn to the question of "cultural appropriation" and whether this has any meaning outside a critical theory context. Finally, we look at the question of continuing poverty and violence in some Indigenous communities, and whether or not additional compensation or "reparations" would be helpful at this juncture in history.

IV

CONTEMPORARY ISSUES

CHAPTER 18

DID EUROPEANS COMMIT CULTURAL GENOCIDE?

*It is true that I did not use the word because I didn't think
of it...but I described genocide. I apologized, I asked
forgiveness for these actions...which constituted genocide.*

—Pope Francis condemns the Indigenous school
system in Canada as "genocidal," July, 30, 2022[136]

Between roughly 1860 and 1996, about one hundred and fifty thousand Indigenous children across Canada were taken from their families and sent to what were known as "residential schools." The stated goal of this system was to provide a basic education for Canadian Indigenous children, which would put them on a par with the rest of Canadian children. The creation of the residential school system was part of a late nineteenth-century vogue for creating public school systems, which spread across the developed world. These systems formed the basis of the public education system that is standard in most countries across the globe today.

---

[136] "'You Can Change the Pope': Pope Francis Says He'll Slow down or Retire." *Euronews*, 30 July 2022, https://www.euronews.com/2022/07/30/its-not-a-catastrophe-you-can-change-the-pope-pope-francis-says-hell-slow-down-or-retire.

For all their obvious flaws, the creation of public school systems across the globe has been one of the most unalloyed policy successes in human history. Study after study shows that every year of education increases a child's lifetime earnings and their IQ, and dramatically increases their life expectancy. An educated populace radically increases national GDP, lowers crime, increases equality, and fosters technological innovation. Education, as almost every politician will aver, is a win-win scenario.

Of course, some schools are run better than others, and the experience of individual children can vary widely. In the late nineteenth century, discipline was apt to be harsh to the point of sadism; school buildings served as vectors for incurable and deadly diseases, and sexual abuse was sometimes rife. These criticisms are true of public school systems across the world, whether we are speaking of Japan, India, the UK, the US, or Canada.

The Canadian residential school system, for its part, was open to these types of abuses for a number of reasons. First among these was an attitude among school authorities toward Indigenous people that has been described as "patronizing, feckless, ill-considered, and generally ineffectual benignity."[137] In other words, while most school officials were well-meaning, their attitudes contained a great deal of condescension, coupled with occasional nastiness and abusiveness. It did not help that the system was chronically underfunded and that many of the individual schools were located in truly remote areas. The schools were set at a considerable distance from the children's homes, because school officials found that when children were located within walking distance of their parents, the children tended to abscond in the night in a (sometimes ill-fated) attempt to return home.

By the later 2010s, the Black Lives Matter movement was galvanizing Indigenous activists across the globe to take advantage of the favorable shift in public sentiment. To this end, some Indigenous activists

---

[137] Conrad Black, "Centuries of Failed Policy Does Not Equal Evil Intent," op-ed in Canadian *National Post*, July 17, 2021, https://nationalpost.com/opinion/conrad-black-centuries-of-failed-policy-does-not-equal-evil-intent.

gained state funding to search for the bodies of children who—it has been alleged—were murdered and "disappeared" from various Canadian residential schools. Like the California missions, the Canadian residential schools were rebranded as "concentration camps," in which children were deliberately housed in inhumane conditions, until they died and were disposed of with nary a whisper to family and friends.

Then, in May 2021, a "war graves expert" using ground-penetrating radar at the behest of various Indigenous groups claimed to have found about two hundred unmarked graves on the site of the Kamloops Indian Residential School in British Columbia. The effect of the report was immediate and explosive. Though no actual remains had yet been found—and in fact it was subsequently concluded that there were no bodies at the area in question—Prime Minister Justin Trudeau immediately denounced the residential school period as a "dark and shameful chapter" in Canadian history. British Columbia Premier John Horgan said that he was "horrified and heartbroken" to learn of a burial site with 215 children, and he claimed that this highlighted the violence and consequences of the residential school system.

By May 30, 2021, the Canadian federal government lowered all flags to half-mast and later instituted a new holiday to honor "missing" children and survivors of residential schools. Before a single body had been confirmed, the United Nations urged Canadian authorities to conduct a "thorough investigation," and Amnesty International demanded prosecutions of those responsible for the missing people. The Chinese government had a field day with the news, broadcasting the supposed sins of the Canadian government on *China Daily* and other websites.

Meanwhile, in June and July 2021, a series of historic buildings associated with residential schools—mostly churches—were burned to the ground in a wave of arson and iconoclasm that gripped Canada. Once again, Prime Minister Trudeau all but approved, noting that the arsonists' actions were "understandable." At the height of the hysteria, the ten-member board of the Canadian Historical Association got in on the act, declaring on the day before "Canada Day" (July 1) that:

> The Canadian Historical Association, which represents 650 professional historians from across the country, including the main experts on the long history of violence and dispossession Indigenous peoples experienced in what is today Canada, recognizes that this history fully warrants our use of the word genocide.

While Pope Francis initially resisted calls to condemn the Canadian residential school system as "genocidal," he eventually relented, and by July 2022, he publicly endorsed the use of the term "genocide."

MASS HYSTERIA VS. HISTORICAL REALITY

The case of the Canadian residential school system shows that mass hysteria is alive and well in the twenty-first century. A few years ago, we believed that this sort of thing belonged to the seventeenth-century era of the Salem witch trials, or at least to totalitarian states such as Nazi Germany and Maoist China. We now know that modern Western countries remain just as susceptible to versions of mass psychosis as any historical society. Most of us are aware that the internet has created a new golden age for the spread of disinformation, but as of now, there seems precious little anyone can do about it that would not do more harm than good.

By calling the residential school system genocide, Pope Francis and the Canadian Historical Association create a very dangerous precedent. Not only does this sort of pronouncement fall right into the laps of modern-day, genuinely genocidal totalitarian governments and their propaganda machines, but they also set the bar for "genocide" shockingly low, as we will now demonstrate.

In comparison with the more violent history of Indian-settler relations in the United States, the history of Indian-settler relations in Canada was demonstrably tame. The Wikipedia page recording "massacres in the history of Canada" contains only a dozen incidents in the entire three hundred years between 1600 and 1900. Almost all involve less than a few dozen victims. Moreover, about half of these were perpetrated by Indians on settlers. There are numerous military engagements and raids that one could add to this list, including among the Dutch, French, and English and their allies in seventeenth-century Acadia, as well as many smaller incidents that go unrecorded. But even if this list is somehow missing 90 percent of the Indian-settler massacres in the history of Canada, the Canadian Left has a tough job making a case for actual genocide.

With few actual massacres to publicize, the Left-wing Canadian Historical Association turned to another weapon in the arsenal of victimhood—so-called cultural genocide. This is what Pope Francis had in mind when he spoke of the residential school system as genocidal—and although it employs the same word for political ends, it is already a far cry from genocide of the physical, murderous type.

The idea behind cultural genocide is that a dominant group (usually Europeans) intentionally tries to snuff out the culture of a "subaltern" group (usually Indigenous people). The Canadian Historical Association alleges that most of this cultural genocide took place from the 1870s onwards, when the Canadian government decreed that Indigenous children would have to go to public school. As this was the Victorian era, these schools were often strict, suffused with Christian messages, and served as hothouses for the spread of disease. Children therefore died at the schools in what we would today consider shocking and tragic numbers, just like they did at every boarding school during that time period.

As has been shown by several writers familiar with the subject, the intention behind the residential school system was never to eradicate or exterminate Native Canadians or their culture. The Canadian professor Jacques Rouillard of the University of Montreal called the whole affair "a genocide without victims," referencing the fact that no murders or suspicious deaths had ever been proven at the hands of residential school officials, despite a massive search.[138] Canadian publisher and author Conrad Black likewise argued that just because the school system ended up a semi-disaster by some measures does not mean that the intentions behind it were evil.[139] Almost everyone involved believed that their primary mission was to educate Native children: to teach them to read and write so that they could get jobs, improve their lot, and become full-fledged members of Canadian society.

There is nevertheless a kernel of truth behind the cultural genocide argument, despite the fact that the term "genocide" represents a gross distortion of what really went on. In the early 1800s, many Native Canadians and Native Americans were living largely traditional lives. By the early 1900s, most of these traditions were gone or rapidly fading. Much of the blame for this loss does lie with mass education systems created by Western governments and propagated by nineteenth-century missionaries. But is it fair to call it "genocide"? Or is this purposely—and damagingly—inflammatory?

A BRIEF HISTORY OF INDIGENOUS EDUCATION

The crux of the cultural genocide argument hinges on the question of whether it is wrong to educate Indigenous people in traditions that are not their own. This sounds like an easy one to answer: of course it is wrong! But almost immediately, the ship of cultural purity runs aground.

For example, there are many who insist that anyone who educates Indigenous people in the language of the colonizers is committing cultural genocide just by using the wrong language. Irish nationalists have been arguing this for centuries, and some Indigenous activists continue

---

[138] Professor Jacques Rouillard, "A 'Genocide' without Victims? Is the Latest 'Woke' Offensive against Canada about to Collapse?" *History Reclaimed*, January 19, 2022, https://historyreclaimed.co.uk/a-genocide-without-victims-is-the-latest-woke-offensive-against-canada-about-to-collapse/.

[139] Black, "Centuries of Failed Policy Does Not Equal Evil Intent."

to argue this today. The obvious downside of educating someone in a language with few speakers—as for example Welsh speakers sometimes find today, however, is that it can be a recipe for isolation, poverty, and intractable social problems.

Thankfully for today's hundreds of millions of descendants of historical Indians, Europeans did not set up an educational apartheid system, where they attempted to shelter Indigenous people from the knowledge that Europeans had inherited from previous civilizations. Instead, they made thousands of attempts across the centuries, usually stemming from humanitarian impulses, to help Indians improve their lives and their communities through education.

Long before the residential schools and their American equivalent were set up in the later nineteenth century, thousands of European settlers had been attempting to better Indigenous lives through education. A glance at some of the many schools run by Europeans for Indigenous people over the course of colonial history reveals not merely a history of stern taskmasters and cruel patriarchs but also of concerned educators and teachers who often treated Indigenous children like their own. The products of those schools went on to become some of the most celebrated Indians in North American history. Nineteenth-century educational reformers were well aware of centuries of success emanating from the education of Indigenous children, many of whom became leaders in the Indigenous community. To accuse these educators of cultural genocide is not only wrong, it's desperately ignorant.

In Quebec City, a school was set up for Indian girls as early as 1639 by a pair of Ursuline nuns named Marie de l'Incarnation and Madeleine de la Peltrie. This school was independent from most church oversight and run by women, so it can be seen as a major step in feminine empowerment in the history of Canada. The women did all they could to clean and feed the Indian girls who were left in their care. They report that most girls came in covered from head to toe in lice.

The teachers learned Indian languages and taught Indian children to write in their Native tongues as well as French. They wrote dictionaries and books of religious instruction in multiple Native languages including Montagnais, Algonquin, Huron, and Iroquois. Far from attempting to eradicate the Indian languages, they assumed that these languages would be active in perpetuity—just like Arabic or Chinese. They believed that teaching the Indians to read and write their own languages would empower them to negotiate on the same level as the French, thus protecting their property rights and their political sovereignty. The Ursuline School survived until recent times.

In New England, missionaries such as John Eliot not only learned Native languages but also spent a good deal of time teaching Natives how to read and write in their own languages. Eliot and others wished to give Indians title to their own lands by setting up so-called Praying Indian villages, which were administered by Native councils. Cynics call this "eliminating indigeneity," but reading the letters left by these missionaries and activists, a sympathetic reader recognizes that their goal was often to augment and empower indigeneity, not to eliminate it.[140] One goal was to educate them as preachers and lawyers as a way to provide them with weapons to be eloquent in the defense of their land against the possible encroachments of white settlers.

In Boston, Eliot founded a school for Indians, African Americans, and European children that survives to this day as the Eliot School for Fine and Applied Arts. Eyewitness accounts show that Indians were commonly seen in the streets of Boston and other English settlements in early colonial America, and Eliot assumed this would continue to be the case. A provision in Eliot's will specified that Indian and African American children should be admitted to the school without prejudice.

---

[140] According to Pekka Hämäläinen, Eliot and others like him were "trying to peacefully eliminate Indigeneity." Is that fair? Is that sweeping, cynical assessment the best we can say about him? Could we perhaps say that he was trying to help the Indigenous people of New England cope with the realities of a rapidly globalizing world, in a way which would most redound to their own benefit? "Indigeneity" was bound to disappear or at least alter profoundly as soon as contact with the rest of the world was sustained. Nor should it be forgotten that many Natives—perhaps the majority—wanted this contact to be sustained. See Hämäläinen, *Indigenous Continent: The Epic Contest for North America*, Chapter 11.

Peter Folger of Martha's Vineyard was the maternal grandfather of Benjamin Franklin. He was also a passionate educator, who ran a local school in which Indian and European children were educated side by side. The children grew up together under the Puritan code that all souls were created equal. Folger was a pacifist, a poet, and an interpreter of local Indian languages; his poem the "Denunciation of War" chastened the colonists, encouraging them not to go to war even in the face of recent massacres instigated by the Indians.

One of Folger's students was Caleb Cheeshahteaumuck, who later graduated from Harvard Indian College. Before attending Harvard, Caleb moved from Martha's Vineyard along with his fellow Indian pupil Joel Hiacoomes, where he attended a grammar school in Cambridge, Massachusetts, run by Elijah Corlet. In Corlet's school, as in Folger's, Native American pupils were instructed in the same curriculum as European children.

Designed to cater to American Indian needs at the northern colonies' only university, Harvard Indian College was founded in 1656, only twenty years after Harvard itself. The building and the students were maintained through charitable benefactors from across England and New England, who wished to further the improvement of Indian lives. Beginning in 1663, the college printed the Eliot Indian Bible, translated by John Eliot into the Massachusetts tongue.

Caleb Cheeshahteaumuck graduated from Harvard Indian College in 1666. Another graduate was John Wompas, who had been born among the Nipmuc Indians of central Massachusetts. Wompas was adopted by an English family in Roxbury and married an Indian girl named Ann Prask in 1661. Prask had inherited a significant chunk of land from her father, and Wompas used this patrimony to launch a successful career as a land speculator.

Wompas eventually attended Harvard from 1666–68 and, perhaps lured by the tales of faraway lands that he encountered in his reading, became a merchant sailor. He used some of the money from his land speculation to purchase trade goods, including African slaves. Many

Indians took to a maritime life in early New England. One researcher has recently uncovered mention of dozens of Amerindian sailors in the New England fishing and merchant fleets in the seventeenth century.[141] It is likely that these records are only the tip of the iceberg.

At various times Wompas served as an advocate for Indian rights to Massachusetts land, although one imagines him being primarily self-interested. He even managed to obtain an audience with King Charles II of England. While in London, Wompas received from the king a letter ordering the governors of Massachusetts to respect the property rights of the Indians. Wompas later died in London while seeking a second royal audience. At his death, he left a fair amount of New England land to various associates, most of them Englishmen. However, he did leave some to his Nipmuc kinsmen John Awassamog, Norwaruunt, and Pomhammell. Some of their descendants and beneficiaries still own the land today.

It is difficult to argue that Wompas would have been better off without any European-style education. On the contrary, his story is typical of thousands of Indians who were born in the woods but subsequently built and navigated a hybrid Indian-European culture in colonial America. Wompas' life was successful by any measure—even compared with the biographies of most European-American settlers. And yet modern "pro-Native" activists see it as a source of shame.

By the later eighteenth century, a substantial portion of the most influential Indians in American history would be profoundly impacted by Old World ways of thinking. Leaders such as Tecumseh, Sequoia, John Ross, and Major Ridge would never have cut the towering figures they did without access to European-style education. Such life stories only hint at the positive effect that Western-style education has had, and continues to have, on Native Americans and their descendants.

Like the mestizo of Mexico and the métis of Canada, the Indigenous people of the United States are a hybrid both physically and culturally.

---

[141] Pulsipher, Jenny Hale. "The Digital Archive of John Wompas." (2017). https://scholarsarchive.byu.edu/data/2/.

To pretend otherwise, is as disingenuous as to suggest that the Canadian residential schools were a bad idea at their core.

WAS IT GENOCIDE?

To call the education of Indigenous children "cultural genocide" is to ignore the complex history of cultural interaction that had often been occurring long before any formal educational regimes were set up in a given region. Throughout the history of European settlement in America, many Europeans dedicated their lives to the education of Indigenous children, because they believed fundamentally in the value of education to empower and transform Indigenous lives, and to help them become productive members of the global community. Modern-day activists will call this shortsighted, and in various ways it undoubtedly was. But overall, one would be hard-pressed to argue that the average experience of Indian children in Western-style schools made them worse off in the long run. To pretend that the entire school system was fundamentally a bad idea is not only to misunderstand these historical people's motives but also to misconstrue or ignore the universally proven power of education itself.

It seems as though modern critics of the residential school system would have preferred Indian children to grow up illiterate, with hardly any chance of getting a mainstream job or of impacting modern culture through writing, teaching, or advocacy. Such criticism ignores the abuse and poverty that might have occurred at the hands of parents and relatives on the reservation, and ignores the fact that schools often provided better nourishment and health care than might have been available at home. The "genocide" crowd's silence on these fundamental points is deafening. Indeed, what would Pope Francis, or the Canadian Historical Association, have proposed in place of the residential school system, and would it stand any realistic chance of improving children's lives?

Rather than kowtow to political faddism such as the #CancelCanadaDay hashtag that trended on Twitter in the summer of 2021, august institutions such as the Canadian Historical Association and the Catholic Church must take the responsible route of refusing to play fast and loose with historical truth. Politicians too, especially prime ministers and premiers of Canadian provinces, should observe a bit of decorum and respect for the history of their own institutions, in the face of those whose principal goal is to make the government of Canada look bloodthirsty and rapacious beyond all historical reality. When major institutions lose sight of historical reality and reason, the world slips rapidly into anarchy.

Meanwhile, the Left commits another fundamental error by pretending that cultural hybridization is one-sided. As we will see in the remaining chapters, the impact of American Indians on mainstream American culture has been far greater than the large population disparity between the two groups might suggest.

CHAPTER 19

IS USING NATIVE AMERICAN NAMES "CULTURAL APPROPRIATION"?

Far from being a trivial issue, the trend [of wearing Indian headdresses at music festivals] reminds indigenous peoples of all the more serious crimes and indignities they have been subjected to over the past 500 years. Even after their land was stolen and vast numbers were killed, the remaining Native Americans were not granted full citizenship until 1924, and their religious rights were not protected until 1978. Tribal chic treats them as other: exotic creatures in their own land.

—Dorian Lynskey, "This Means War: Why the Fashion Headdress Must Be Stopped," *Guardian*, July 30, 2014

By the mid-2010s, news outlets began to decry the newly fashionable sin of "cultural appropriation." According to Britannica.com, "Cultural appropriation takes place when members of a majority group adopt cultural elements of a minority group in an exploitative, disrespectful, or stereotypical way." According to Leftist cultural pundits, when a non-Indian wears an Indian headdress to a party, this triggers Indigenous people into remembering all the "serious crimes and indignities that they have been subjected to for 500 years." The *Guardian* journalist Dorian Lynskey—who so far as one can tell is of European descent—"whitesplains" to us that headdress-wearing also leads to stereotyping. It does so by erasing distinctions between various Indigenous groups, as it disrespects Indigenous culture in general.

By the late 2010s, the cultural appropriation movement drove the United States into a full-scale erasure of any and all vestiges of Amerindian culture. Insider.com ran a list of "things you should never say to a Native American," alleging that saying things like "powwow" or "spirit animal" within earshot of your Indigenous friend might cause them grievous psychological harm. Schools banned "Indian" Halloween costumes—long a staple of the holiday—and Thanksgiving parties were likewise nixed. As one mother on romper.com put it:

> Last year, my daughter's preschool decided to have a Thanksgiving party. I reached out to the director of the school to let her know that our family is Indigenous and that I would love to come talk to the class about what that means. I anticipated a smooth interaction, one woman of color to another, but she told me that as she herself was "part Indian" (1/30th Cherokee, she said), she did not need my input or guidance around what the children need to know or what would be considered offensive. Needless to say we took my daughter out of that school and they proceeded to have their Thanksgiving party, complete with construction paper headdresses, tomahawks and facepaint. This isn't an unusual occurrence—these kinds of "parties" happen every

year—but parents need to understand why it's not
OK to dress kids up as "Indians" for Thanksgiving.

Pressure from busybody parents and activist groups forced many
venerable sports teams to change their names. The Cleveland Indians
first dropped their decades-old Chief Wahoo logo in 2018, and continuing pressure forced them to change their name to the "Guardians" as of
2021. The Washington Redskins likewise were forced to drop their name
in 2020, changing it to the "Commanders." Across the United States,
dozens of colleges, high schools, and primary schools with Indian names
or logos felt pressured to drop any representation of American Indians.

Before we assess the validity of these arguments, it might be instruc-
tive to turn our attention to the question of cultural appropriation in
Mexico and other Latin American countries.

CULTURAL APPROPRIATION IN MEXICO

The Mexican Day of the Dead has become famous the world over for its
combination of macabre skull imagery and vivid Indigenous costumes.
These symbols clearly mark the Day of the Dead as a survival of Aztec
religion. At the same time, the Day of the Dead is celebrated on the eve-
nings of November 1 and 2, which is centered on All Soul's Day in the
Catholic calendar. Like much else in Mexico, the Day of the Dead represents a unique fusion of Catholic and Indigenous religious practices.

Is it cultural appropriation for Mexicans to celebrate the Day of the
Dead? The first challenge arises because it is difficult to determine who
is "dominant" and who is being "oppressed" by this holiday. Clearly, the
Catholic religion became dominant over Indigenous religions in Mexico,
so it could be argued that the Day of the Dead is a Catholic appropriation of Indigenous culture. At the same time, one could argue that the
Day of the Dead is respectful of the Indians, because it actually took care
to incorporate Indigenous symbolism and many other subtle elements,

rather than riding roughshod over Native religion altogether. (This was also true of Catholic expansion into other regions of the globe.)

The ethnic mix of Mexicans today adds further difficulty to the problem of determining who is "dominant" or not. Since the majority of Mexicans are mestizos, it makes good sense for them to celebrate a hybrid holiday such as the Day of the Dead. Meanwhile, Indigenous Mexicans living separately sometimes preserve elements of their own culture that are more local and not nationally celebrated like the Day of the Dead. Furthermore, there are fully European Mexicans and mestizos who might choose to celebrate the Day of the Dead because it is something their community does—or they might not.

According to the standard American logic on cultural appropriation, Mexicans should divide themselves up by race in order to determine whether or not it is appropriate for members of their particular group to celebrate the Day of the Dead. Presumably, our activist friends would argue that a European Mexican who celebrates the Day of the Dead is guilty of appropriating Indigenous customs, while for a mestizo Mexican it is okay. What an Afro Mexican is supposed to do is anybody's guess. The situation becomes a reductio ad absurdum if we begin to take into account each individual's unique racial mix.

The same thing applies in the United States. Who, for example, should be allowed to wear a Native headdress? Could a half-Indian wear one? Even if they are not a member of a tribe? Must they only wear them for official religious ceremonies? What percent of Indian blood does one have to have in order to use words like powwow, wampum, or tipi? Once more we run into a reductio ad absurdum. The only real choice we have is either to allow Indian symbolism to proliferate because people find it fun and/or meaningful in their own ways or attempt to squelch the proliferation of Indian symbolism by claiming racism, colonialism, and the like. At present, at least in the United States, the killjoy faction is winning the battle, but it's not at all clear that this is good for anyone.

WHO INVENTED CULTURAL APPROPRIATION?

Before turning to the history of Indian representation in United States culture it behooves us to spend a moment digging up the origins of the concept of cultural appropriation. No points will be awarded for guessing when and by whom it was invented. Like most of the problematic concepts we have addressed, the idea of cultural appropriation first started kicking around academic circles in the late 1970s or early '80s, coming into vogue as part of a subgenre of critical theory known as "postcolonial theory."

Postcolonial theory is based on the (originally Marxist) idea that society neatly divides into camps of oppressed and oppressor. As we have seen, critical theory believes a priori that "the system" is predicated on the oppression of a minority by a dominant group. It therefore assumes that any cultural action by the dominant group must further the oppression of the minority.

But what happens if we don't accept postcolonial theory and its Marxist assumption of a "system" based on the oppression of a minority by a dominant group? What if we imagine instead that democratic society is plural, a place where many groups act as vectors of power and influence, and where individuals of different groups play many different roles? What if we recognize that every person may be "privileged" in some ways, relative to some people, while at the same time being less privileged in others?

As soon as we reject the ham-fisted Marxist logic that lies behind cultural appropriation, the idea that a "white chick wearing a headdress" is necessarily bad is no longer a priori true. Like a breath of fresh air, the sweeping away of Marxist cynicism and empty Leftist rhetoric opens the possibility that if Lana Del Rey wants to wear a headdress, then it might just be cool, or symbolic, and indeed, even respectful of Indian culture and a reminder of what has been lost in the American West. The alternative, as we shall see, is the complete erasure of Indian culture from the

United States—ironically the same kind of erasure that activists accuse Western civilization of fostering.

This more realistic approach also reminds us that what happens in the real world is usually more a question of cultural amalgamation rather than cultural appropriation. When the Left cries "cultural appropriation!" it reifies culture as though it were a permanent and unique expression of a particular race or ethnic group. But as we have demonstrated in the previous chapter, culture in the real world is in a permanent state of flux; it always involves give-and-take and adaptation. Indians in America continually changed their styles of dress, for example, as new contacts introduced them to new materials and concepts. Who is to say that what Mohawks were wearing in the 1700s (after European contact) was any less "authentic" than what they were wearing in the 1500s (after direct and indirect contact with groups across large parts of North America)? Language, toolmaking, religious beliefs, systems of kinship, food, styles of dress, all of these things are forever being spread and borrowed by various groups, to varying degrees. Although each human group may have distinctive traditions that it may wish to preserve, it is in the nature of culture not to be fixed but fluid and adaptable. Contrary to much critical theory essentialism, culture does not exist to express an immutable essence of fixed identity but to facilitate commerce and interaction between human groups.

The United States has long been a premier adopter of culture as a tool of political unification. As a country with immigrants from every corner of the globe, America has a genius for embracing and incorporating different aspects of its immigrant cultures into the mainstream. This is a mark of respect and inclusion, not of racist domination. To read it otherwise is to fetishize Indigenous culture in a way that is profoundly unhistorical.

A BRIEF HISTORY OF INDIAN REPRESENTATION IN AMERICA

Many will argue that the American adoption of Indian names and iconography is merely a psychological defense mechanism—a way expiating guilt and justifying crimes. They argue that the Thanksgiving myth, for example, was spun primarily to "whitewash" settler atrocities and to make it look as though the Indians were willing participants in the takeover of their continent. This narrative can sound convincing on the surface, which goes a long way toward explaining its popularity in recent years. A deeper look at how Indian names and imagery became an iconic part of mainstream American culture, however, reveals this narrative to be yet another gross simplification.

One of the first major representations of Indians in American popular culture was the Indian Head penny, which was the most common coin in the United States between 1859 and 1909. The coin was an instant hit with the public and has remained one of the most popular American coins of all time. Featuring a noble Indian woman in a feathered headdress with the word LIBERTY across its band, the coin was designed in 1858 by the engraver James Barton Longacre. Prior to 1859, most American coins featured a bust of Lady Liberty with a freeman's cap, taken from classical Greco-Roman models. In justifying his novel design, the engraver Longacre wrote the following:

> From the copper shores of Lake Superior, to the silver mountains of Potosi from the Ojibwa to the Araucanian, the feathered tiara is as characteristic of the primitive races of our hemisphere, as the turban is of the Asiatic. Nor is there anything in its decorative character, repulsive to the association of Liberty.... It is more appropriate than the [Roman-inspired] Phrygian cap, the emblem rather of the emancipated slave, than of the independent freeman, of those who are able to say "we were

never in bondage to any man." I regard then this emblem of America as a proper and well defined portion of our national inheritance; and having now the opportunity of consecrating it as a memorial of Liberty, "our Liberty", American Liberty; why not use it? One more graceful can scarcely be devised. We have only to determine that it shall be appropriate, and all the world outside of us cannot wrest it from us.

A couple of points stand out. First, Longacre (correctly) believed that the feathered headdress was common across large parts of the United States—not only in a few tribes as is often claimed today. Feathered headdresses can be found not only across North America proper, but they were also integral parts of Aztec and Incan iconography as well. Secondly, Longacre intentionally rejected European symbolism (the Phrygian cap) as being inappropriate to the New World. He wanted to see Indigenous culture represented in mainstream America—precisely what many of today's activists accuse European Americans of failing to do. Thirdly, Longacre meant the coin to immortalize the perpetual independence and freedom of the Indians, which could even be read as a pro-Native political statement.

The end of the nineteenth century saw a massive upswing of interest in Indian culture. The first studies on Indian ethnology, including those of Clinton Hart Merriam, began to appear in the decades before 1900. The opening of the Smithsonian in 1846 led to a bourgeoning interest in collecting Native artifacts and stories, and the Smithsonian was already employing Native American ethnologists such as Francis La Flesche by the 1880s. Meanwhile the National Park movement and photographs by the likes of Carleton Watkins inspired many Americans to travel out west and see the beauties of the country for themselves. Fascination with the Indian past (and present) built as a result of this and other factors, inspiring many people to dedicate their lives to preserving what they could of Indian culture.

The fighting skills of the Indians also attracted the interest of a number of British and American officers, most famously Robert Baden-Powell, the founder of the Scouting movement. Baden-Powell was influenced by another Indian enthusiast, Ernest Thompson Seton, who founded a group called the Woodcraft Indians. Seton was born in England and immigrated to Toronto in Canada; he later traveled west before settling down in New York and Connecticut. As director of the Boy Scouts of America between 1910 and 1915, Seton was responsible for including many Native American elements in the philosophy and habits of the Boy Scouts. Today, of course, this is considered an egregious sin, and write-ups of the early Boy Scouts are full of claims of "appropriation" and "stereotyping." Indiancountrytoday.com ran an article in 2019 claiming that the Boy Scouts have been "one of the worst culprits" of cultural appropriation in American history.

From the earliest editions of the Scout manuals, Indians feature as guides and role models. Indians are credited with knowing the location of the pole stars, seldom getting lost in the woods, making fires without matches, being athletic, being expert hunters and bowmen, purifying water, practicing good hygiene, being experts at canoeing, being expert trail blazers and markers, being expert soldiers, being as courageous as a Roman soldier, being able to face death with a smile, being fiercely loyal to allies, and dozens of other skills that were thought to be lacking in European American boys and girls. The Boy Scouts arguably set up a racial and/or cultural hierarchy, in other words, in which the American Indian was superior to the European.

The perceived martial prowess of the American Indian was incorporated into the symbolism of the United States armed forces as they rose to world prominence during the early twentieth century. The US Army's 45th Infantry is known as the Thunderbirds; the First Battalion, Fifth Marines are known as Geronimo; this was also the cry of paratroopers as they jumped out of planes into combat. Most US military helicopters are named after Indian tribes; the Tomahawk cruise missile is an icon of modern warfare. During World War II, the Navajo Code Talkers fought alongside the US Marines in numerous campaigns across the Pacific, providing invaluable service. From the Civil War to the present day, the warrior ethos of Amerindian culture has led an above-average number of Indians to enlist, meaning that American Indian people are overrepresented in the US military relative to other groups. Today's poisonous liberal narrative threatens to break that long-held tradition—and to deprive many Native Americans of a major historic avenue of social mobility.

THE ERASURE OF THE AMERICAN INDIAN?

With the rise of America to global dominance in the mid-twentieth century, the American Indian became an icon of global culture. People in Asia, Africa, Europe, South America, and Australia all became familiar with the stereotype of the rugged, stoic, tough warrior-scout who used to roam the American west. For a numerically tiny people, this arguably amounted to a major public relations coup—and a tremendous mark of honor and respect. To this day, American Indian symbolism is common throughout Europe, even among students and householders who seldom set foot outside urban areas.

One of the greatest complaints made by the Left regarding Indigenous history is their claim that too many people want to "erase" Indigenous people from historical narratives. But is it not possible that the activists who complain about the erasure of American Indians from history are complicit in the greatest PR disaster that could ever befall any group: the destruction of a hugely important, respected, and ubiquitous image? The American Indian once beloved and revered the world over is rapidly becoming invisible in mainstream culture—the result of the too-liberal application of the questionable doctrine of cultural appropriation.

Ironically, it is mostly non-Indian, self-proclaimed "allies" of Native Americans who vociferously push this movement to erase the Indian from mainstream American culture. By erasing popular reference points such as the Cleveland Indians and Halloween costumes, they risk relegating the American Indian to even greater historical obscurity and cultural irrelevance.

American Indians should think twice about the rush to embrace this particular application of critical theory. The majority of Indian-related symbolism in American culture was intended to portray Indians in a positive light. In the absence of such symbolism, popular memory fades fast. In twenty years' time, it seems likely that Indians will have evaporated from mainstream culture altogether—except perhaps as hapless, perpetual victims.

CHAPTER 20

ARE NATIVES OWED REPARATIONS?

*This is all stolen land.... We are landless Indians in our
own territory. The only compensation for land is land.*

—Corrina Gould, spokesperson for the
Confederated Villages of Lisjan/Ohlone

O
pportunists across the world are using the distortion of global
history to agitate for the redistribution of wealth, land, and
political power to "indigenous tribes." They recognize that the
wave of guilt spread by critical theory has created an historic opportunity
for personal gain that might never be seen again.

As Canadian professor Frances Widdowson chronicled in her 2008
book *Disrobing the Aboriginal Industry*, most of the people who benefit
from this redistribution are not even (majority) Indigenous themselves
but rather a gaggle of lawyers, opportunistic politicians, contractors, and
bureaucrats who stand to gain from politicized efforts to "make repara-

tions" for perceived historic wrongs.[142] Of the Indigenous people who do benefit, many are wealthy business owners and tribal leaders who fail to redistribute gains to the majority of their constituents.

Of those who do not stand to benefit directly from the transfer of huge sums of federal money, many who advocate are non-Indigenous pundits and academics who have taken up the cause out of intellectual curiosity and political zeal. Many of these advocates are not even historians, but political scientists and lawyers who, in their ignorance of historical complexity, take the stolen land narrative as gospel.

The weaponization of history by identity activists stands to gain a handful of people trillions of dollars' worth of capital to the detriment of nearly everyone else.[143] Before irreversible harm is done to the public purse, it behooves us to look at the history of Indian reparations, and the possible repercussions of ceding land and political power to individual tribes.

REPARATIONS IN THE UNITED STATES

Native Americans make up about 1.5 percent of the American population, though the borders of this population are very fuzzy due to questions

---

[142] Widdowson was, until recently, a tenured professor at Mount Royal University in Calgary, Canada. She has written many books and articles about the Canadian Indigenous industry and remains a lonely voice who aims to detail precisely who benefits from the political opportunism surrounding Indigenous rights. She is on record criticising BLM and also suggesting that the Canadian residential school system had provided at least some benefits to its pupils. In the aftermath of the George Floyd riots, however, she was fired despite holding tenure. In a subsequent interview with the *Montreal Gazette*, she said that although she was not surprised that she was fired, she was nonetheless "shocked at how much the university had deteriorated over the past year and a half for that to happen." Jessica Mundle, "Calgary Tenured Professor Critical of Black Lives Matter Has Been Fired," *Montreal Gazette*, January 5, 2022, https://montrealgazette.com/news/canada/calgary-tenured-professor-critical-of-black-lives-matter-has-been-fired.

[143] There is even a website called historyisaweapon.com, which lists Howard Zinn, Malcolm X, Noam Chomsky, Eric Williams, Immanuel Wallerstein, and several other authors featured in this book on its "essential reading" list. It also prominently features the quote "White people scare the crap out of me" by Michael Moore. The irony being that the people who maintain the website accuse mainstream historians of weaponizing history, as an excuse to justify their own militant weaponization of history.

of tribal membership and the prevalence of mixed heritage. Members of this 1.5 percent are about twice as likely to live in poverty as the average North American household.[144] Fertility rates are high, as is often the case with impoverished and under-educated households. Whereas about 80 percent of adult Americans possess a high school diploma, only about 70 percent of Amerindians do. While about 25 percent of Americans hold a bachelor's degree, only about 11.5 percent of Native Americans do so. The education gap also turns into an employment gap; Amerindian households experience more than double the national unemployment rate on average, while in some reservation communities incidence of unemployment is as high as 35 percent.

On the social side of things, Amerindian individuals are particularly likely to experience a "range of violent and traumatic events involving serious injury or threat of injury" to themselves and are also very likely to witness similar traumatic events. Of all American racial groups, Amerindians face the highest likelihood of becoming the victim of a violent crime. This prevalence of crime is also associated with gang involvement, alcohol and drug use, suicide attempts, vandalism, theft, and truancy. Alcoholism on reservations stands at about seven times the national rate. As though this weren't bad enough, Amerindian youths were more likely to be killed in a motor vehicle accident than other teens; they also report the highest incidence of risky behavior related to automobile use such as never wearing a seatbelt (44 percent of youths reported this), and drinking and driving (40 percent reported this).

These are serious and traumatic statistics, and any humane person who reads statistics like these will be moved to, at least, formulate in their minds a plan of action that they would undertake if they were in a position to help. The knee-jerk reaction from those on the Left will be to blame historical racism for these woes, while those of a more centrist

---

[144] Most of these statistics are pulled from the influential 2008 article by Michelle Sarche and Paul Spicer, "Poverty and Health Disparities for American Indian and Alaska Native Children: Current Knowledge and Future Prospects," *Annals of the New York Academy of Sciences* 1136, no. 1 (2008), 126–136, https://www.ncbi.nlm.nih.gov/pmc/articles/PMC2567901/.

or Right-leaning bent will likely blame the government handouts and dependency created by the reservation system.

Given the social catastrophe that is ongoing on so many Indian reservations, anyone not beguiled by the CRT racism narrative will find themselves wondering whether the reservation system was a good idea after all. The question becomes: What price cultural identity? Would it not have been better for today's descendants of Indigenous Americans if the US government had broken up the tribal system altogether and insisted on Western-style education for Indigenous children? From the perspective of millions of women, children, and other victims of violent crime and trauma on reservations, the answer is most likely: Yes, they would have been materially better off growing up in mainstream society.

Those who call for reparations and additional compensation for Amerindian households often point to these appalling statistics as a rationale for shoveling more money into tribal pockets. But these advocates ignore a major gap in their reasoning: Amerindian households experience the greatest number of social problems of any racial group in America, at the same time that they have long been far and away the most compensated group in American history. In other words, all that money has so far done nothing—except perhaps to cause more problems.

Reparations and support for the Indians began in the seventeenth century, when hundreds of churches and charitable groups set up foundations to provide food, clothing, shelter, education, legal representation, and political sovereignty to Native Americans. This represents a massive outpouring of resources and goodwill—the extension of a massive pro-Indian safety net by the so-called colonizers—which today goes almost entirely unrecognized. We have seen hints of this in the numerous schools and charities that were set up in every US colony and state, wherever Indians could be found. We have seen further hints in the efforts of missionaries and intellectuals to sway public opinion against the Indian removal policy of the 1830s through the 1850s.

Meanwhile the United States Bureau of Indian Affairs was created in 1824 with the purpose of protecting the Indians from settler encroachment and helping them to achieve peace and prosperity. Though there are many reasons to view this mandate cynically, the bureau nonetheless did a lot of good as its role continued to expand, and it continues to be a positive presence in the lives of many Amerindians today.

The bureau's main function was to administer federal transfer payments (welfare) to American Indians, and arguably, in the later nineteenth and early twentieth centuries, this helped to avert a much greater humanitarian disaster than we in fact witnessed.[145] Of course we can find countless instances of corruption, graft, paternalism, indifference, and inefficiency in the long history of the bureau, but nevertheless a good deal of food, medicine, education, shelter, and other benefits have been enjoyed by millions of Amerindians as a result of its existence. Many commissioners over the decades have been competent and even zealous in their desire to protect and ameliorate the condition of the Indians.[146]

By the end of the nineteenth century, private charitable groups actually took the lead in spearheading efforts to raise Indians out of poverty. The goodwill of these "friends of the Indians" is hardly to be doubted, though we now consider many of their ideas outdated and even counterproductive.[147] Suffice to say that the benevolent efforts of well-meaning Europeans we have mentioned remain the tip of a charitable iceberg stretching back to the time of Columbus.

The financial compensation of Amerindians by the US federal government began in earnest during the nineteenth century. Much of this history has been chronicled by Stephen J. Rockwell in his book *Indian Affairs and the Administrative State in the Nineteenth Century*. Though Rockwell's book is predictably critical of US Indian policy, between the lines what emerges from his study is a picture of a very robust system

---

[145] As a Keynesian economist, I am not averse to the notion that government intervention is sometimes a useful fix when an economy or group gets into a tight spot.

[146] A good reference point for how the US government attempted to work with Indians in the aftermath of the creation of the reservation system is chapter 18 of the abbreviated edition of Francis Paul Prucha, *The Great Father: The United States Government and the American Indians* (Lincoln: University of Nebraska Press, orig. pub. in two volumes in 1984; single abridged volume, 1996).

[147] Prucha, 1996, ch 13.

of transfer payments made to Indian people throughout the century. According to a report by the Cato Institute:

> The federal government provided health services, food rations, infrastructure, and farm implements to Indian tribes. It provided courts and police to some reservations, and it made regular annuity payments to tribes as a part of treaties. In 1819, Congress began annual appropriations of $10,000 for a "civilization fund," part of which went to missionary groups to "civilize" Indians. Until 1822, the federal government provided subsidized goods to tribes through the "factory" trading system.

The Dawes Act of 1887 has already been mentioned in a previous chapter. It saw the creation and codification of additional annual payments in cash and kind. Many tribes were already receiving regular annuities from the US government decades prior to this. This has led some to observe that Native Americans were the first Americans to receive regular welfare payments—some sixty years before the New Deal guaranteed basic stipends to every American citizen.

Members of a US tribe were considered members of "domestic dependent nations" and wards of the state until 1924. Since that time, they have been legal citizens of the United States, with all the rights to welfare, Medicare, Medicaid, Social Security, and other benefits that came to entail.[148] In 1934, the Indian New Deal began the process of returning tribal sovereignty—including the lucrative power to adminis-

---

[148] The Indian Citizenship Act of 1924 was meant to express gratitude to all those Amerindians who fought for the United States armed forces during the First World War. Opinion has remained divided as to whether or not it was a good thing for Indians to accept US citizenship; modern activists find it a convenient way to lambaste the US government for either granting citizenship and "stripping Indians of their separate political identities" or else not granting it sooner. The only thing one can be sure of in a democracy is that someone will complain even if leaders take the best available course of action. This is all part of the game, however, and it's better than any alternative.

ter mineral rights—back to various tribal groups. It also allocated additional federal funds to create make-work projects on reservations and helped ensure that Indian culture and language would be incorporated into reservation schools. It created additional funds for health care and farming assistance. It furthered the practice of hiring Indians or part-Indians to run the Bureau of Indian Affairs. While this makes sense on some levels, in other ways this practice has been likened to hiring a fox to guard the hen house. In a relatively small community it is virtually impossible to avoid significant conflicts of interest.

Since the 1970s, the changing attitudes of the American public have encouraged the federal government to pursue a policy of "Indian self-determination." Generally speaking, this has allowed for increasing tribal input in decisions impacting their affairs. This "hands-off" policy has concentrated power in the hands of a few interested individuals, and the result has been predictably high levels of corruption and misappropriation of funds. According to a report published by downsizinggovernment.org:

> In 2011, the Department of the Interior's Inspector General (IG), Mary Kendall, testified to Congress about the "gross program inefficiencies at many levels of Indian Affairs and in tribal management of federal funds." The IG described, for example, how the BIA funded a fish hatchery at a reservation for fourteen years and yet no fish were hatched. Eventually, a BIA official visited the reservation and found that the alleged hatchery was actually a real estate development that the tribes had been funneling taxpayer money into.

> In another incident, the BIA spent $9 million for public ferryboat service in Alaska, but the money was redirected to a private tour boat operation. And in Montana in 2011, ten people—including

BIA employees—were indicted for a decade-long scheme that embezzled $1.2 million from a tribal lending program operated by the Fort Peck Tribe.

The IG found that in one BIA region, millions of dollars were wasted on road projects that were never completed. She noted that "internal management controls were so broken down that wage-grade employees were earning over $100,000 a year, with overtime, without explanation." On one of the road projects, $2.4 million had been spent, but the IG couldn't find any of the work that was supposed to have been done.[149]

In modern America, the public is well aware that being a member of an Indian tribe can bring significant economic benefits. The Google search bar brims with questions such as "How do I get money for being Native American?" "How do I claim Indigenous status?" and the like. Many people perceive their Indian heritage as a sort of golden ticket to a free ride at the expense of the US taxpayer.

In addition, members of Indian tribes benefit from the enormous budgets of the modern Bureau of Indian Affairs and its sister organization the Bureau for Indian Education. Both of these exist to provide additional welfare to registered tribe members and, in some cases, other people who can claim Indian ancestry. According to Indian Country Today, the total budget allocated to American Indians comes to more than $20 billion per year, equivalent to about $20,000 allocated per Indian in the United States.

During the Obama administration, more than $3.3 billion was given out by the federal government in response to longstanding lawsuits with various tribes. For example, in 2016, a payment of more than $492

---

[149] Chris Edwards, "Indian Lands, Indian Subsidies, and the Bureau of Indian Affairs," *Downsizing the Federal Government* blog, February 1, 2012, https://www.downsizinggovernment.org/interior/indian-lands-indian-subsidies.

million was awarded to seventeen Amerindian tribes, many of which have only a few thousand members. The awards per member are therefore often substantial. These lawsuits were expressly settled as reparations payments to make up for the breach of historical treaties and the historical mismanagement of tribal resources.

Other disputes are still ongoing, such as the Black Hills case of the Great Sioux Nation. In this case, the Sioux claim about six thousand square miles in the Black Hills region of South Dakota, based on the 1868 Fort Laramie Treaty. Some Sioux subsequently went to war with the United States after the treaty was signed, inflicting defeat on US forces in the Battle of Little Bighorn, which caused Congress to revoke the treaty. Acting on changed sentiments in the 1970s, the Sioux sued the United States for the abrogation of Fort Laramie, and in 1980 they won a Supreme Court case upholding their right to the land. The court awarded a cash settlement in lieu of the land, but the Sioux opted not to settle, since this would terminate their land claims.

Meanwhile, the money has been accruing compound interest in a bank account and is estimated to be worth well in excess of a billion dollars. Despite this, the Sioux have been busy pursuing their land claims and have managed to secure nearly one-third of the six thousand square miles in question. It is hoped by many tribe members that they might eventually gain both the land and the compensation awarded in 1980.

In addition to these federal payments and subsidies, members of many tribes are eligible for payouts and dividends from the management of tribal land, casinos, mining rights, and so forth. As of 2015, about one-fifth of American tribes had annual casino revenue of between $10 and $25 million, which for many tribes enabled per capita payments in the thousands of dollars.

It is estimated that about one-fifth of all Americans receive welfare benefits and that the average payout is about $35,000 per year. Welfare programs tend to be run at the state level. Meanwhile, Indians living on reservations are eligible for a combination of state-level welfare plus the federal and tribal benefits accorded above. The total package of Native American benefits, even for those who are not eligible for state-level welfare, can easily exceed the compensation received by non-Native welfare recipients.

On the flip side, those who live on reservations often do not own their own land or even their own houses. This renders many of them perpetual renters, with all the incentives to neglect property that this entails. Many have theorized that this "enslavement through welfare" at the national, state, and tribal level is to blame for persistently high levels of poverty, alcoholism, mental illness, and other social issues detailed above.

The land controlled by American Indian tribes today is often dismissed as negligible, but this is mere posturing. As the reservation system was finalized in the later 1800s, Native Americans remained in possession of some 2.3 percent of all United States land, even though they numbered less than 0.3 percent of the US population at the time. Despite a bourgeoning population since 1900, tribally registered Native Americans remain in possession of more land per capita than non-Native Americans of any other background. That land, at over 2 percent of the US property market, is today valued at $700 billion. Hardly a drop in the bucket.

In all, there seems to be little need or rationale for further monetary compensations for Native Americans—certainly not for compensation driven by journalistic sensationalism and political agitation. What legal claims remain on the books can and should be decided through the courts. By far the majority of actionable claims already have been adjudicated, and there should be the end of it.

Meanwhile, Natives have been and continue to be the recipients of enormous welfare programs at the federal, state, and tribal level for the better part of two hundred years—far longer than any other group. Every year, they receive far more benefits than, for example, black Americans on a per capita basis, not least because of the wealth built up by some tribes. The pressing need, as many administrators have recognized, is for this great wealth to be managed in a way that maximizes benefits to individuals, incentivizes social improvement, and minimizes corruption. That is a laudable goal that should be pursued in lieu of political opportunism.

NOT STOLEN: TOWARD A BALANCED HISTORY OF EUROPEAN COLONIZATION

The arrival of the Spanish caused a massive demographic collapse in the population centers of the New World, particularly in greater Mexico and greater Peru. A century later, the arrival of the French and the English caused similar population collapses on the East Coast of North America, which gradually spread west across the continent. The Spanish administration of Hispaniola and other Caribbean islands proved an unmitigated disaster for the Indians of the region, as these were subjected to forced labor, forced relocation, wanton cruelty, and even enslavement at the hands of ill-governed adventurers. The Spanish conquest of the Aztecs and the Incas was a civilizational disaster that permanently derailed the autonomous development of New World culture. In the Spanish conquest of Mexico, easily one hundred thousand people died from the direct consequences of war and the real number might have been double or triple this amount.

From the first arrival of English traders in North America, the English were prone to be suspicious, standoffish, and supercilious toward various Indian groups. Individual merchants attempted to cheat Indians whenever they thought they could get away with it, and double-dealing was a frequent fact of life when it came to treaties with the Natives. Sometimes, outright frauds such as the Walking Purchase were perpetrated in order to strip Indians of their land claims. Settlers took advantage of their higher concentrations of population, their political organization, their access to firearms, their literacy, and their desirable products in order to gain the upper hand in negotiations with the Indians throughout the colonial period.

Continuous encroachment and occasional bad behavior sparked periodic conflicts with the Indians, conflicts that might result in a massacre of settlers but that usually turned out worse for the Indians. While colonial governments attempted to maintain a separation of the two peoples and a political status quo, in the longer run the simple fact of overwhelming colonial population meant that the Indians were inexorably pushed over the Appalachians. In the south, the US government signed treaties with the Five Civilized Tribes, while in the north and west, the Iroquois and other tribes were slowly driven before the encroaching settlement by a process of squatting, land purchases, and occasional open warfare.

The discovery of gold in North Carolina and Georgia in the 1820s put tremendous pressure on the southern governments to "remove" the Indians across the Mississippi, where for a generation it was naively believed they would find a permanent home. The election of Andrew Jackson in 1828 saw the triumph of the Indian-removal party, which precipitated the series of forced migrations on the southern tribes that came to be known as the Trail of Tears. Meanwhile, the purchase of greater Louisiana in 1803 sped up the Americanization of the greater Mississippi River basin. The rapid advance of technology led to massive overland migrations in the 1840s and '50s, which now began to reach the US West Coast, meaning that the remaining Indian population was increasingly surrounded, isolated, and continually harassed by settlers and soldiers alike.

The discovery of gold in California in 1849 brought a tremendous influx of ruffians and adventurers into California, and after these provoked a handful of skirmishes with the local Indian population, a series of "wars" erupted that were often little more than Indian-hunting expeditions. It took some fifteen or twenty years for the massacres and bloodshed to be brought under control by the US federal government, partly due to the Civil War draining resources from Indian-protection operations, but by that time most of the Indian population of California had scattered or been assimilated. The Civil War saw an uptick of violence across the west, and a number of massacres and forced marches resulted.

On the Great Plains, some of the last remaining groups of "free" Indians survived by hunting buffalo—until the advance of firearms technology in the early 1870s saw the entire American bison population wiped out in a few years. After this time, a few decades of desultory warfare saw the last Indian groups subdued by the US Army, and the reservation system was forced on the Amerindian. Many Indian children were forced to go to public schools where the avowed goal was to "kill the Indian," i.e., to remove all vestiges of Indian language and culture from the student, replacing it with the dominant English-speaking Christian and Western ideology.

This is hardly a glorious track record, and there is much about it to lament. That being said, we have sought to demonstrate that there are virtually no grounds—at any time in the five-hundred-year history of European settlement in the New World—for declaring European policies or actions against the Amerindians to be "genocidal." This is—at best—a metaphor; at worst an inexcusable exaggeration that diminishes the victims of actual genocide. Nor is there historical justification for arguing that the United States or any Western Hemisphere *country* is fundamentally illegitimate on the grounds that it was "stolen" from Indigenous peoples. Even if some land was stolen or conquered in war, a great deal of it was purchased and sold voluntarily. Such a simplistic view also ignores inescapable realities such as demographic reality and the necessity of switching from a hunter-gatherer to an agricultural lifestyle after the introduction of firearms.

Another thing that this lamentable history does not justify is the accusation that either Europeans or their culture was particularly depraved in comparison with other global cultures. Most Western Hemisphere countries where there were substantial Native populations in 1491 are today majority Indian or mestizo. The same holds true throughout the Old World to an even greater extent. All this gives the lie to the myth of settler colonialism as a consistent policy or systemic feature of European civilization. Looking at global history as a whole, it is abundantly clear that Europeans were no more prone to violence, hierarchy, patriarchy, or slavery than any other people on Earth. In fact, the last few centuries have demonstrated nearly the opposite: Western civilization has been the overwhelming force behind the triumph of human rights in modern global society. This includes the abolition of slavery, women's rights, gay rights, minority rights—in short, every form of equality that most modern people hold dear. This human rights revolution was made possible through the advance of European learning and technology—the same learning and technology that are lamented so bitterly by those who criticize European expansionism and colonization.

In a further irony, the theoretical framework that paints Europe as particularly depraved is itself a brainchild of the European tradition of scientific and Enlightened self-criticism. Only in the West has radical self-criticism evolved the fine heights that we see today. Already in the nineteenth century, the European penchant for self-criticism reached new heights with the spread of Marxism; unfortunately, nearly every modern theory that is critical of Europe continues to use an outdated Marxist paradigm of "inevitable struggle between two opposing groups" as its basis. Critical race theory is a direct descendant of this line of thinking as it evolved in the 1960s and '70s. Any theory that posits that Europeans are a priori worse than any other historical group is likely to be based upon this hoary reasoning and should be exposed by critically minded historians for the lazy, derivative wish fulfillment that it is. Until we do so, policies that treat underprivileged groups as victims rather than as potential success stories will continue to fail our societies and prolong tragic achievement gaps among Indigenous populations and certain other minority groups.

THE CASE FOR OBJECTIVITY IN HISTORY

One of our major goals has been to present a case for objectivity in our portrayals of history. Traditionally, the public holds historians to the same high standards they apply to courtroom judges. An ideal historian will look dispassionately at the evidence, the sources, and the probable facts of a case, and write a narrative interpretation based on reason, logic, and a well-honed sense of judgment. Personal preference—including political opinions—is supposed to be relegated to secondary status.

This is particularly important in a democracy: only when the public has access to value-neutral information about the past can citizens be expected to make rational, informed decisions about what to do in the present and future.

In the West, we traditionally tolerate a plurality of views, in the knowledge that plurality and open debate form the basis of both the scientific method and the democratic process. Most of us realize that since no one person can be perfectly objective or knowledgeable, the closest humans can get to objective truth is by averaging the opinions of several experts. This is how science (and history) has been operating in the West since the Renaissance. There is immense value in the fact that Howard Zinn and Noam Chomsky are allowed to air off-beat and one-sided interpretations of history; this is one of the glories and greatest strengths of our Western system.

In a dictatorship, censorship is imposed from above. The problem we are currently facing in the Western academy is a new species of censorship driven by social-media mobs—the same social media mobs who savaged the president of the American Historical Association for making the same argument I am making here. The ability of a single student's tweet to spark campus action, which sparks bad press and spooks administrators into silencing errant faculty, is novel, and our system has not yet worked out the problems this creates for the concept of open scientific debate.

It would be one thing if most faculty members bravely fought against such conformism, but the sad fact is that most academics find it more expedient simply to go along with social media fads. This is why the likes of J. K. Rowling, Noam Chomsky, Margaret Atwood and Salman Rushdie had to sign the letter on "Justice and Open Debate" that was published in Harper's Magazine in July 2020.[150] The sobering conclusion is that even a PhD is not enough to foster an ability to stand up against popular social trends, no matter how fleeting or irrational.

It is okay if a minority of historians abandon the ideal of objectivity in pursuit of an activist agenda, but when too many do this at once, then history quickly loses its status as a branch of scientific knowledge. The value of ideologues such as Howard Zinn or Noam Chomsky lay in the fact that they were minority, opposition voices, who were understood to have a challenging but idiosyncratic interpretation of the facts. The history of the twentieth century taught us that when extreme views become mainstream, society can rapidly fall apart.

If one is concerned about the proliferation of conspiracy theories on both the Right and Left, then one of the surest long-term bulwarks against them is a commitment to objectivity on the part of professional historians. By giving in to the zeitgeist and writing lopsided narratives in order to score social media points with activist peers, historians such as Benjamin Madley and David Silverman merely feed the public's susceptibility to sensationalism and unreason. Their books contribute to the unraveling of democratic society and the debasement of the scientific method.

Another reason historians have abandoned objectivity in recent years has to do with the polarization of American media. Here I blame Ronald Reagan's deregulation of American television news—particularly the FCC's abolition of the 1949 Fairness Doctrine. It certainly seems that since the later 1980s, mainstream "news" has become more polarized than it was in the days of Walter Cronkite in the 1970s and early 1980s. We know that Americans have become politically more polarized

---

[150] This remains one of the most powerful indictments of cancel culture—and proofs that it is real—that is ever likely to be written. https://harpers.org/a-letter-on-justice-and-open-debate/

at the same time. If they grow up in such an environment, how can we expect young history students to learn and maintain an air of neutrality? Sadly, liberal Americans are more than ready to lecture conservatives for a retreat from reality, while failing to recognize that they are lecturing from the bow of a sinking ship.[151]

The predictable result of this folly is a crop of young historians for whom the concept of historical neutrality is a foreign concept. They enter the profession aiming at activism rather than truth, and their professors do precious little to correct them.

Some will object that this book has been anything but "neutral" in its interpretation of European adventurism in the New World. To which I would respond: yes, I have intentionally portrayed European adventurism in a more positive light than the majority of modern analyses.

My purpose in doing so should be obvious: to help restore balance to our narratives. While I have no quarrel with modern historians who wish to correct Eurocentric readings of history, the trend toward Euro-bashing has now become so dominant, so shrill, and often so unmoored from historical reality that someone has to step in and present a corrective to their excessive revisionism. Only when facts balance propaganda can we hope to return to a more objective record of what actually happened in the past.

And there is a deeper, more specific purpose behind my defense of Western culture and American institutions. Though few on the Left will believe it, my motivation has little to do with my own particular race or gender, and everything to do with the safeguarding of human rights for humanity as a whole.

If Marx and his New Left successors were proven wrong in any one thing over the course of the twentieth century, it was that there *is* a fundamental difference between democracy and autocracy. Democracies *do* respond to the will of the people, and—slowly but surely—provide increasing prosperity and freedom over time. Autocracies, on the other

---

[151] See for example, Kevin M. Kruse and Julian E. Zelizer, *Myth America: Historians Take On the Biggest Legends and Lies About Our Past* (Basic Books, 2023).

hand, become stuck in the paranoias of their leaders. They remain corrupt, breathtakingly unequal, unresponsive to environmental emergencies, reckless with regard to human rights, and bellicose, and they generally provide far inferior opportunities for the mass of their people. Contrary to what the critical theorists want us to believe, autocracies are the major stumbling block to world peace and environmental justice in the world today.[152] China, for example, emits fully 27 percent of the world's greenhouse gases every year (250 percent more than the United States), with little sign of stopping.

The United States remains the major political, economic, cultural, and military bastion of democracy in the modern world. Almost every good enjoyed by human beings today results to some extent from the United States and its institutional foundations in Europe. This is a self-evident truth. If the United States were to become dysfunctional as a democratic and military power, wise people recognize that the collapse of democracy across the globe would be swift, and the collapse in global living standards even swifter.

Historians have much more power than they imagine, and they must therefore be extremely careful what they wish for. It is fine and good to criticize the West, but it is another thing to distort the past to such an extent that we no longer recognize the true origins of the blessings we enjoy or the institutional foundations that sustain them. If we refuse to study the architects of the Renaissance, the Scientific Revolution, and the Enlightenment because they were guilty of being European males; if we instead make up false histories because they make us feel good, then our ability to defend the downtrodden across the world today, and to defend our institutions against threats from autocrats and strongmen,

---

[152] The ambiguity felt by many prominent liberals towards democracy is shocking. See for example Simon Tisdall's "Outdated and out of time: Biden's crusade for global democracy is doomed to fail" in the Guardian, Feb 26, 2023. Tisdall finds Biden's promotion of democracy around the globe distasteful, saying that it smacks of "neo-imperialism" or a new colonialism. I sincerely wonder what he would prefer instead. https://www.theguardian.com/commentisfree/2023/feb/26/biden-crusade-for-global-democracy-is-doomed-to-fail

will be crippled by ignorance and false knowledge. Such a course is foolish in the extreme.

Genocide historians and the "stolen ground" chorus imagine that they are championing justice for the historically downtrodden. What they do instead is enable modern-day genocide and human rights abuses on a far larger scale, by baselessly removing one of the most important weapons in the democratic arsenal against tyranny: the truth that, despite their faults, America and its democracy will continue to warrant a prominent place on the moral high ground of history.

ACKNOWLEDGMENTS

This book has been two years in the making. During that time, it has matured into an exposé of the influence of dogma on our interpretations of history and a heartfelt attempt to rebalance our understanding of how Europeans behaved vis-à-vis the Indigenous People of America.

I have many people to thank for inspiring me to take this journey into the public sphere, fraught with danger though it may be to my erstwhile life as an historical researcher. First on the list must be my editors at the *Spectator*, Mary Wakefield and Will Moore, who recognized the value of my "Myth of the Stolen Country" essay and increased its potency with breathtaking efficiency. Among those who helped me to spread the word, Michael Medved stands out as having taken the time to appreciate the details of my project and giving insightful advice at a key juncture.

Numerous scholars and public figures have reached out to talk with me and provide encouragement; most valuable of all have been those who provided correctives to my understanding. I cannot mention many of these, since acknowledgment here might cause them social or professional difficulty; however, Steven Pinker, Nigel Biggar, Bruce Gilley, John Bonnett and Muriel Newman stand out as particularly insightful. Of my thousands of academic critics on Twitter, only Jeff Ostler has taken the time to engage with me scholar to scholar, and I am sincerely appreciative of his professionalism in that regard. My History Reclaimed editors Robert Tombs and David Abulafia have also been tremendously encouraging; I thank them immensely for providing a professional space where one can take a moment's shelter from the maelstrom.

Among the numerous readers and editors who have helped with the manuscript, Rachelle and David Boger provided invaluable feedback on an earlier draft. My wife, Jennifer, has likewise provided valuable assistance as an editor and exacting grammarian, and my activist daughter Persephone—although she is skeptical of the entire project—has done her best to keep me "from sounding too much like a jerk." I hope she has succeeded, at least in part. My son Patrick, with his natural chill, has made it that much easier to keep an even keel throughout this process. My mother, Revelly Ann Paul, provided a good deal of criticism and moral support, though she and my father find it difficult to conceive how quickly things have degenerated in the academy since they retired. I must also (anonymously) thank several students at Leiden and other Dutch universities who prepared the maps and tables, together with several students and colleagues who provided feedback on issues covered here.

The highest thanks must be reserved for Adam Bellow of Bombardier Books, who not only encouraged this project from the beginning but who has also provided world-class editorial expertise and shape to the project far above the call of duty. For his tireless efforts and friendship, I will be forever grateful.

Index